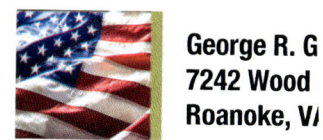

George R. G
7242 Wood
Roanoke, V/

MW01566865

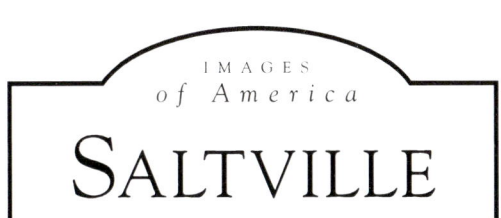

IMAGES
of America

SALTVILLE

ON THE COVER: GONE FISHIN'. This Depression-era photograph shows several men fishing along the banks of the North Fork of Holston River. At least one of these fellows has had a very successful day. While the Great Depression did not cause wholesale economic disaster for Saltville or Mathieson Alkali Works, work schedules were cut. Some chose to hunt and fish to supplement their food supply. The railroad and the plant are on the opposite shore.

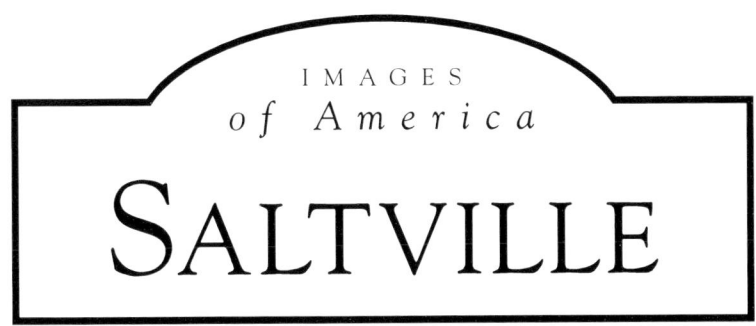

IMAGES
of America

SALTVILLE

Jeffrey C. Weaver
in cooperation with
The Museum of the Middle Appalachians

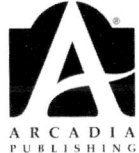

ARCADIA
PUBLISHING

Copyright © 2006 by Jeffrey C. Weaver
ISBN 978-0-7385-4211-9

Published by Arcadia Publishing
Charleston, South Carolina

Printed in the United States of America

Library of Congress Catalog Card Number: 2005938520

For all general information contact Arcadia Publishing at:
Telephone 843-853-2070
Fax 843-853-0044
E-mail sales@arcadiapublishing.com
For customer service and orders:
Toll-Free 1-888-313-2665

Visit us on the Internet at www.arcadiapublishing.com

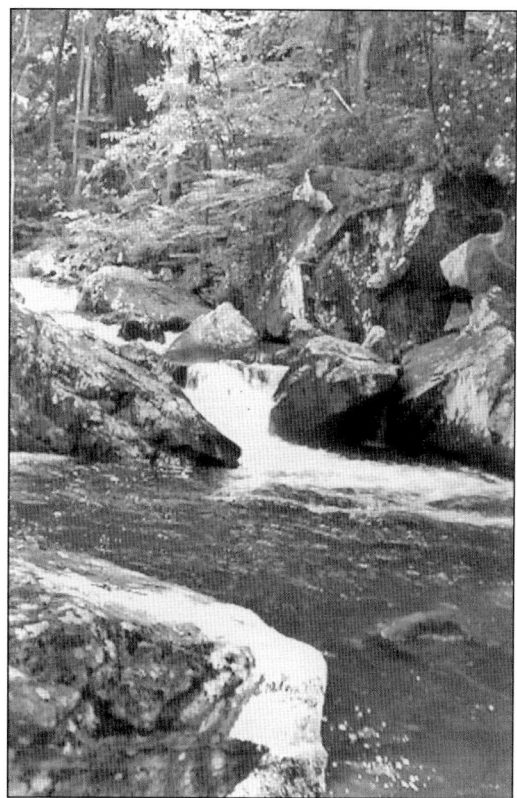

TUMBLING CREEK FALLS. This scene, located about four miles west of the center of Saltville, is an often-visited local attraction. It is located near the Clinch Mountain Wildlife Refuge. Also nearby is Laurel Bed Lake, located very near the top of Clinch Mountain. This spring-fed body of water is a popular attraction for naturalists and locals alike. (Photograph by J. Weaver.)

Contents

Acknowledgments	6
Introduction	7
1. Environment and Archeology	9
2. Old Saltville	15
3. Mathieson Alkali Works	33
4. New Saltville	49
5. Saltville Suburbs	69
6. Disasters	81
7. Transportation	87
8. Education	93
9. Civic Life	99
10. Recreation	109
Bibliography	128

ACKNOWLEDGMENTS

Most of the images contained in the following pages are from the collection of the Museum of the Middle Appalachians. This museum, located on Palmer Avenue in Saltville, Virginia, was established in 1998. The facility has served as a repository for ice-age fossils, Native American relics, Civil War finds, and a large collection of photographs documenting the history of the town of Saltville. This book represents a small fraction of this photographic collection. Some exhibits are changed on a regular basis at the museum. Enlargements of the images of America contained in this book may be obtained from the museum.

Identification of the photographs is more difficult than acquisition. Several people who have made Saltville's history a life's avocation have provided invaluable assistance in captioning of these images. Those who went above and beyond what one could reasonably expect include:
Roger Allison, newspaper man for the *Saltville Progress*
Helen Barbrow, president of the Saltville Foundation
Janice Barbrow, manager of the Saltville Public Library
Jerry Catron, historian of Madam Russell United Methodist Church
Rick Davidson, citizen of Saltville
Andrew Frye, neighbor and former railroad man
Harry Haynes, manager of the Museum of the Middle Appalachians
Hugh Helton, neighbor and former Mathieson Alkali Works employee
Loretta Hodgson, editor of the *Saltville Progress*
Ed Sheets, who digitized many of these pictures
Fred Singleton, businessman and next-door neighbor
Tom Totten, photographer and photograph collector

Special thanks are tendered to Roger, Jerry, Helen, Hugh, and Harry for assisting in correcting the captions in this book.

INTRODUCTION

The present size of Saltville belies the community's importance in history. The present community, first occupied by Europeans in the mid-18th century, is only the latest chapter of a very long history.

The abundance of animal life attracted hunter-gather aboriginal peoples to the valley. Archeological evidence indicates human habitation in the Saltville Valley for over 14,000 years. These first settlers have been generally denominated "pre-Clovis" people. Aborigines occupied the Saltville Valley for millennia. This is shown by an abundance of artifacts found throughout the area. These peoples discovered the value of salt. Through some unknown process, either evaporation or boiling, they reduced the brine to the mineral form and traded it with other Eastern American tribes.

First European contact with the peoples in the valley came in 1567. An expedition of Spaniards under Juan Pardo left their camp near Morganton, North Carolina, marched north for four days, and attacked the Native American village called Maniatique, located on the present-day site of Saltville, Virginia. They left a written account of the expedition. These documents, discovered in a Spanish archive in the 1990s, yield some detail about the native people, called Xuala by the conquistadors but who identified themselves as Yuchi. When the first settlers arrived 200 years later, the natives were gone.

In 1745, King George II granted Col. James Patton 120,000 acres of land west of the Blue Ridge Mountains. Patton was surveyor of Augusta County, which encompassed all of Virginia west of the Blue Ridge Mountains all the way to the Mississippi River. Patton and his son-in-law, Col. John Buchanan, led an expedition in 1748 that discovered the Cumberland Gap. A member of their party, Charles Campbell, had a survey made of the "Salt Lick" in 1748. Campbell obtained a patent on the land in 1753. When he died, these lands passed to his son, William.

After the Revolutionary War, the western frontier became more settled. By the 1790s, several families were located in the Saltville area with good land titles. Perhaps the most famous of these settlers was Madam Elizabeth Henry Campbell Russell. She was born Elizabeth Henry, sister of Virginia's famous governor Patrick Henry. Elizabeth married local hero William Campbell in 1776. Campbell brought his bride to what must have seemed like the end of the earth in Southwest Virginia. Campbell led the patriot forces at Kings Mountain in October 1780 and a contingent of mountaineers to Eastern Virginia before the siege of Yorktown. Campbell fell ill and died there in 1781. Arthur Campbell, cousin of the general, was appointed guardian for the children of William and Elizabeth in 1782 and immediately began the commercial manufacture of salt. Elizabeth Henry Campbell, after a very brief courtship, married Gen. William Russell, another Revolutionary War hero, in 1782. In 1782, Russell began a second salt manufacturing operation in the valley. Russell and Elizabeth moved to Saltville in 1788. Madam Russell became a staunch supporter of the Methodist church. The Russells hosted American Methodist bishop Francis Asbury 13 times over the next several years.

Francis Preston, son-in-law of Elizabeth Henry Campbell Russell, leased his wife's property to William King for the then-unheard-of sum of $12,000 per year in 1795. This is the date at which serious industrialization began in the Saltville Valley.

Gypsum deposits were also discovered near Saltville at an early date. In 1808, Col. Francis Smith chartered the Buena Vista Plaster Company. This company operated in the southwest end of the valley. It eventually operated under the name U.S. Gypsum. Southern Gypsum, which operated in North Holston, was later acquired by Mathieson Alkali Works.

Just before the Civil War, George Palmer, a New York industrialist, along with a series of partners that included Benjamin K. Buchanan and William A. Stuart, acquired the title to the saltworks. Their company, the Holston Salt and Plaster Company, operated until the early 1890s. Mathieson Alkali Works began operation in the valley in 1892. They merged with Olin Corporation in the 1950s, and the company was called Olin-Mathieson. Sometime later, the name was shortened to just Olin. After Olin announced the closure of the facilities in Saltville in 1970, the village suffered a severe economic downturn. The town is still recovering.

As you browse the following pages, you will learn how Saltville's environment, industry, and people have combined to create a unique culture in the southern Appalachian highlands.

One

ENVIRONMENT AND ARCHEOLOGY

Geologic processes eons ago laid salt deposits in the Saltville Valley in northwestern Smyth County and northeastern Washington County, Virginia. The limestone formations that underlie the village were eroded by water over time. This water also dissolved the salt. The resulting brine filled the voids of the karst geology below the surface. This saltwater percolated to the surface. These ponds were fed by the Saltville River, forming a lake in the lowest section of the town. Sodium chloride is a basic necessity of animal life. All kinds of prehistoric animals were attracted to these salt ponds; many lost their lives, and their bones sank into the mud along the shores of the lake. Paleontological excavations have uncovered remains of mastodons, mammoths, stag moose, elk, deer, musk oxen, and other animals common in North America during the last ice age.

The fragile ecosystem in Saltville is something to behold. In the town or close by are salt marshes with sea birds—300 miles inland from the Atlantic. Plants found here include some commonly only found along the coast. Other features include the Tumbling Creek falls and Clinch Mountain, which rises to about 4,400 feet above sea level and over 2,600 feet above the village on the valley floor. The alpine environment here is typically Appalachian, with stands of hemlock and rhododendron.

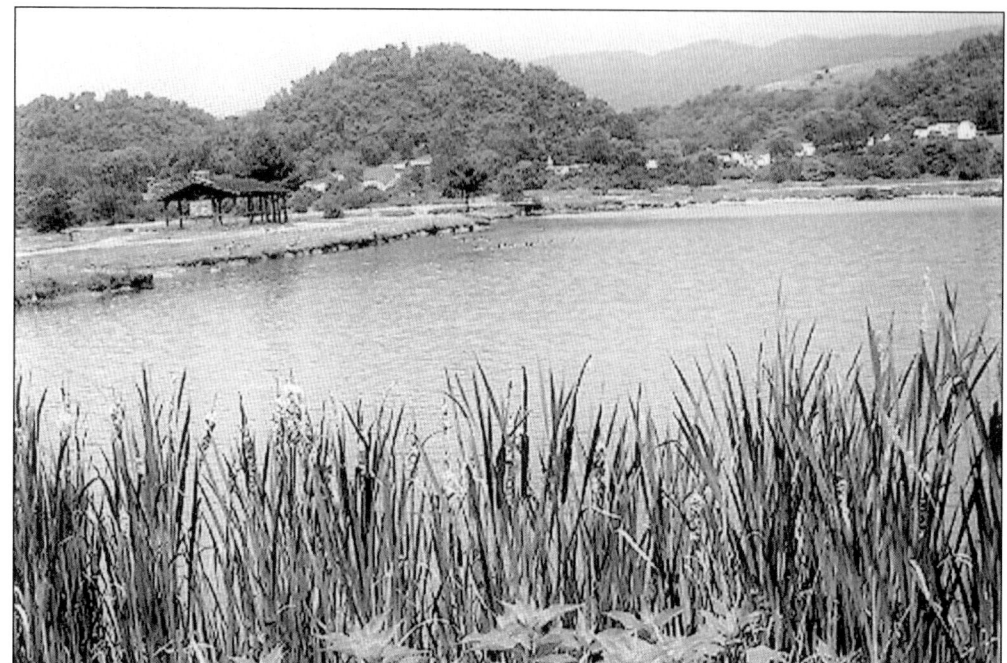

THE WELL FIELDS. This photograph shows one of the ponds located in Saltville. These bodies of water have accumulated in the last several years and are reminiscent of the lake that once covered the lower part of town. These ponds are home to ducks, geese, sora, herons, and other birds. The town is a bird sanctuary. (Photograph by J. Weaver.)

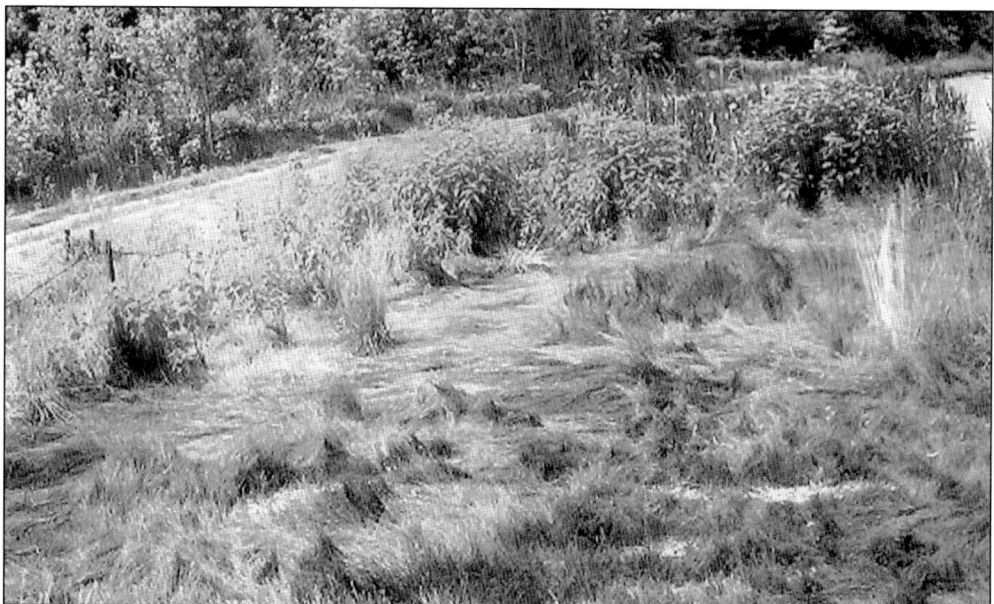

COASTAL ENVIRONMENT. Grasses and other plants commonly associated with a coastal environment are found in or around Saltville's well fields. These ponds are incredibly beautiful when the marshmallows are in full bloom. Sea birds migrating over Saltville are attracted by the ponds and leave seeds behind, creating this unique ecosystem 300 miles from the Atlantic. (Photograph by J. Weaver.)

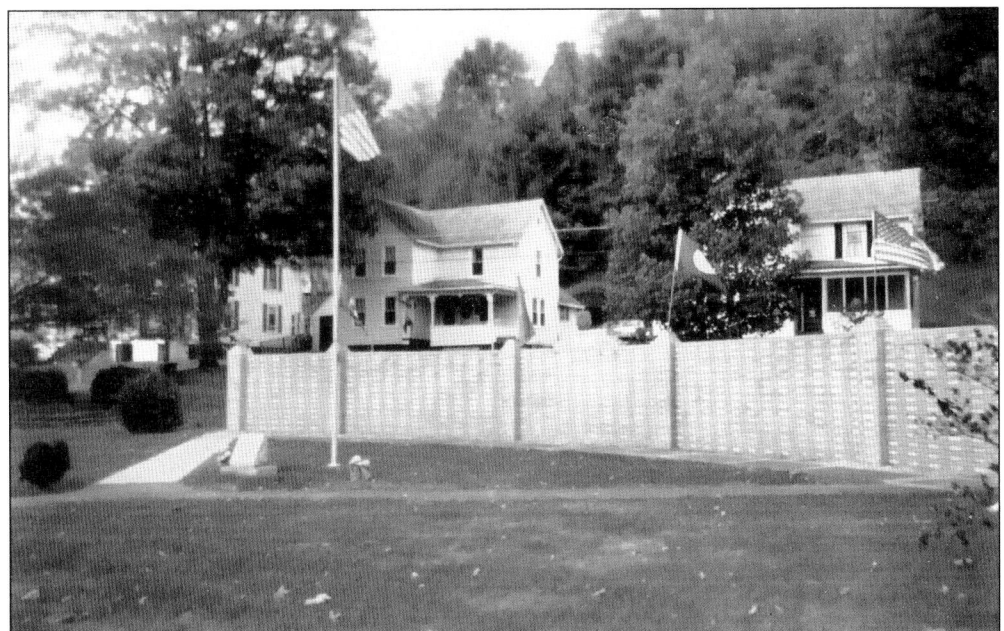

VETERANS WALL OF HONOR. Saltville has had a long history of service in the military. This wall recognizes the sacrifice of local men in America's wars. This wall is the backdrop for Memorial and Veterans Day observances in the town. It is maintained by the Hardy Roberts Chapter of the Veterans of Foreign Wars.

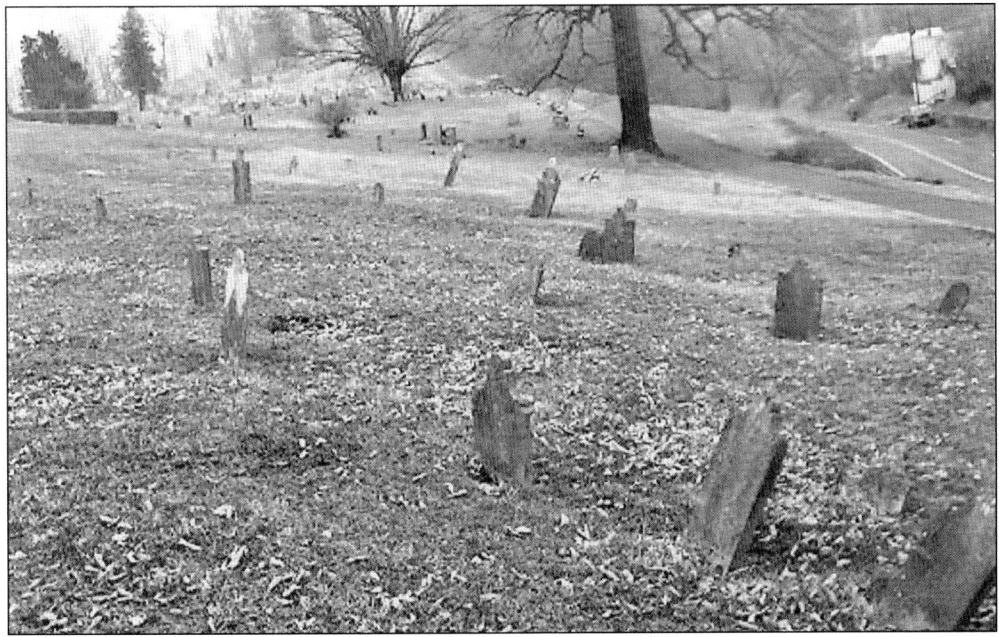

ELIZABETH CEMETERY. Elizabeth Cemetery, located in the east end of town, is the resting place for many of the town's beloved dead. This fog-shrouded snapshot shows the older section of the cemetery. Many of the grave markers were destroyed during the First Battle of Saltville on October 2, 1864, when Union general Stephen Burbridge attempted to take the town. Elizabeth Chapel Methodist Church stood near this spot before the Civil War.

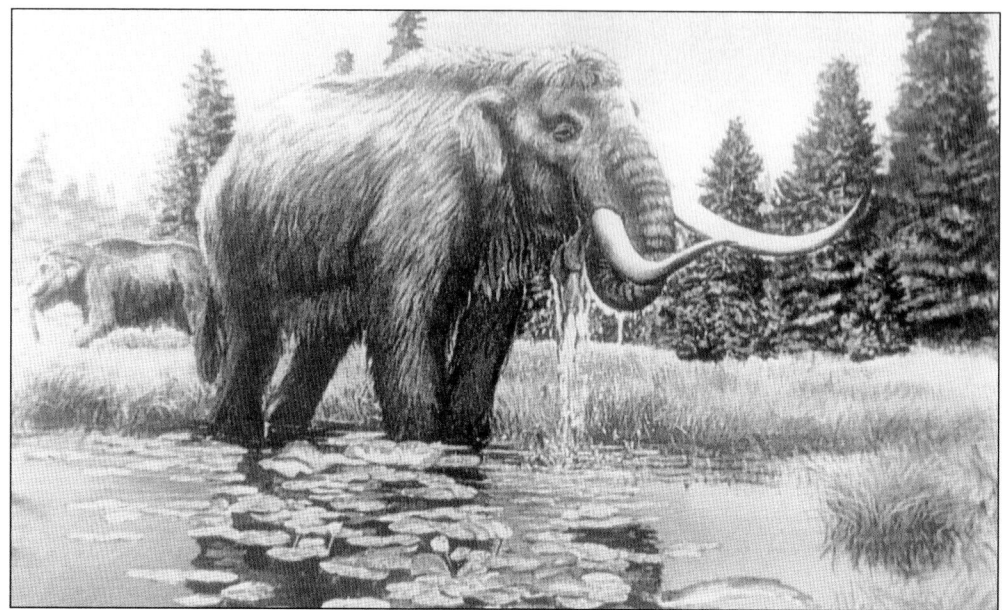

MASTODON. This is an artist's conception of what the Saltville Valley must have looked like 15,000 years ago. These ancient animals were the models for the Museum of the Middle Appalachians' mascots, Woolly and Little Salty. Woolly and Little Salty are celebrated annually with Woolly Day. The reproductions of Woolly and Little Salty also participate in parades in town and neighboring communities.

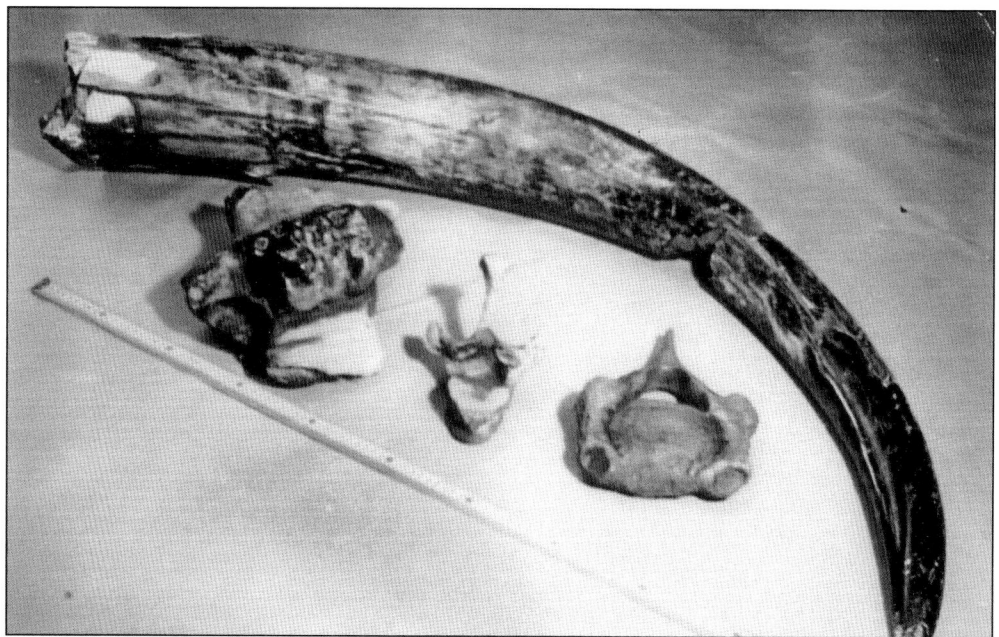

SALTVILLE FOSSILS. Mastodon and woolly mammoth bones have been discovered in Saltville. This image shows a shows a tusk, a tooth, and vertebra. Note the yardstick in the foreground, which gives some indication of size. These bones and many others are on display at the Museum of the Middle Appalachians. In addition to the bones of these ancient relatives of the elephant, fossils of stag moose, giant beavers, and other ancient animals have been found.

PALEONTOLOGY. This paleontologist is examining a fossilized hip bone of either a mammoth or mastodon discovered in Saltville. This image was made in the mid-1960s. Fossils have been found regularly for over 200 years, and samples were sent to Pres. Thomas Jefferson for his collection of natural artifacts.

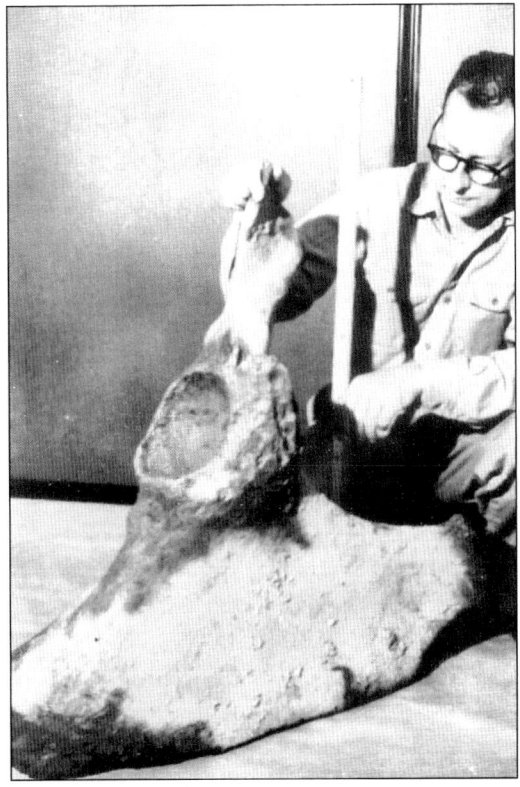

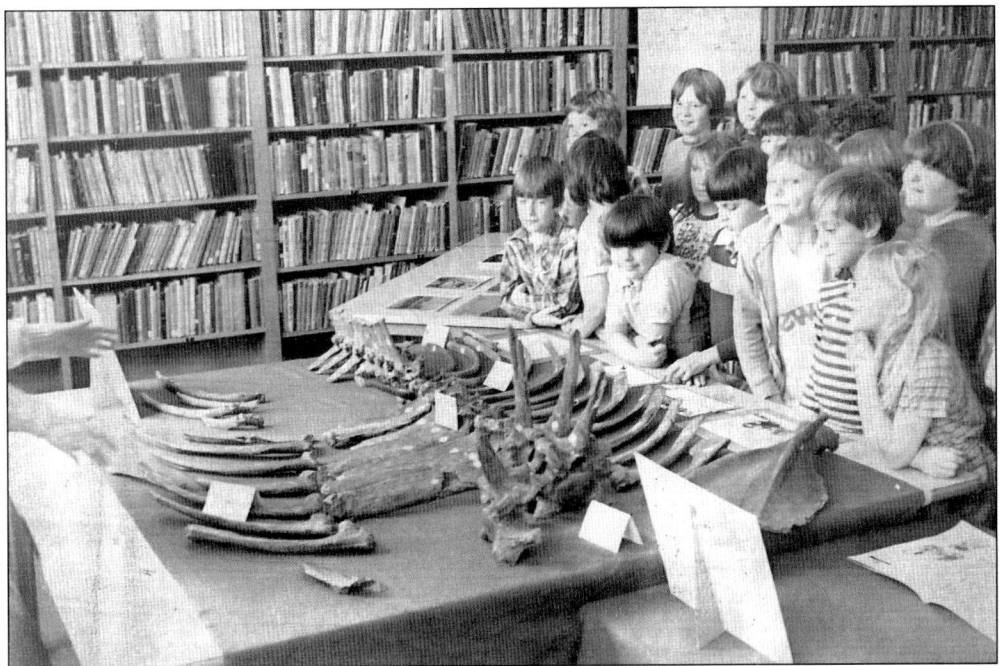

KIDS AND BONES. This image shows the display of the fossilized remains of over 40 bones of an ancient musk ox. The children appear to be fascinated by the display. This program took place in the mid-1980s in the library at the Saltville Elementary School. (Courtesy of Roger Allison.)

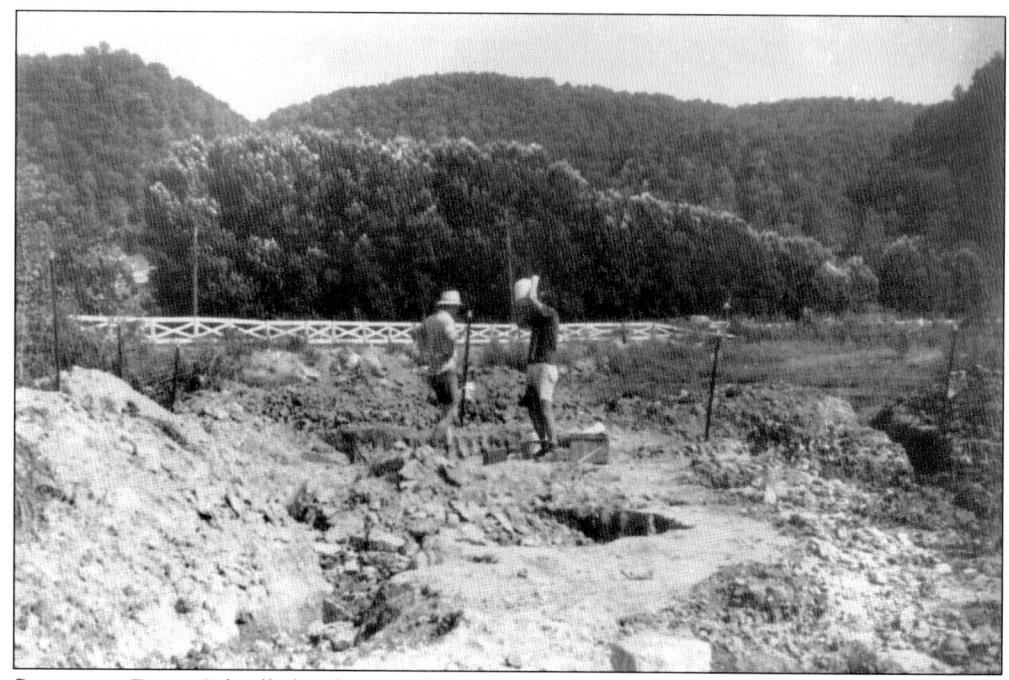

SALTVILLE DIGS. Saltville has been and continues to be a significant source of Ice Age fossils. Excavations have been conducted by Virginia Polytechnic Institute, the Smithsonian Institute, the Virginia Museum of Natural History, and more recently by East Tennessee State University. This photograph was taken in the mid-1960s.

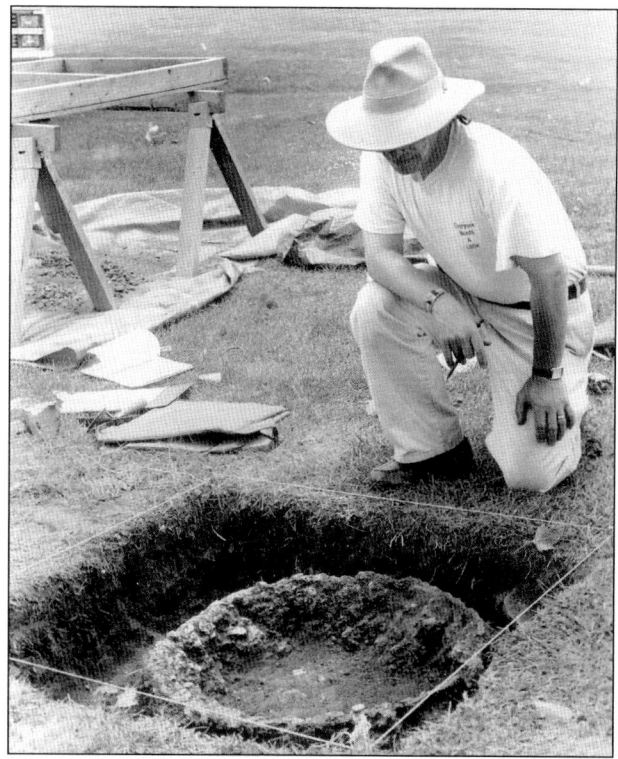

SALT KETTLE FIND. Ancient animals are not the only discoveries in the digs around town. This image shows a salt kettle discovered near the seventh green at the Saltville Municipal Golf Course near the site of the original Arthur Campbell salt well. The kettle dates from the 1780s. (Courtesy of Roger Allison.)

Two

OLD SALTVILLE

Old Saltville is located at the western end of the present town. It is the location of the first discoveries of salt, and it was here that most of the residents lived until the coming of the Mathiesons in 1892. The first salt wells were dug here in the 1780s. These wells brought prosperity and famous visitors like Andrew Jackson in 1804, James Madison in 1808, and Confederate president Jefferson Davis in 1863. Bishop Francis Asbury was a 13-time visitor.

A Confederate garrison was located at Saltville from very early in the American Civil War. This post was commanded for a time by John C. Breckinridge, former vice president of the United States, and generals John Hunt Morgan, Humphrey Marshall, Samuel Jones, and William Preston. Many other Confederate officials visited Saltville. The salt works were the object of several planned Federal army raids. Two were actually carried out, resulting in battles. The first of these raids was led by Kentucky's Gen. Stephen Burbridge and ended in a convincing Confederate victory on October 2, 1864. The second raid, led by U.S. Army general George Stoneman, succeeded in defeating the Southern forces defending the town in December 1864.

William Alexander Stuart, brother of Confederate general J. E. B. Stuart, lived here, as did General Stuart's wife, Flora. Virginia governors Wyndham Robertson and Henry C. Stuart called Saltville home for part of their lives.

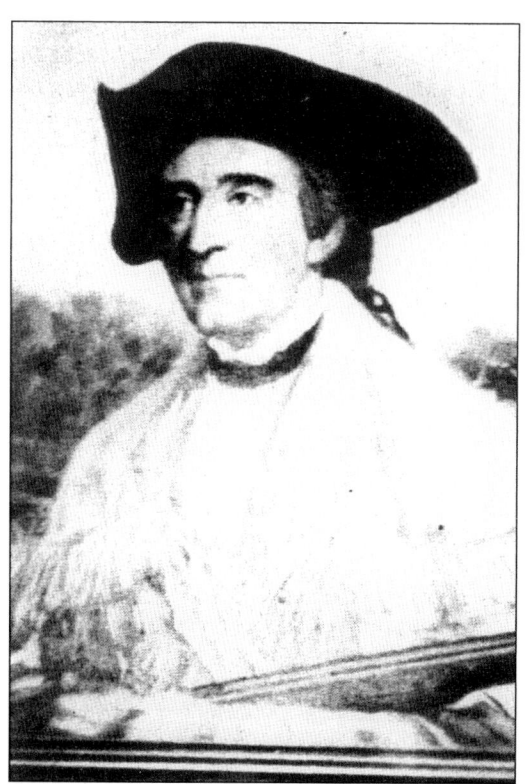

COL. WILLIAM CAMPBELL. This conjectural portrait shows Colonel Campbell, who was considered by many of his contemporaries "the Hero of Kings Mountain." He was the second owner of the "Salt Lick." He married Elizabeth Henry in 1776 and died in 1781, before the close of the American Revolution. (Courtesy of Kings Mountain National Military Park.)

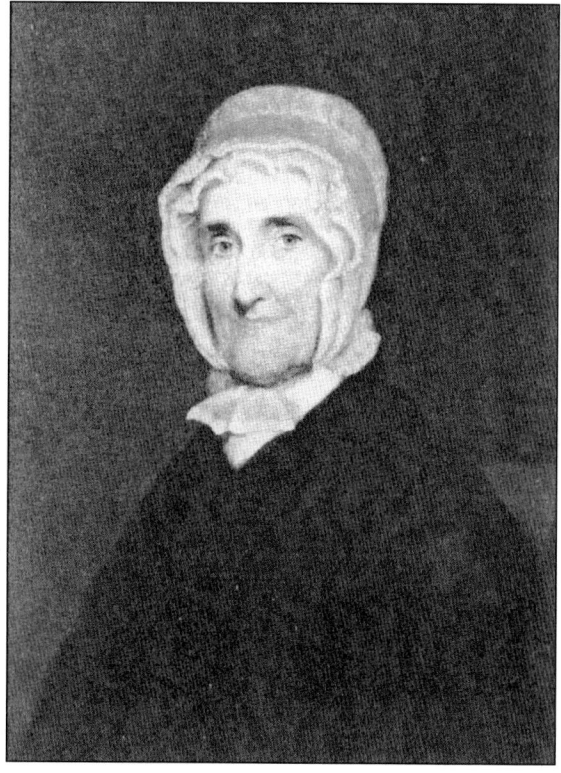

ELIZABETH HENRY CAMPBELL RUSSELL. Born in 1749, Madam Russell, as she was known, was the sister of Gov. Patrick Henry. She first married Colonel Campbell (above) and then Gen. William Russell (next page). She is known as the mother of Methodism in Appalachia and often entertained traveling Methodist ministers. (Courtesy of Roger Allison.)

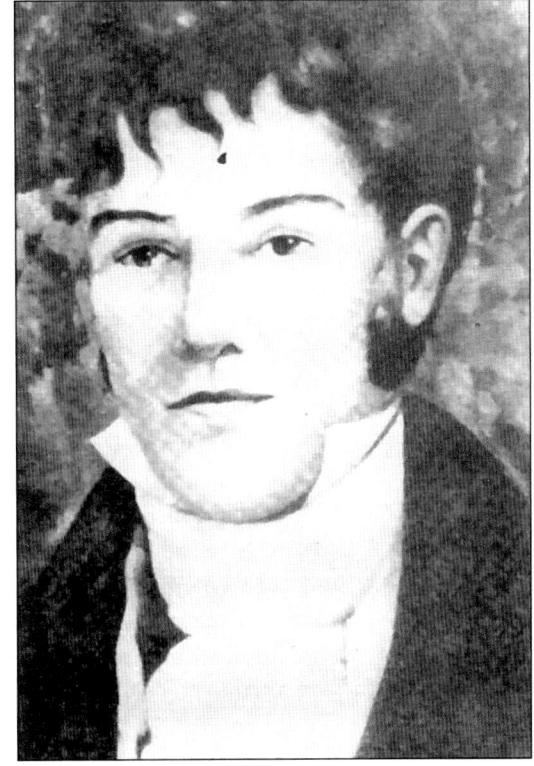

GEN. WILLIAM RUSSELL. A Revolutionary War hero, Russell came to Saltville with his second wife, Elizabeth Henry Campbell Russell, in 1788. He was the first to truly exploit the commercial possibilities of Saltville's salt. He served in the Virginia legislature but died fairly young in 1793, before his full potential was realized. Russell is buried in Arlington National Cemetery. (Courtesy of Jerry W. Catron.)

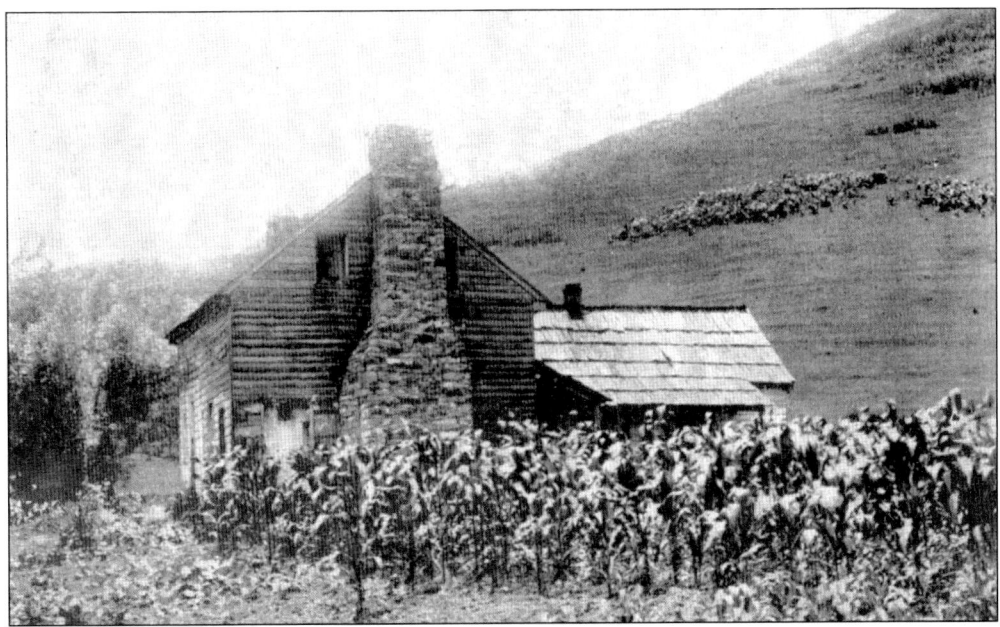

THE RUSSELL CABIN. This cabin was constructed about 1788, when General Russell moved his family to the "North Garden Salt-Works," as he called it in his correspondence. This building was demolished in the early 20th century, but a replica stands in the Madam Russell Methodist Church yard. This photograph of the original cabin is from c. 1896. (Courtesy of Jerry W. Catron.)

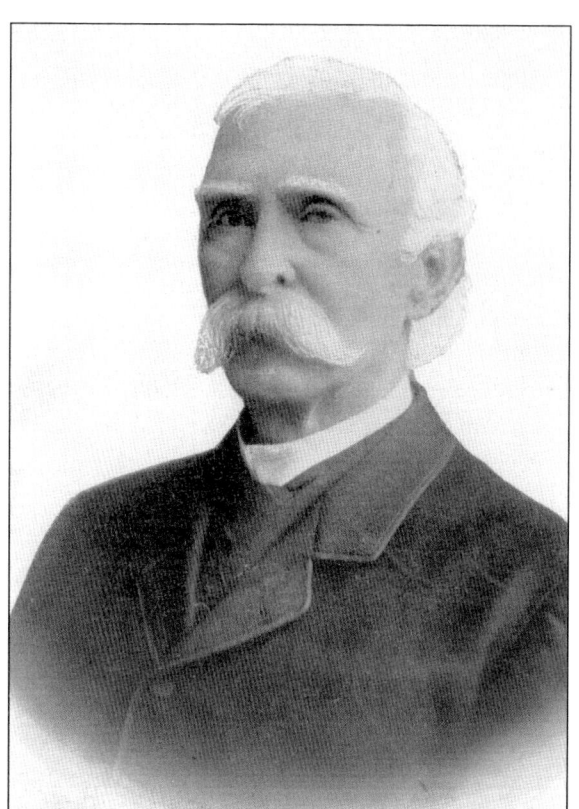

THOMAS L. PRESTON. Thomas L. Preston operated the saltworks before the Civil War. According to the 1850 Federal Census for Smyth County, Preston was worth over $500,000 on paper, making him one of the wealthiest men in America. He was actually heavily in debt at the time. (Courtesy of Roger Allison.)

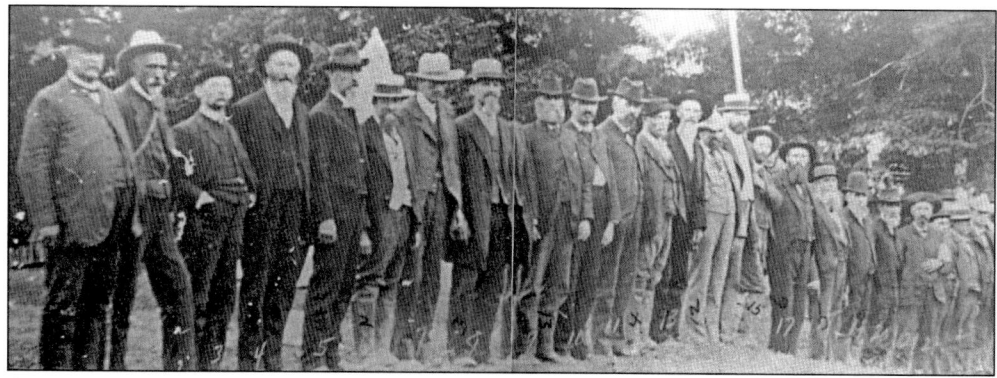

CONFEDERATE VETERANS. This group photograph of gray-bearded Confederates was taken near Saltville c. 1900. Summertime gatherings of these old veterans were a common sight at the end of the 19th century.

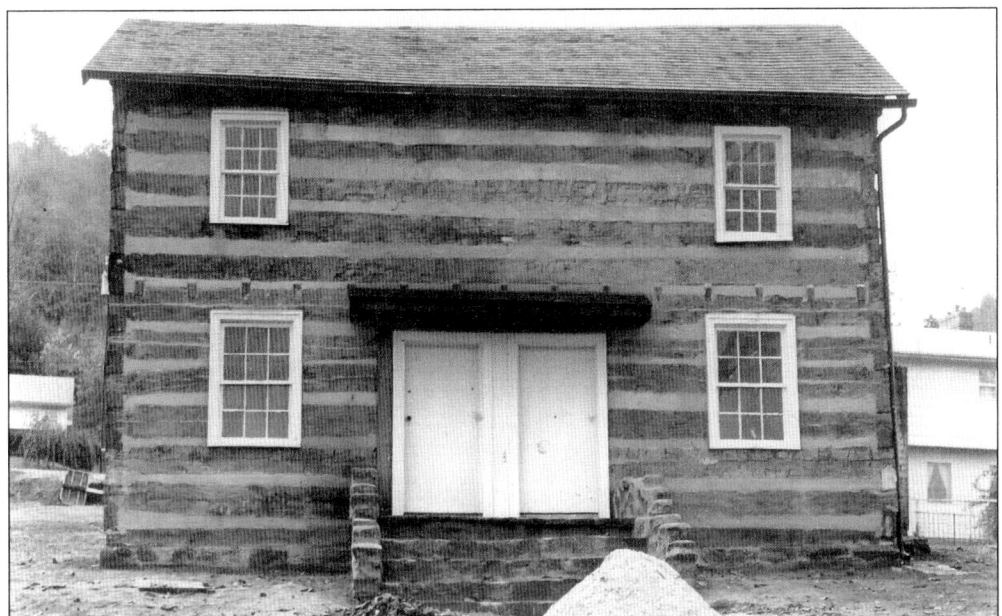

KING-STUART HOUSE. This house, known as the King-Stuart house, was constructed about 1795 by William King "the Elder." King was involved in the early operations of the saltworks. Confederate cavalry major general J. E. B. Stuart's widow, Flora, and their children lived here from 1864 until 1876. The King-Stuart house is located on Smokey Row in Old Saltville.

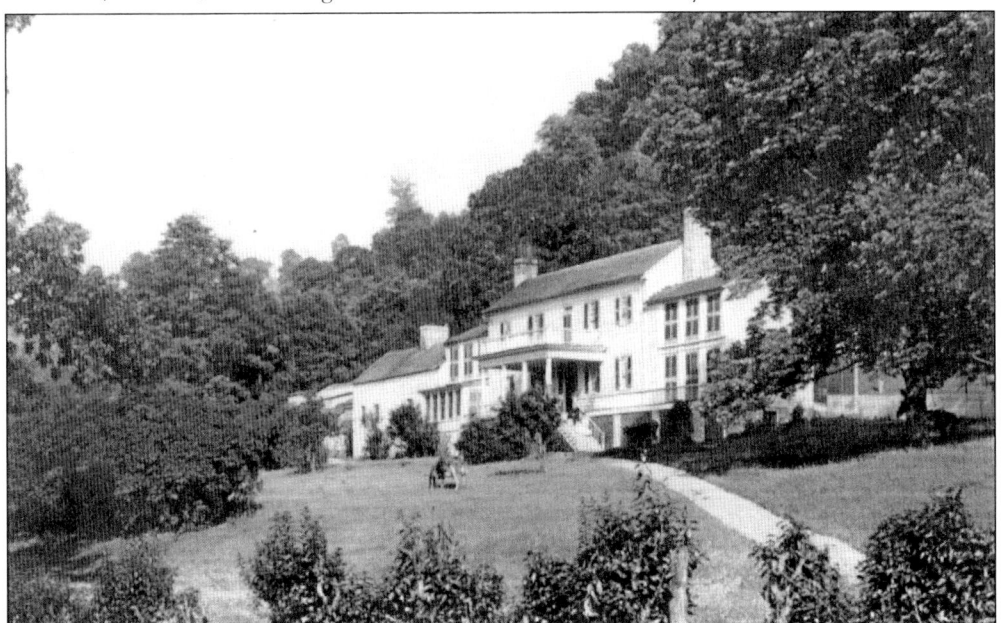

FRANCIS PRESTON HOUSE. The core of the Francis Preston House was built in the late 18th century by Thomas Madison, a cousin of Pres. James Madison. It was expanded in 1808 and enlarged further over the years. Preston entertained numerous members of early America's rich, famous, and powerful in the early 19th century. Two future presidents are known to have visited here, Andrew Jackson in 1804 and James Madison in 1808. In the 20th century, it became a rental property, and it was demolished in 1977.

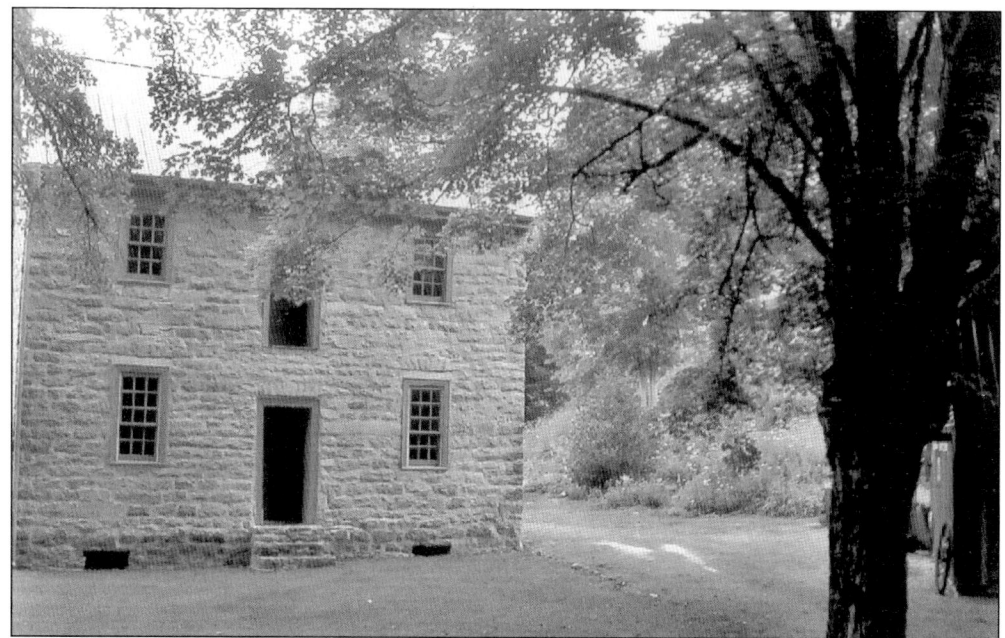

THE SCOTT STONE HOUSE. The Scott Stone House antedates 1790 and was restored about 1990. This house, built in the Pennsylvania German style, is located in Buckeye Hollow about two miles from town. It is believed to be the oldest surviving building in the Saltville Valley. Rumor has it that this house is haunted. (Photograph by J. Weaver.)

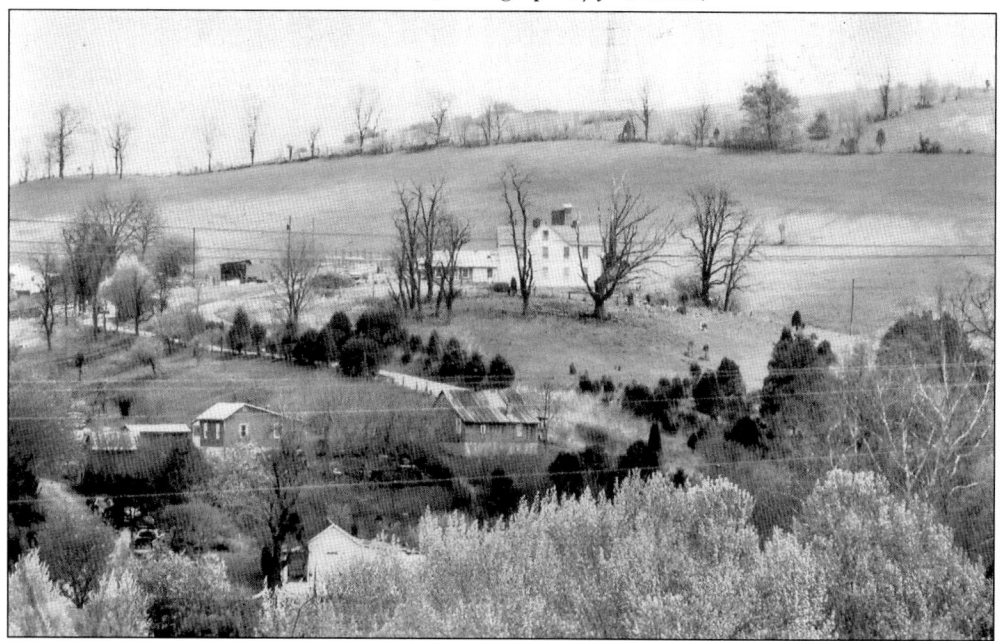

THE SANDERS HOUSE. This building was the home of James Sanders, the 70-something Southern hero of the First Battle of Saltville on October 2, 1864, when he stood in the middle of the river, in full view of the U.S. Army firing at him. This house, located on Cedar Branch, suffered heavy damage during the battle and has since been repaired. Battle damage can still be seen on some of the outbuildings on this farm. (Courtesy of Roger Allison.)

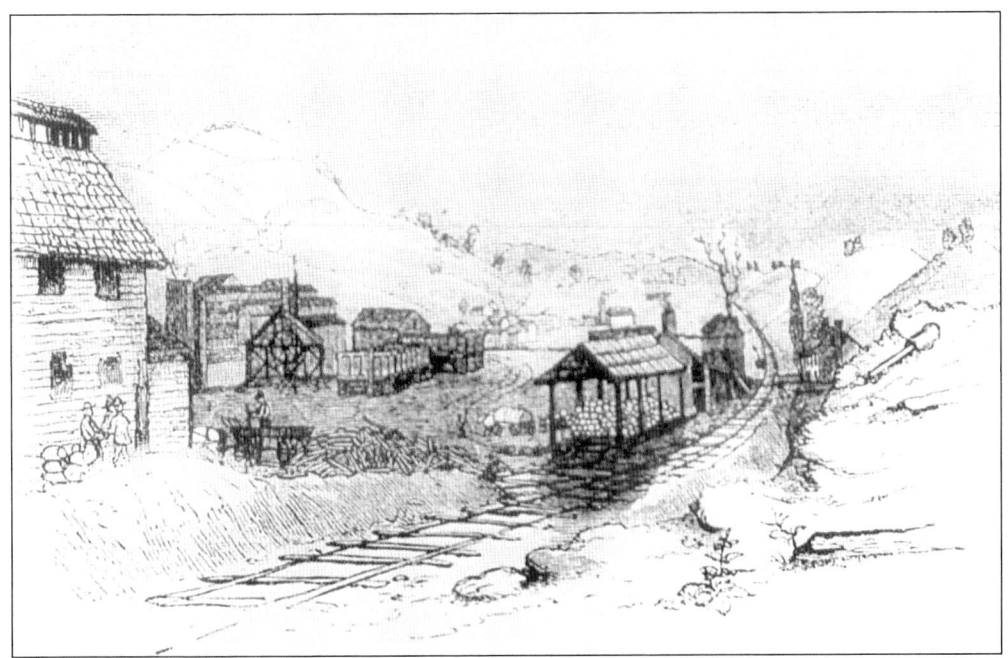

SALTVILLE TRAIN STATION, 1856. This illustration appeared in *Harper's New Monthly Magazine* in March 1857 as part of a serialized travelogue entitled "A Winter in the South." It was sketched in November 1856, shortly after the station was built.

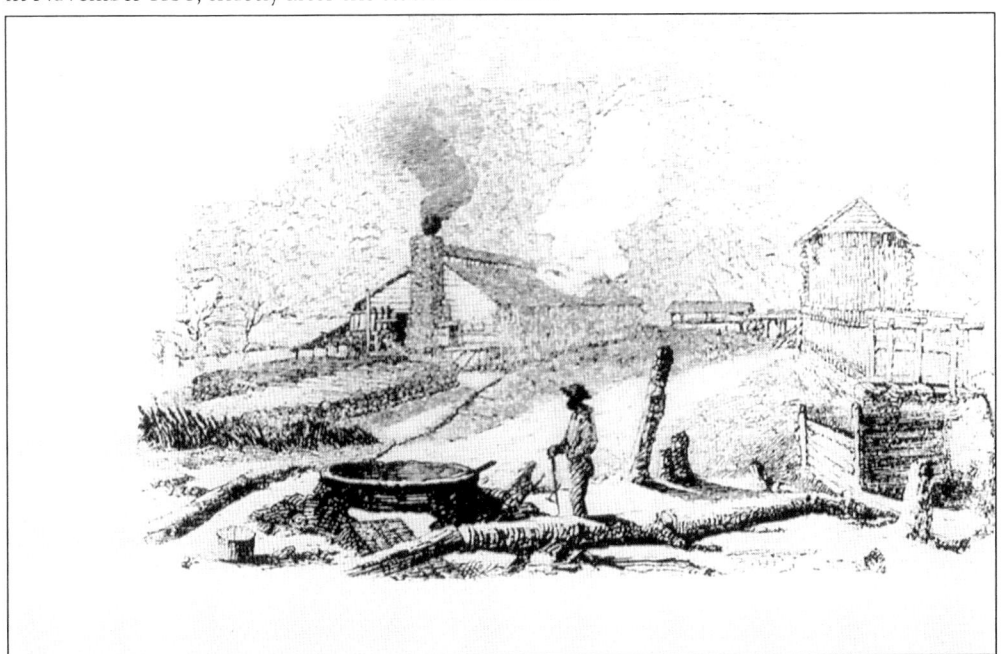

ANTEBELLUM SALT MAKING. This is another drawing from the March 1857 issue of *Harper's*. This scene shows the river furnace and other operations associated with the saltworks in November 1856. Slave labor was used in the salt manufacturing process. The number of slaves varied based on the production requirements, but the total soared during the War Between the States, as other Southern salt supplies were cut off from the Confederate people and army.

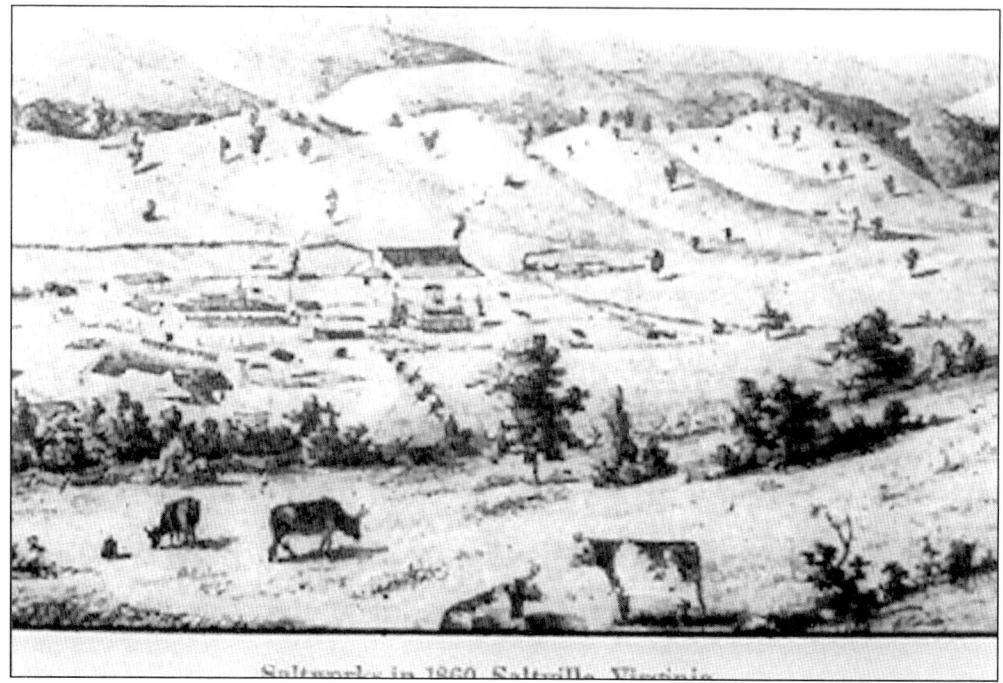

VIEW OF THE SALTVILLE VALLEY, 1860. This sketch is another artist's view of Saltville in 1860. Agriculture and early industry peacefully coexisted at this time. This artwork is a faithful representation of the valley as it appeared. (Courtesy of the Smyth County Museum and Historical Society.)

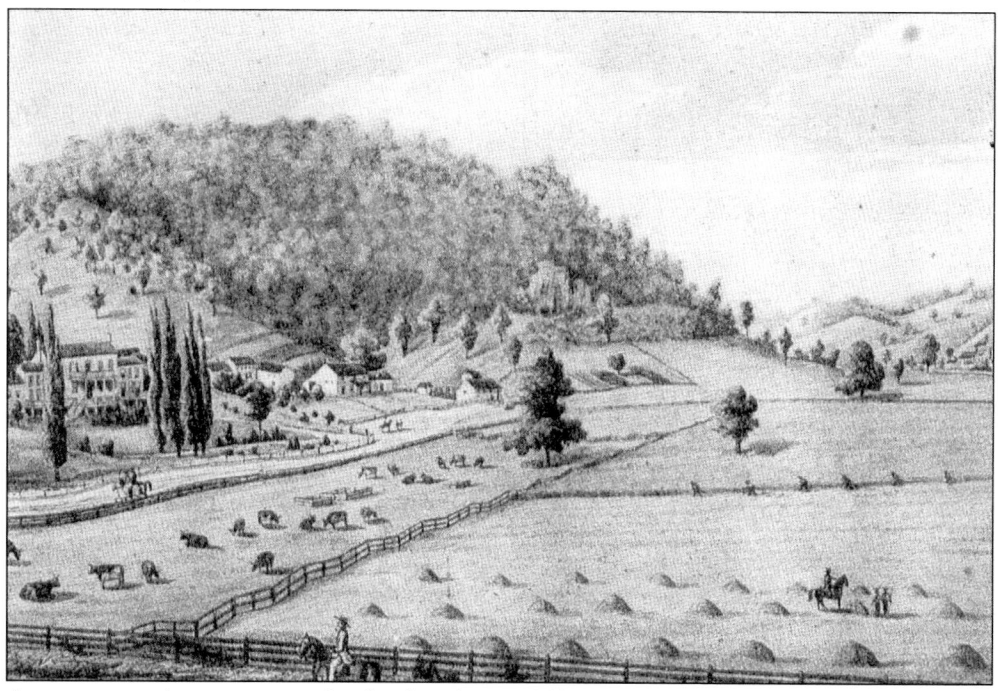

ANTEBELLUM AGRICULTURE. In this bucolic c. 1860 scene, one can see the Francis Preston mansion to the left. The pasture and meadows are now the Saltville Municipal Golf Course.

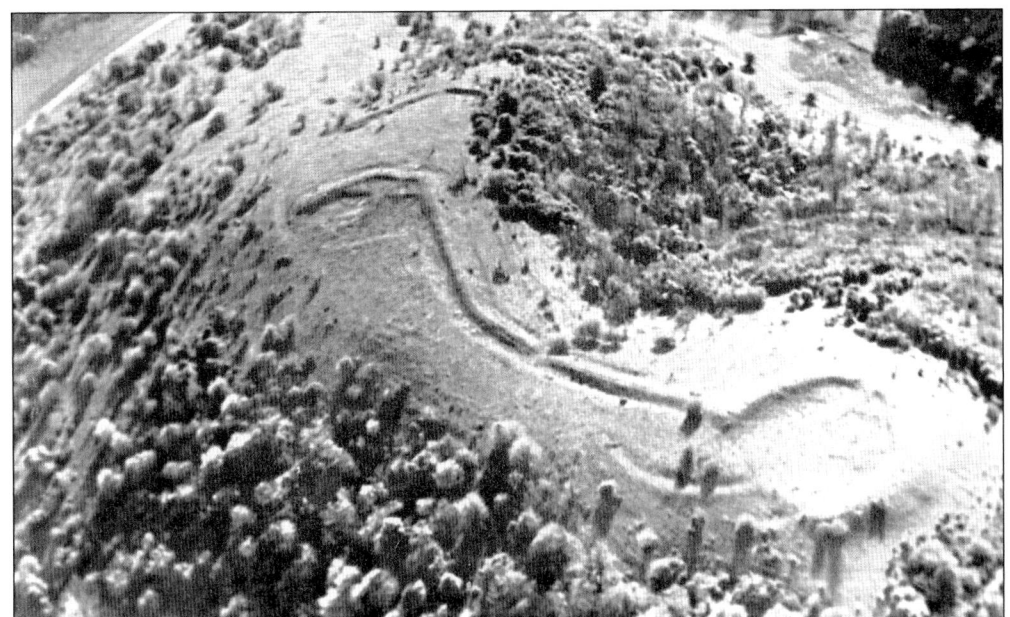

FORT HATTON. During the Civil War, Saltville was heavily fortified. Trenches and gun emplacements were built all over the valley, and nearly every hill had a lunette or artillery-piece earthwork. Many of these fortifications still exist. This is an aerial view of Fort Hatton, located on the western end of town, and it is perhaps the most visually striking of the surviving fortifications. This was the site of some artillery action during General Stoneman's December 1864 raid.

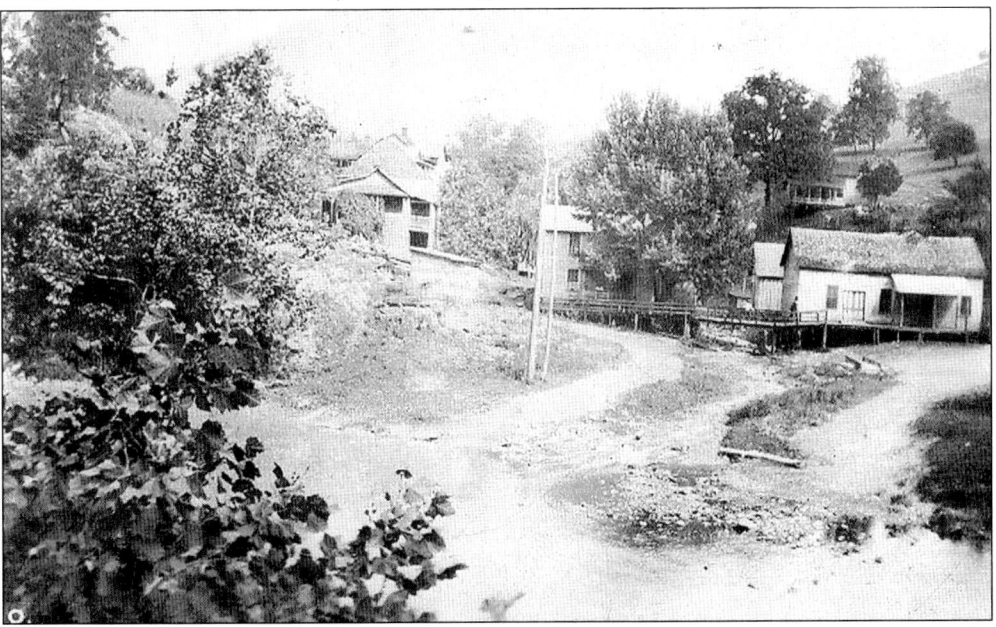

CEDAR BRANCH. This image was made near the beginning of the 20th century and shows Cedar Branch, the site of the heaviest fighting during the October 2, 1864, battle. It is near this site that one of the worst massacres of the war took place, when at least 40 African American soldiers in the U.S. Army who had been wounded were killed after the battle. The *Lynchburg Virginian* newspaper reported the massacre total at over 150, which may have been exaggerated..

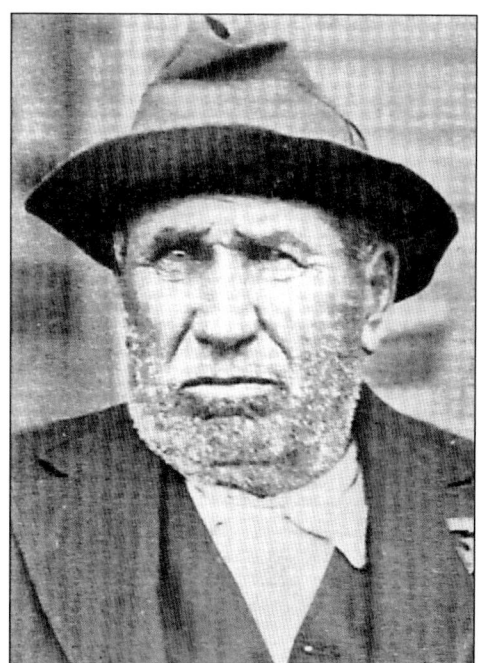 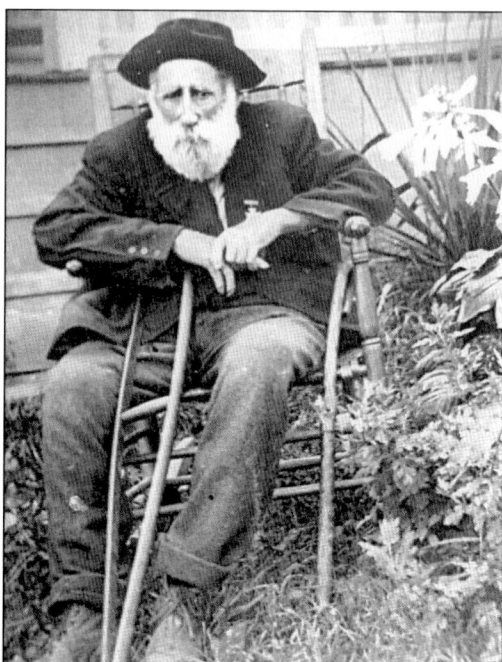

(LEFT) JOSEPH CALVIN LEE. Lee was one of Saltville's last surviving Confederate veterans. He was stationed at Saltville during the Civil War and liked it so much that he stayed. This 1922 photograph appeared in the *Alkalite*, which noted that he had a phenomenal memory. (Courtesy of Roger Allison.)

(RIGHT) UNKNOWN CIVIL WAR VETERAN. It is uncertain whether this man's crutches were a result of the Civil War, an accident, or the infirmities of age. Nevertheless all three problems were common among men of that era.

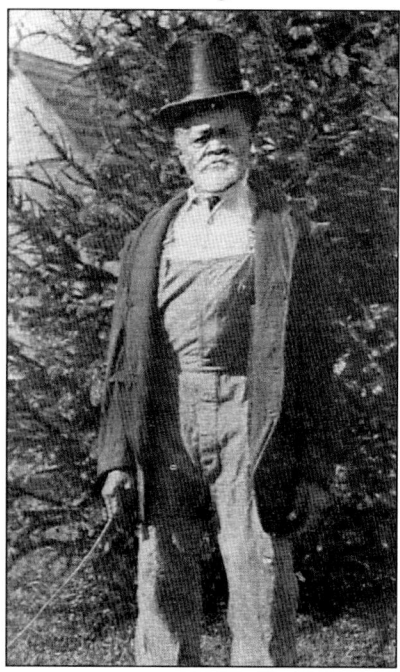

"UNCLE HENRY." Uncle Henry was a former slave who made Saltville his home. This 1922 image is from the *Alkalite*. (Courtesy of the Saltville Public Library.)

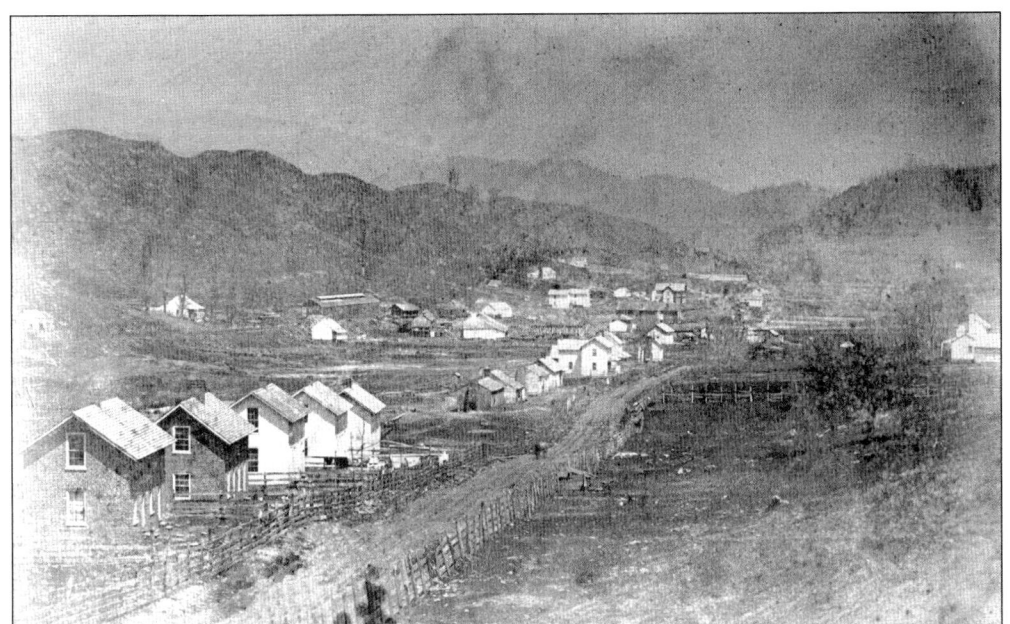

SMOKEY ROW. This 1872 photograph shows the residential section of Saltville just after the close of the Civil War. This section is known as Smokey Row, so named because of the smoke from the furnaces and the trains that drifted into this neighborhood. The road, now West Main Street, was then known as the Saltville-Abingdon Turnpike. This section was macadamized about 1885.

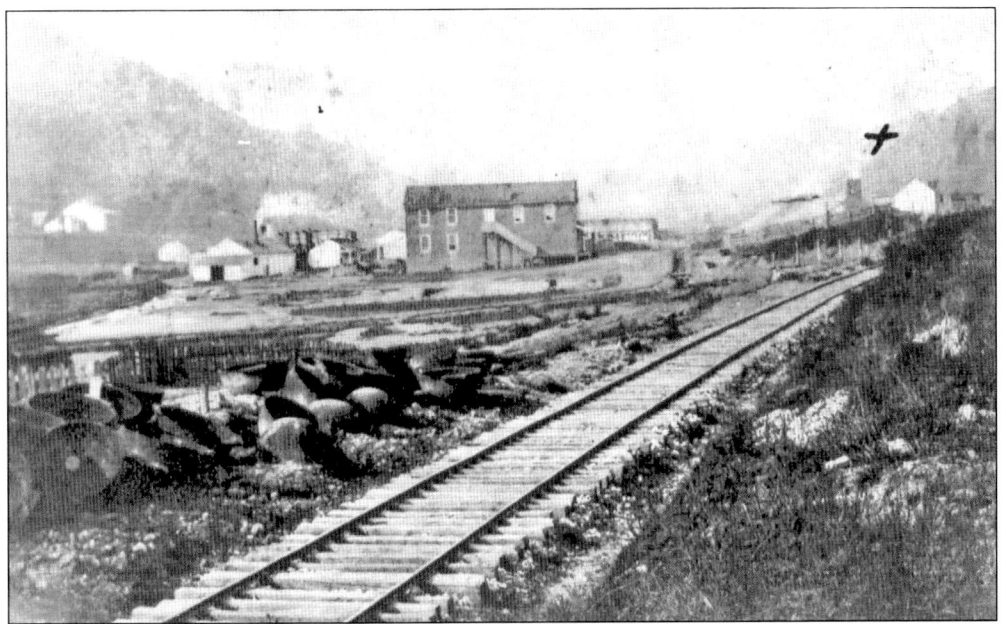

PALMER STORE. Between the 1850s and 1892, George W. Palmer was lord of the Saltville manor. Palmer controlled the saltworks, a store, mill, inn, and many other activities in the valley. The structure in the center of this photograph is the Palmer Store, a mercantile business established in the 1850s. The objects to the left of the railroad are salt kettles, and the "X" denotes one of the salt furnaces in the background.

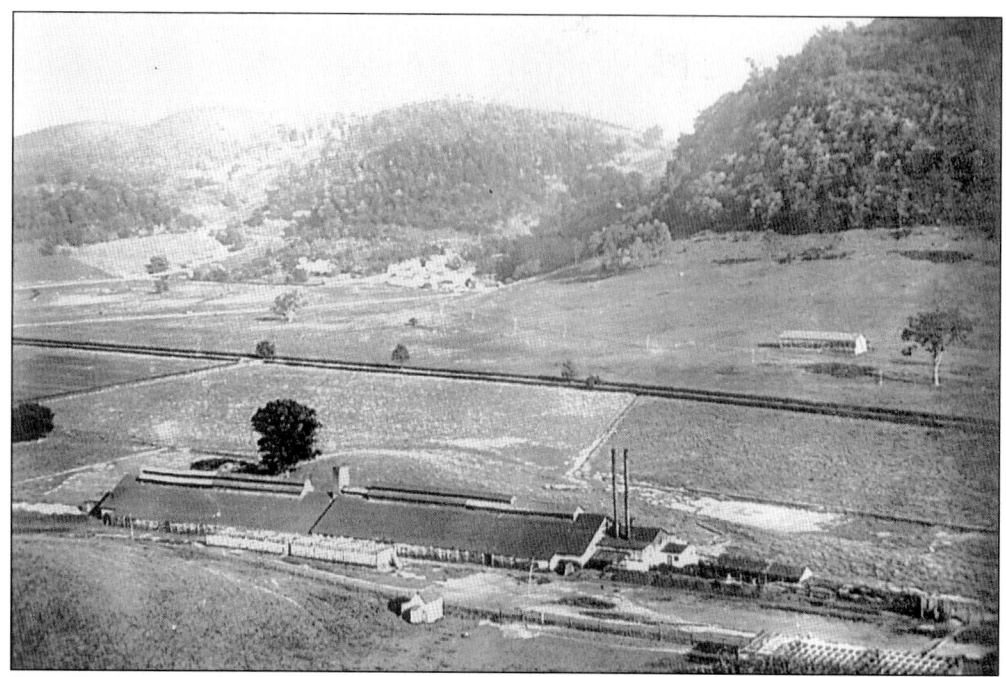

SALT FURNACES. This c. 1892 photograph shows the Alabama Furnace, one of the facilities that had survived from the Civil War. The line shown in the center of the photograph was the macadamized road. It was formerly a toll road between Saltville and Abingdon. Passage rates on the road had been 25¢ for a team and wagon, and droves of cattle were charged 1¢ per head in 1808. Other traffic fell somewhere in between.

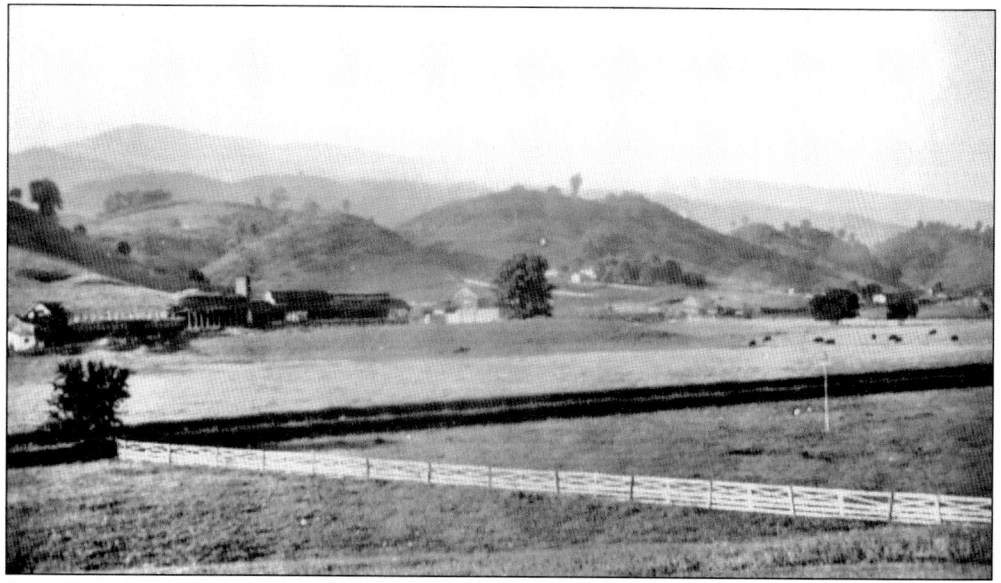

SALT FURNACES. This is another view of the Alabama furnace. Mathieson had acquired the property and was beginning to dismantle it when this photograph was taken in 1892. Note the cattle to the right and Clinch Mountain in the background. Again the turnpike is shown in the center of the photograph. A portion of this road remains as the Old Saltworks Road, which runs between Saltville and Abingdon.

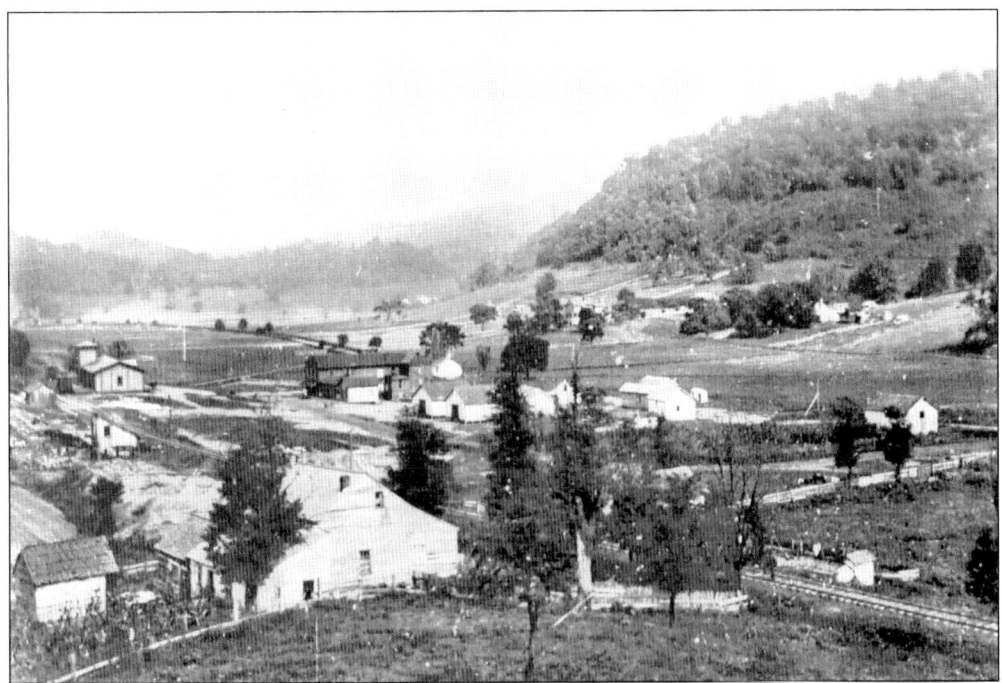

THE OLD TOWN. This 1890 photograph shows the center of Old Saltville. The Palmer Store is shown in the center. The white buildings right of the store were probably livery stable facilities. The Saltville Railroad Depot is shown at center left.

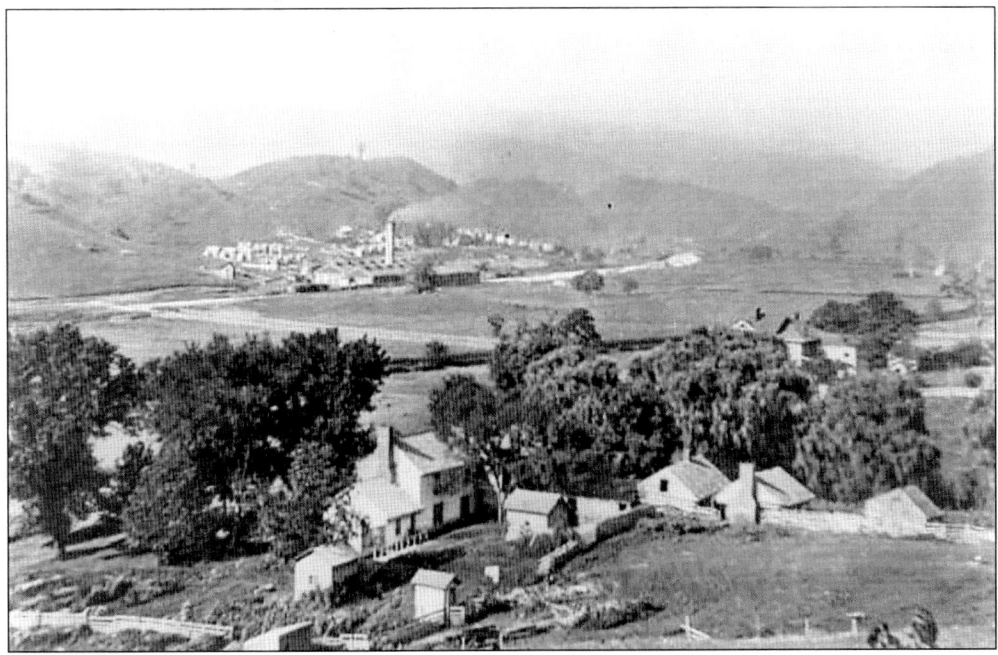

SLAVE QUARTERS. Slavery was an unfortunate fact of history, and the operators of the saltworks used the services of many. This is a photograph of the back of the William A. Stuart house that shows slave cabins to the right of the main house. The Mathieson salt plant is in the center of the background, which dates this photograph to c. 1895.

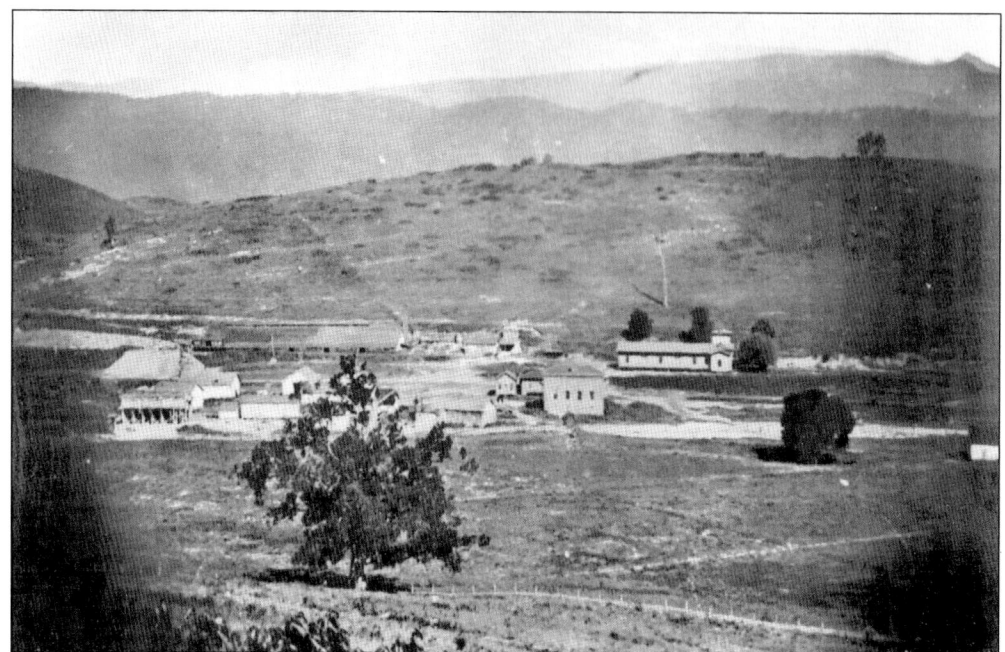

CENTER OF OLD SALTVILLE. This is another c. 1890 view of the center of Old Saltville, showing the back of the Palmer Store in the center and the old depot slightly to the right. The Tennessee Furnace is shown slightly left of center in this photograph. Clinch Mountain can be seen in the distance.

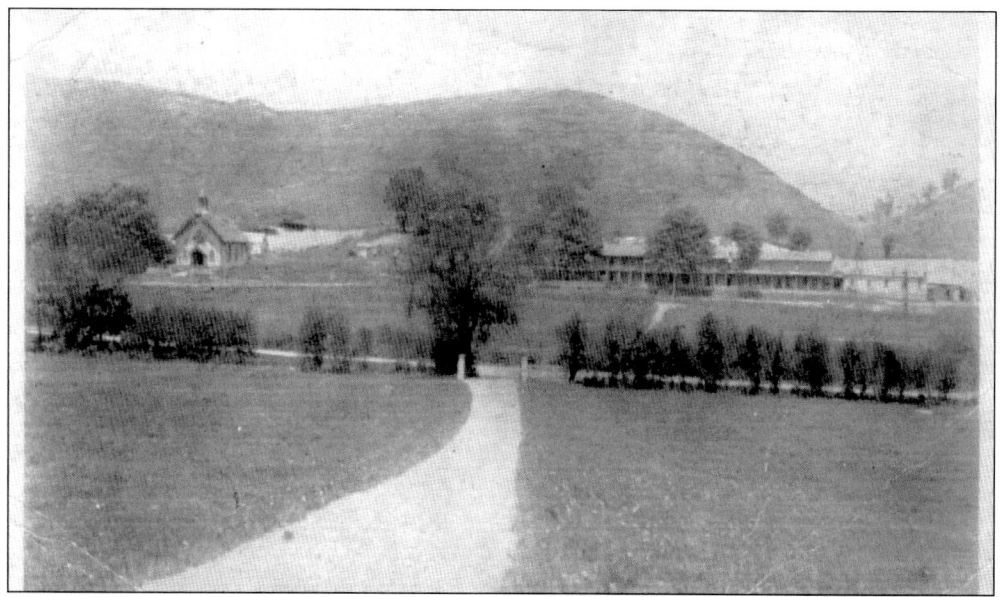

UNION CHURCH AND PALMER INN. This visual record shows the Union Church, built in 1873, to the left and the Palmer Inn, built in 1871, on the right. The Union Church served the Baptist, Episcopal, Methodist, and Presbyterian congregations for about 20 years. In the 1890s, the Episcopal and Methodist congregations built separate structures. When the Union Church burned in 1977, it was still used by the Presbyterians. The Palmer Inn was demolished about the same time. (Courtesy of Roger Allison.)

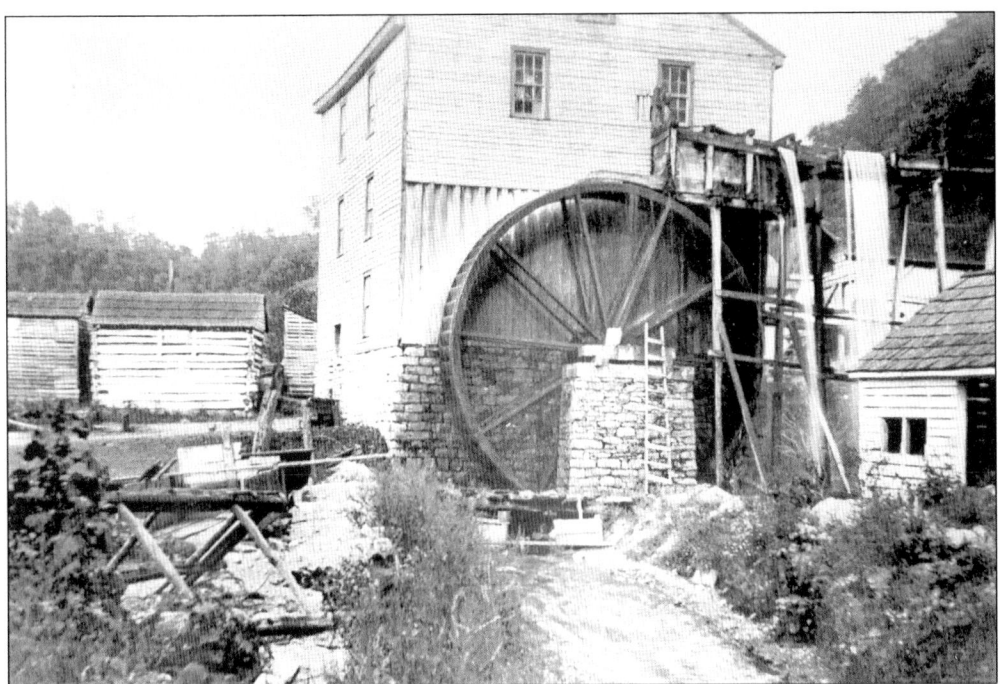

PALMER MILL. The Palmer Mill, located on the western side of town, was an early landmark. It was where the local population had their grain ground. The mill was another of the many businesses operated by George W. Palmer. This c. 1890 photograph shows all of the principal features of the beautiful old mill.

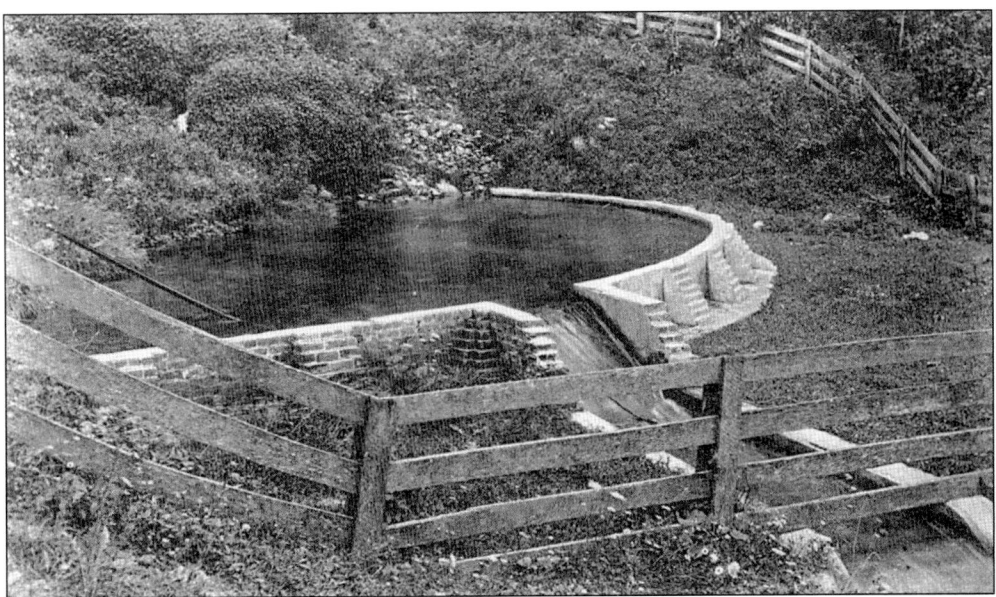

PALMER SPRINGS. Palmer Springs is located on the hill behind Palmer Mill. This containment was the source of water to turn the mill wheel. This site became a popular site for picnics in the early 20th century. Currently it is popular with the teenagers in town. (Courtesy of Roger Allison.)

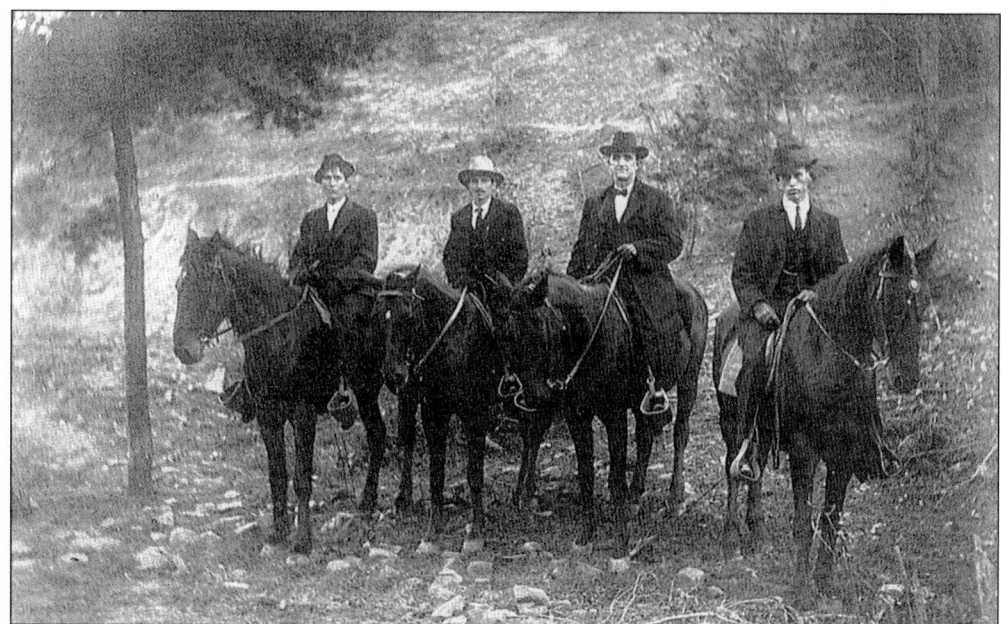

STUART LAND AND CATTLE COMPANY. Another staple of the late-19th-century Saltville economy was cattle. This 1890s photograph shows employees of the Stuart Land and Cattle Company, the largest of several cattle exporting companies in Smyth County and surrounding counties at that time. Cattle were fattened here in the summer and shipped by rail to northeastern markets.

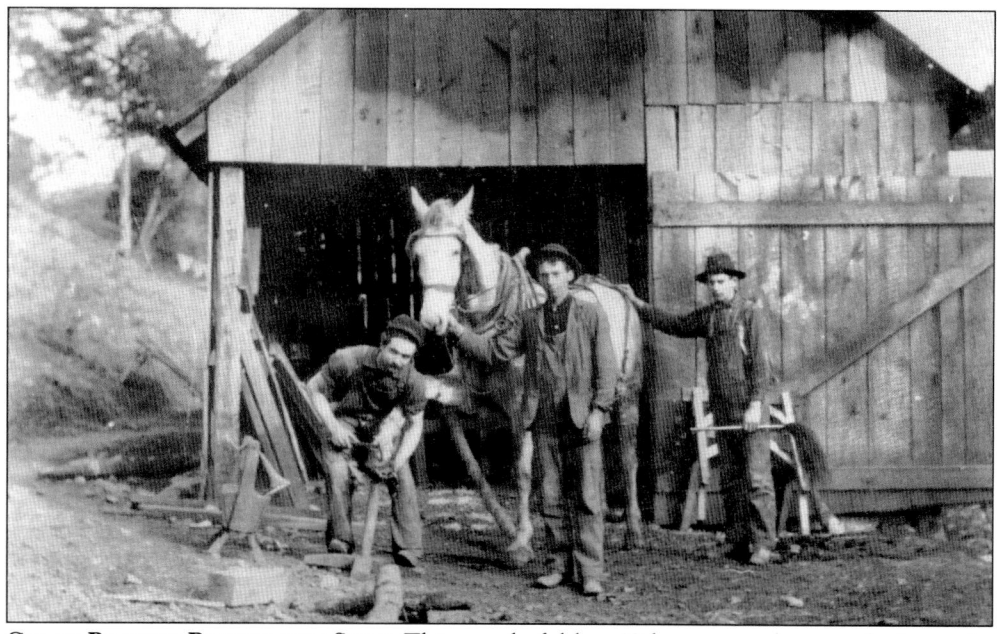

CEDAR BRANCH BLACKSMITH SHOP. This wonderful late-19th-century photograph shows the shoeing of a horse. Rural communities in the South depended on blacksmiths to create things they could not afford to buy in an economy ruined by the Civil War. At the blacksmith shop, one could have his horse shod, his plow repaired, or have any of a number of metal objects fashioned for use at home and on the farm.

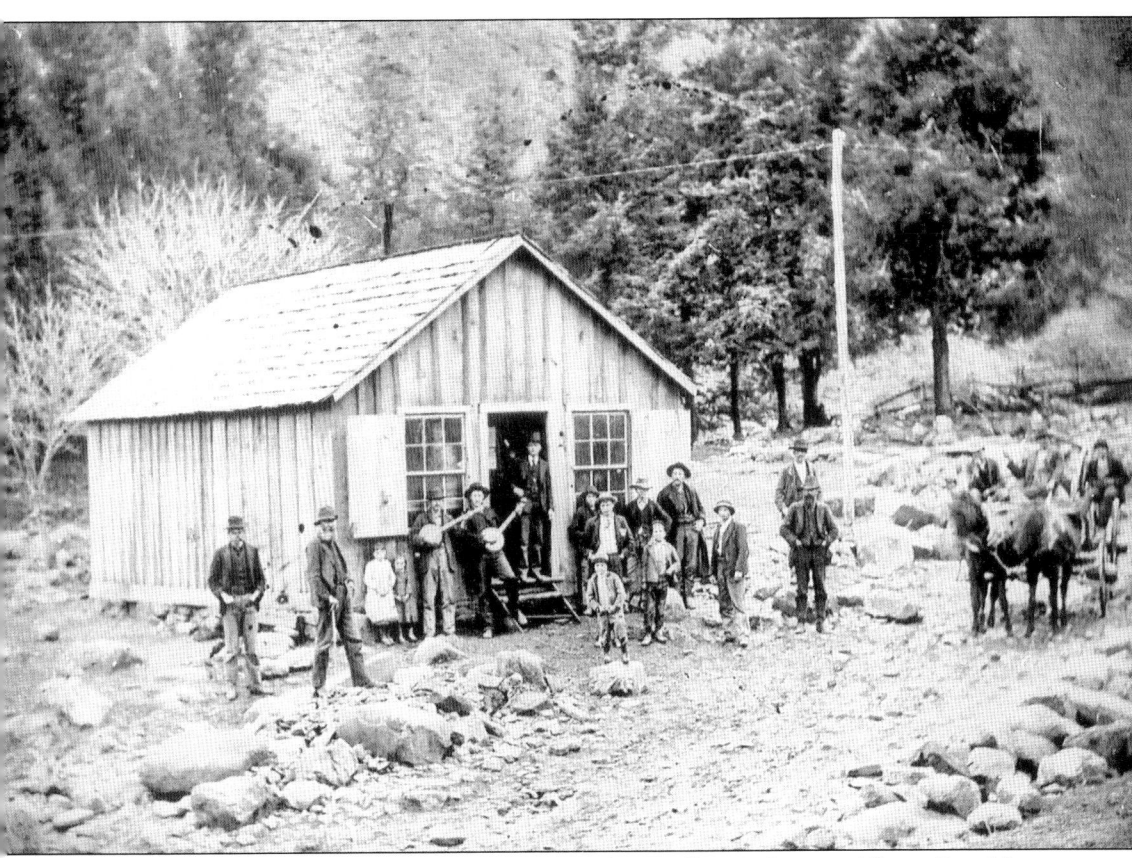

BEN ALLISON'S STORE. This view, made in 1896, is of Ben Allison's Store at Allison Gap. Note the fellows holding banjos to the left of the door. The pole to the right holds the line for the private phone line to the Stuart Land and Cattle Company in Russell County. Ben Allison is standing in the door, and John Allison, a Confederate veteran, is second from the left.

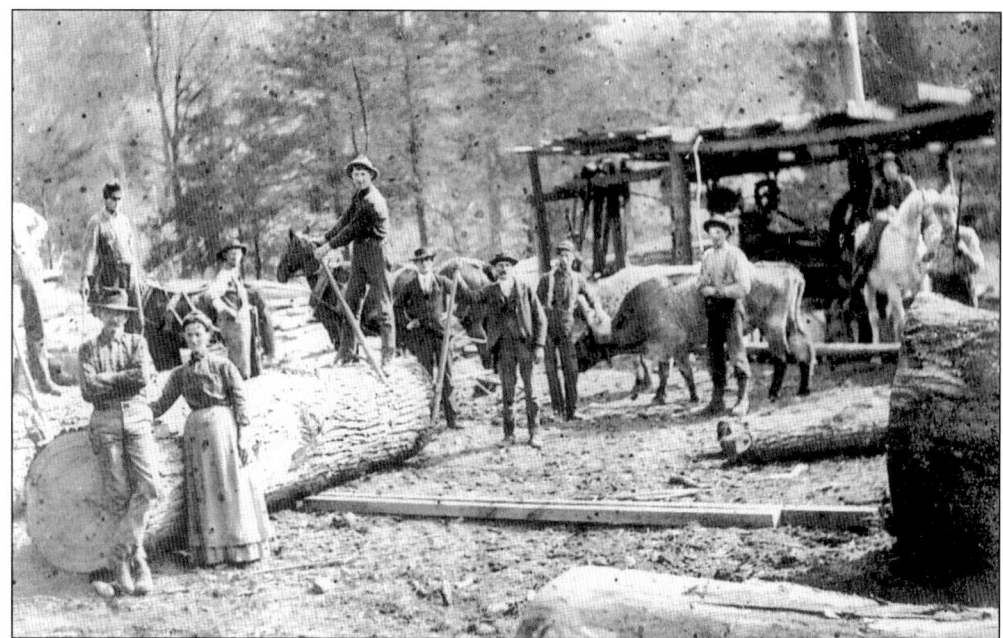

SAWMILL. Although salt making was the dominant industry in the valley, it was not the only one. This is a fairly typical sawmill operation. The mountains around Saltville held vast stands of virgin timber until the coming of the railroad. Lumbering became a significant source of income in the 1880s and 1890s. This sawmill was located in the center of Saltville. The man standing on the right with an eye patch is Goodson Campbell.

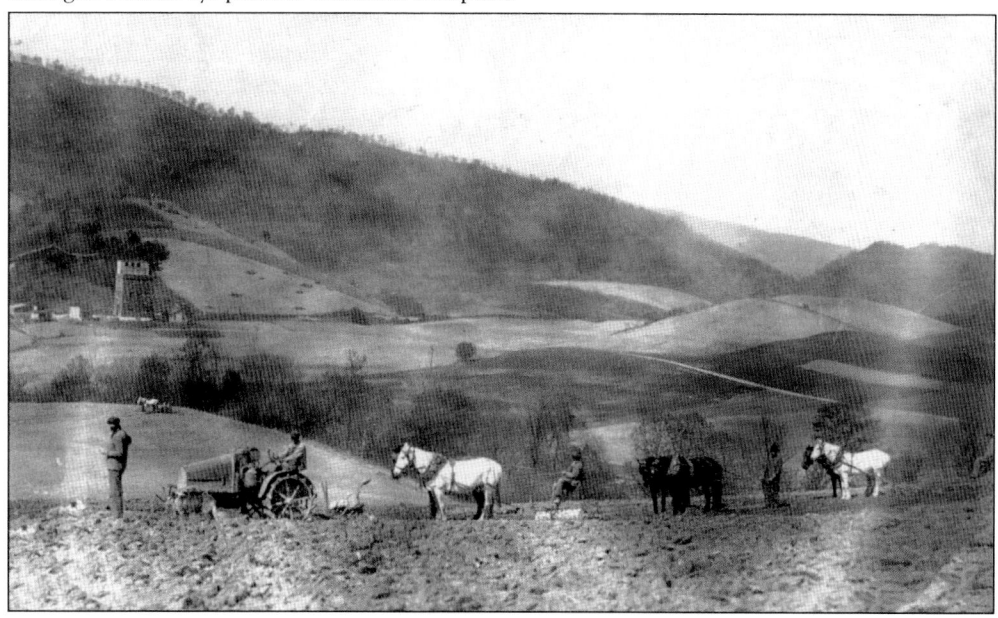

FARM SCENE. This c. 1920 photograph shows a transitional farm scene. The workers are using a mix of draught horses and a tractor to plow fields near Cedar Branch on the east end of town. Note the power station in the left background of the image. Farming was usually a family affair, and in this case, the family canines are ready to assist. This farmland is now part of an expanded Elizabeth Cemetery.

Three
MATHIESON ALKALI WORKS

George Palmer sold the property of the Holston Salt and Plaster Company in 1892, and the title to most of the property in the Saltville Valley was acquired by a group of Northern investors the next year. These men had incorporated as Mathieson Alkali Works in August 1892 in New York. Investigations of the Saltville property and possibilities for a chemical industry had been made in 1890.

Mathieson Alkali Works, as the company was officially known, merged with Olin Corporation in 1954. During its heyday, "the Plant," as it was commonly called, produced a variety of household, industrial, and military products, such as baking soda, caustic soda, and even hydrazine, used to fuel some of the first NASA spacecraft, including America's first manned craft sent to the moon. Olin ceased its Saltville operations in 1971.

In 1894, Saltville was granted a municipal charter, and George W. Palmer was chosen the first mayor. For reasons not entirely clear, the 1894 charter was replaced by a second on February 7, 1896. Even with this municipal government in place, the most powerful man in town remained the plant manager. Mathieson's largesse sustained the municipal government and provided most of the amenities enjoyed by the town and its citizens.

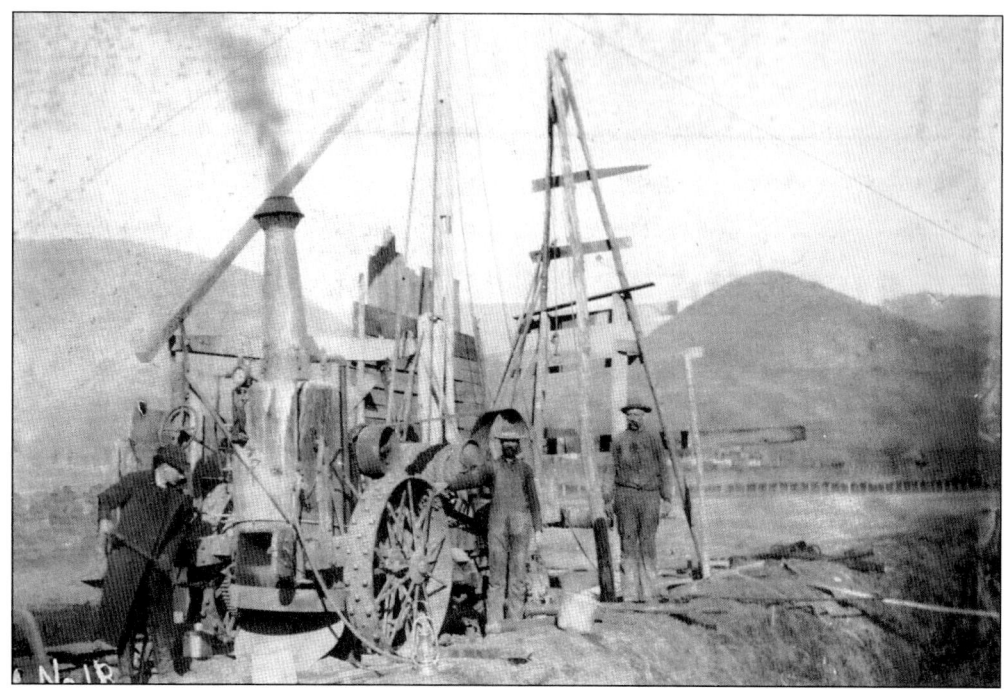

DIGGING A SALT WELL. This photograph shows a horse-drawn steam drill in full operation. This equipment was used to drill wells into the salt deposits under town soon after Mathieson came to Saltville. This image is from the mid-1890s.

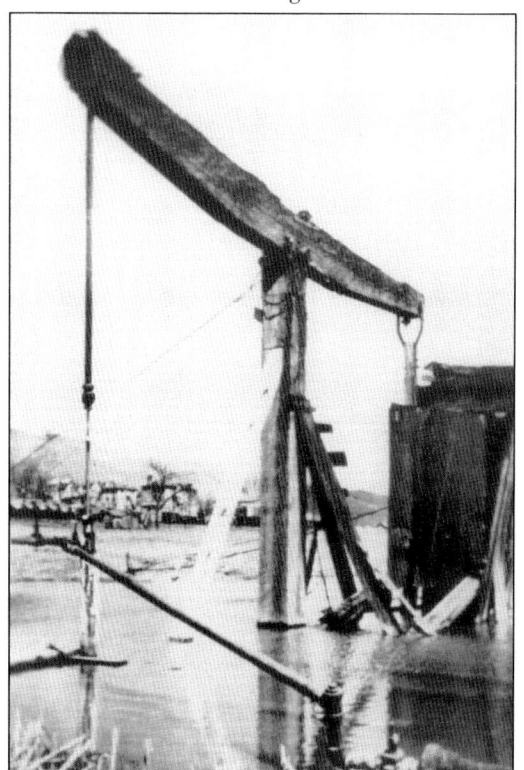

WALKING BEAM PUMP. This mid-1890s image shows a walking beam pump. This type of pump was used to bring brine to the surface, where it was further processed to extract the salt from the solution. A reproduction of this type of pump is on display at Saltville's Salt Park on West Main Street at the Smyth-Washington County line.

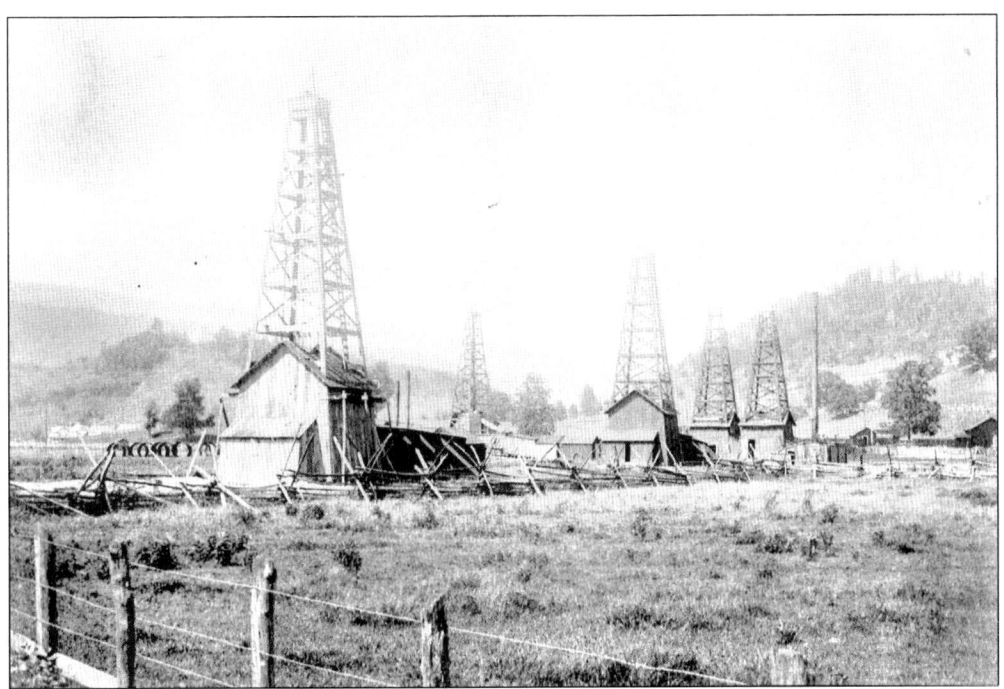

SALT WELLS. This image shows some of the salt wells drilled shortly after Mathieson Alkali Works acquired property in Saltville. This photograph was taken c. 1895.

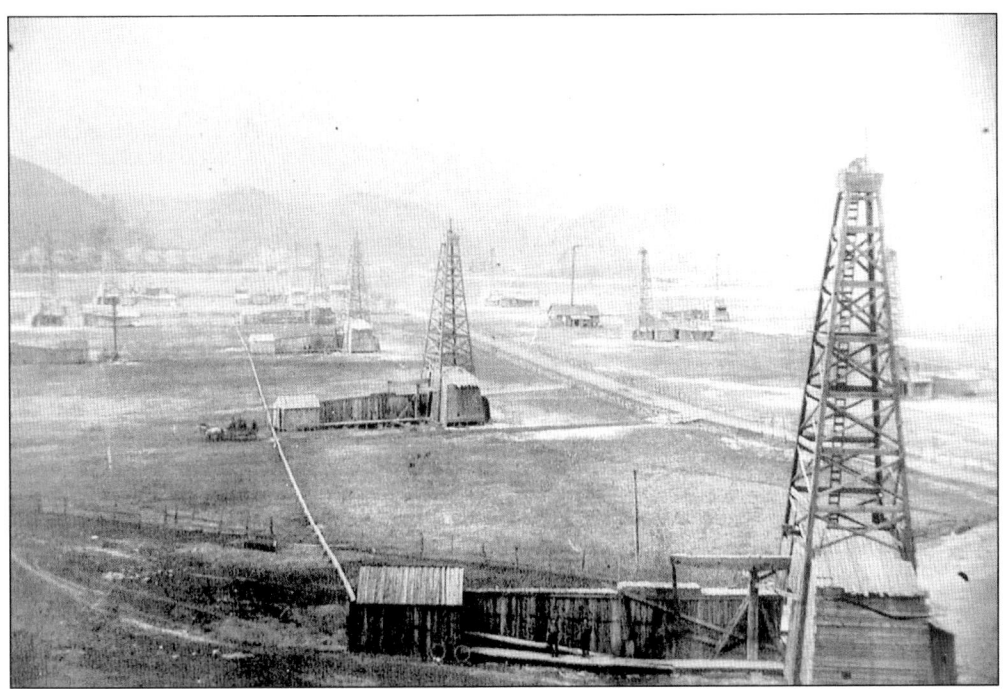

SALT WELLS. This is another view of the derricks over the salt wells, which dotted the western end of Saltville in the late 19th century.

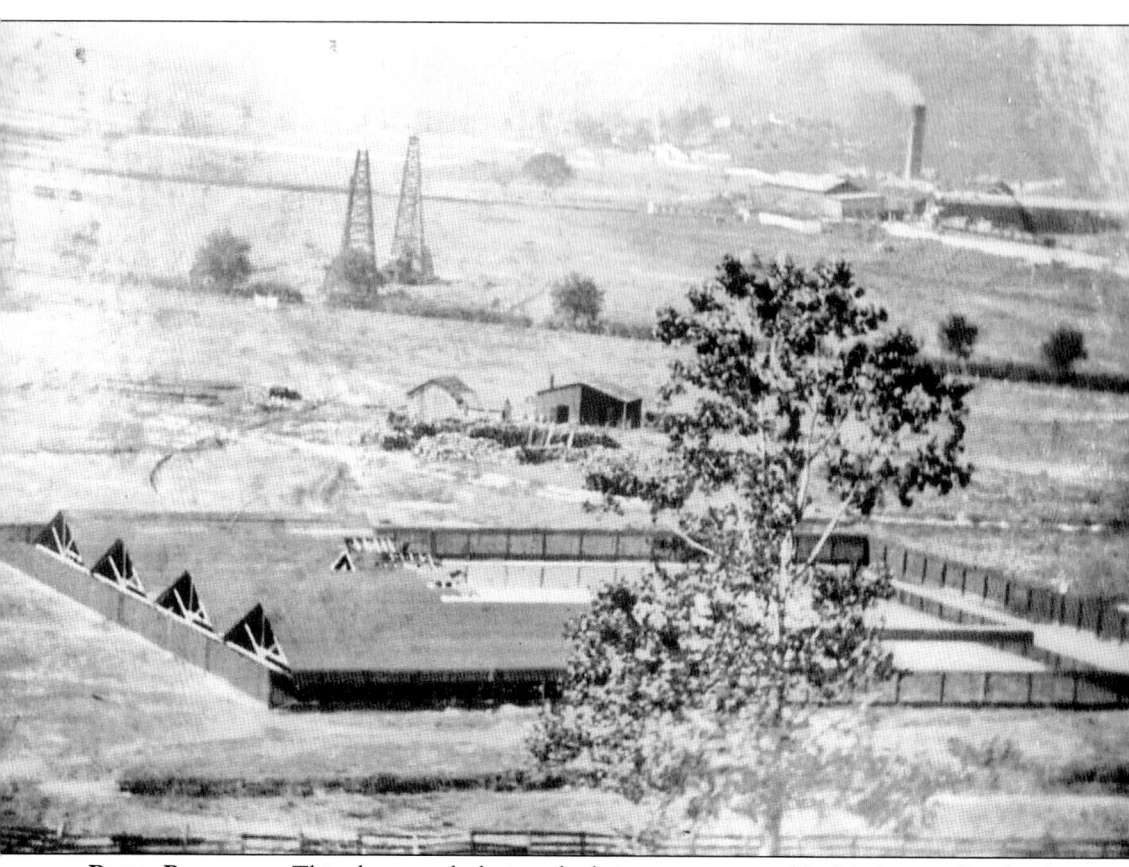

BRINE RESERVOIR. This photograph depicts the brine reservoir used by Mathieson shortly after they acquired the Saltville operation. Mathieson's first salt plant, which operated from 1892 until 1907, is shown in the background of this photograph.

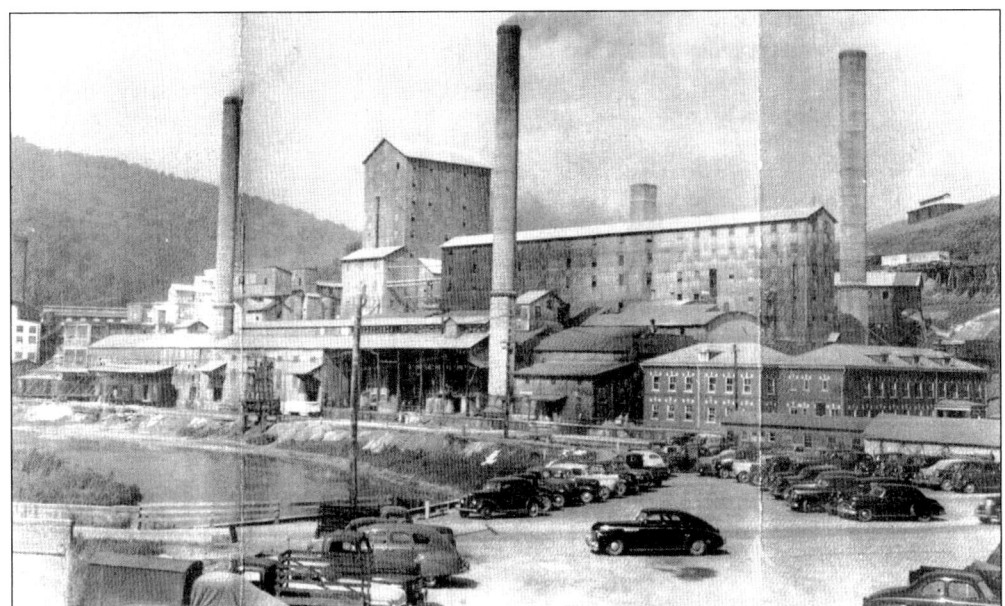

"THE PLANT." Mathieson Alkali Works was a massive facility built on the banks of the North Fork of Holston River in stages beginning about 1892. The first production run at this new facility was held on July 4, 1895. As new facilities were needed, old ones were demolished to make way for the new. This photograph was taken in the late 1940s and is the view most Saltvillians remember.

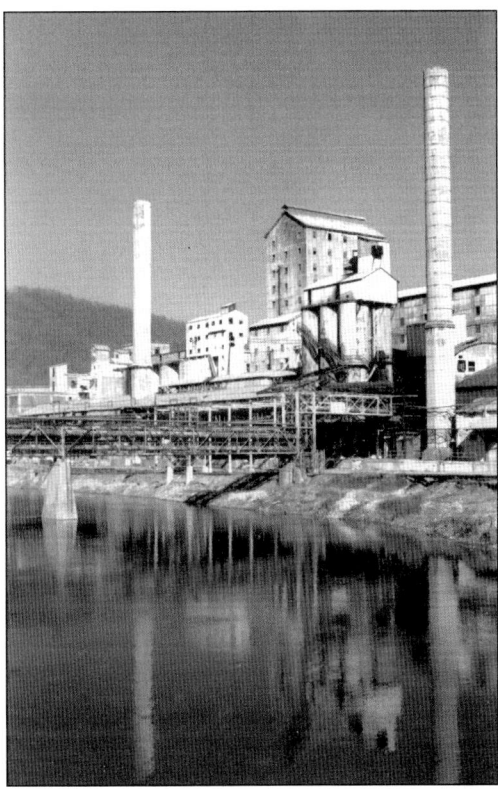

ANOTHER VIEW. This view of "the Plant" was taken in November 1972, after manufacturing had ceased. The tall building in the center of the picture was a 14-story facility called the distiller building or still house. It is believed to be the tallest completely wooden structure ever built in the world. The North Fork of Holston River is in the foreground. Effluent from the plant caused a great deal of mercury pollution in this stream. This plant was demolished shortly after this image was taken. (Courtesy of Roger Allison.)

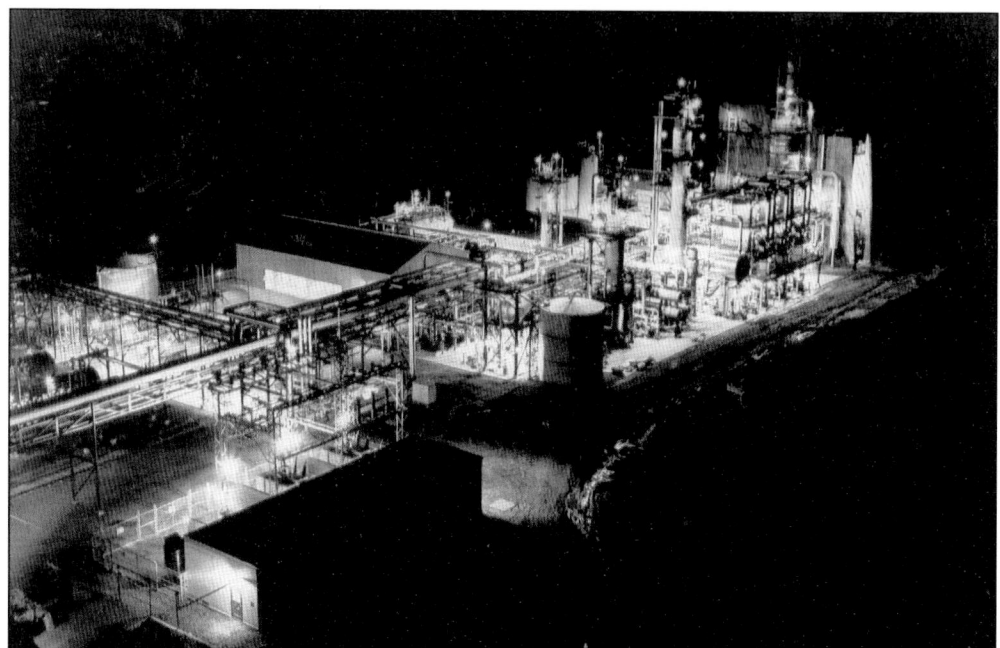

HYDRAZINE PLANT. Hydrazine, H_2N_4, was one of the first propellants for spacecraft. The federal government obtained its supply of this rocket fuel from this Saltville plant. This facility, pictured here at night, produced the fuel to propel the first men to the moon in 1969. (Courtesy of Roger Allison.)

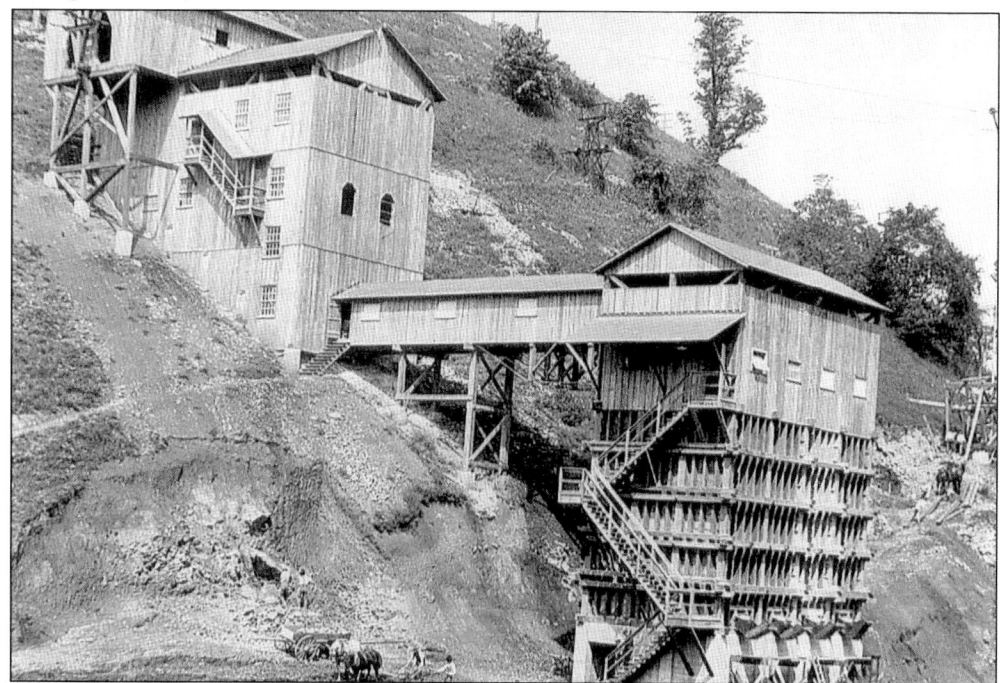

SCREENING PLANT. This facility, in use about 1905, was used to size crushed limestone for various projects. This material was received via the bucket line (aerial tramway) and was sent to the main processing plants the same way. This building burned in 1925.

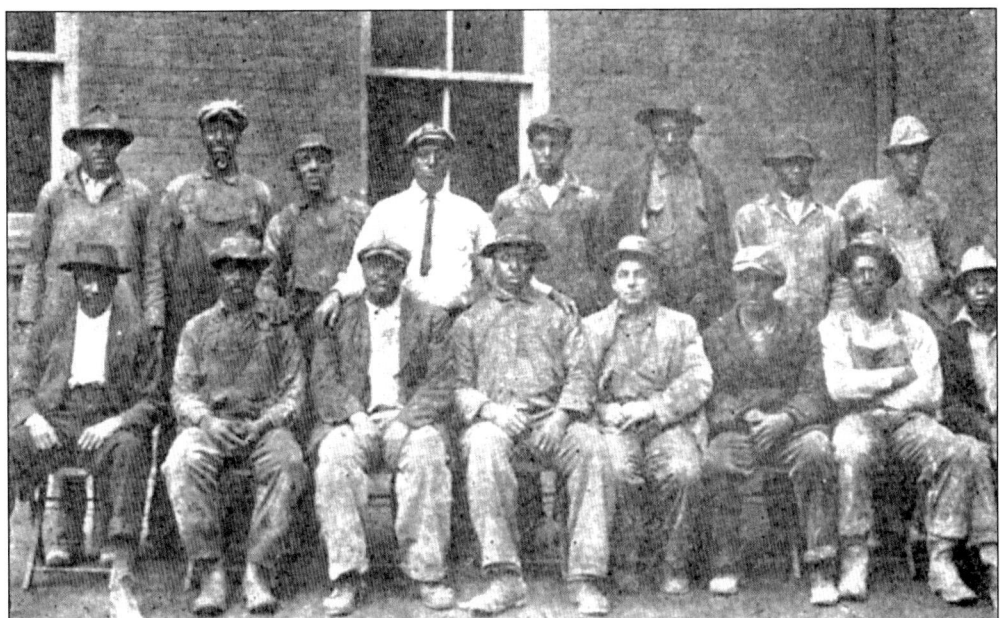

"OLD FAITHFULS." "Old Faithfuls" is the caption this image received in the 1922 *Alkalite*, the company's official publication. There are several groups of workers shown in this edition. From the caption, one might assume these fellows did a little bit of everything and helped out when and where needed. (Courtesy of the Saltville Public Library.)

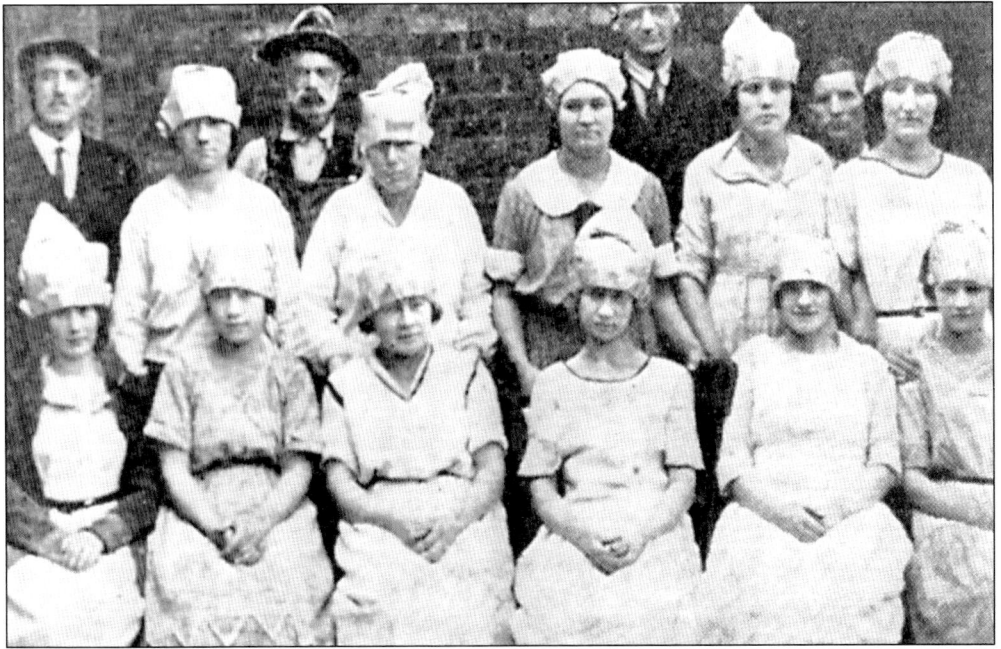

BAKING SODA GIRLS. This 1922 image is of the crew that packed Eagle-Thistle Brand Baking Soda for shipment. There were few women working in the plant in 1922. This was the largest concentration of female workers at Mathieson. The folk-memory tells that these girls wrote notes and packed them in the soda containers in hopes that single men would find their notes and contact them. (Courtesy of the Saltville Public Library.)

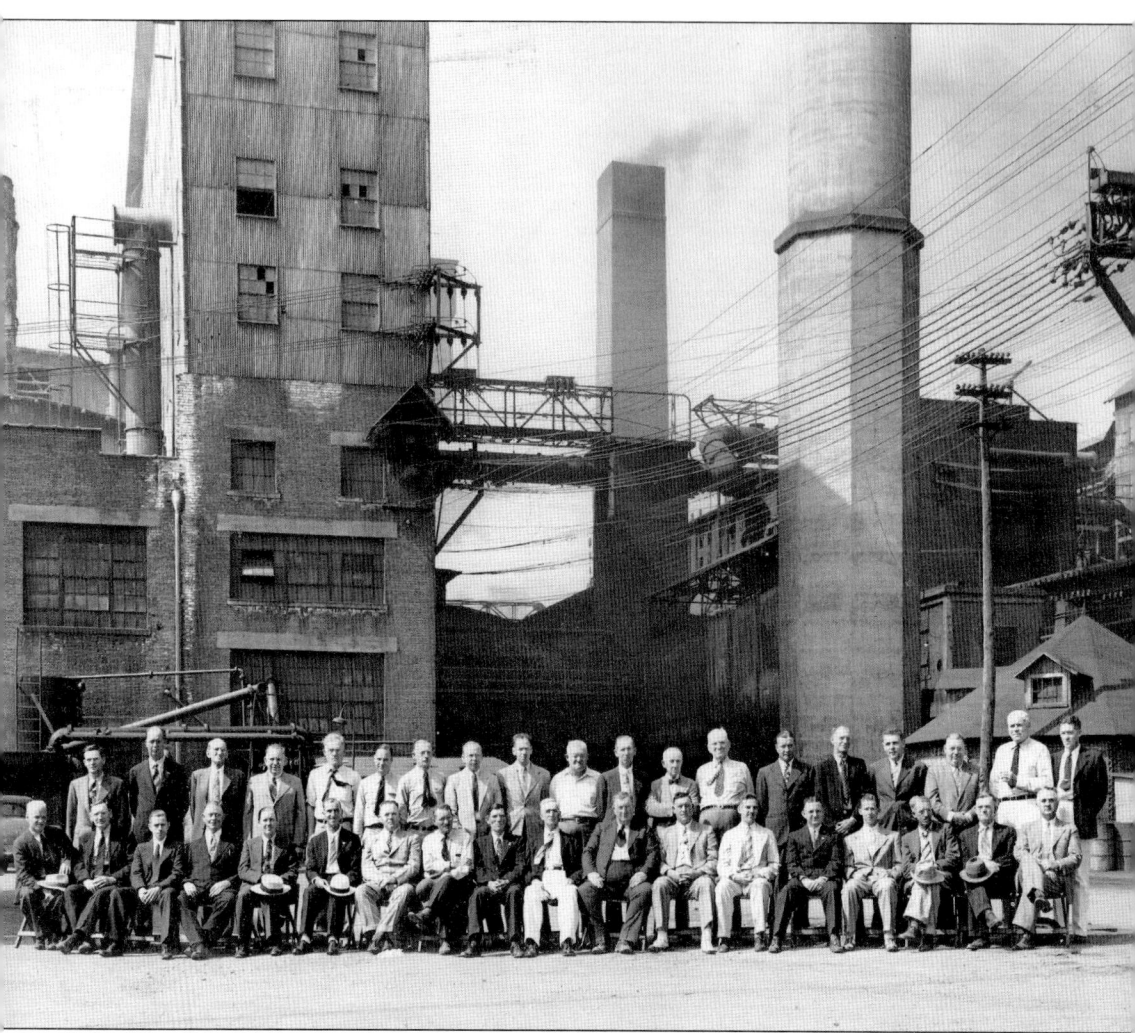

PLANT MANAGEMENT. This c. 1935 photograph shows the white-collar workers at Mathieson Alkali Works in the parking lot of the main plant. This facility produced soda ash or, formally, sodium carbonate. Soda ash is an essential ingredient for glass, detergents, other chemicals, and industrial materials. It is the 11th-most-used chemical used in manufacturing. (Courtesy of Roger Allison.)

REPAIRING A SMOKE STACK. This 1950s-era view shows Native American workers repairing one of the smoke stacks at Mathieson Alkali Works. Some of the facilities required specialized workers to keep them in good order. Some of these facilities were unique. Most of the training provided for the average worker was on the job.

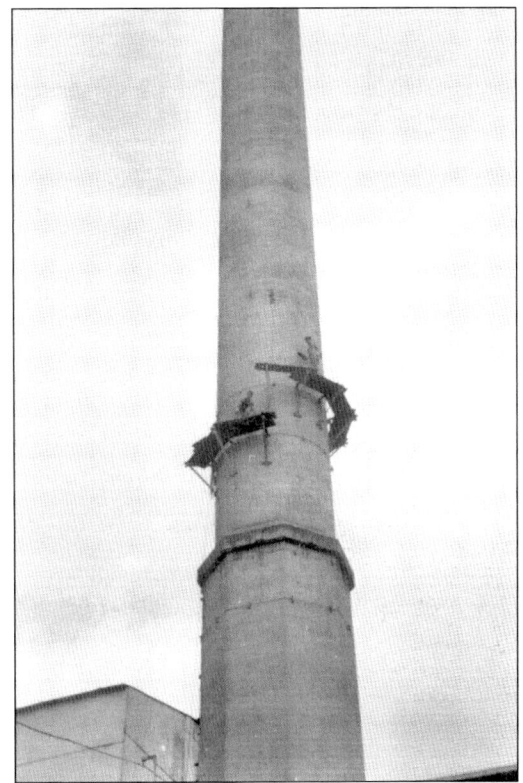

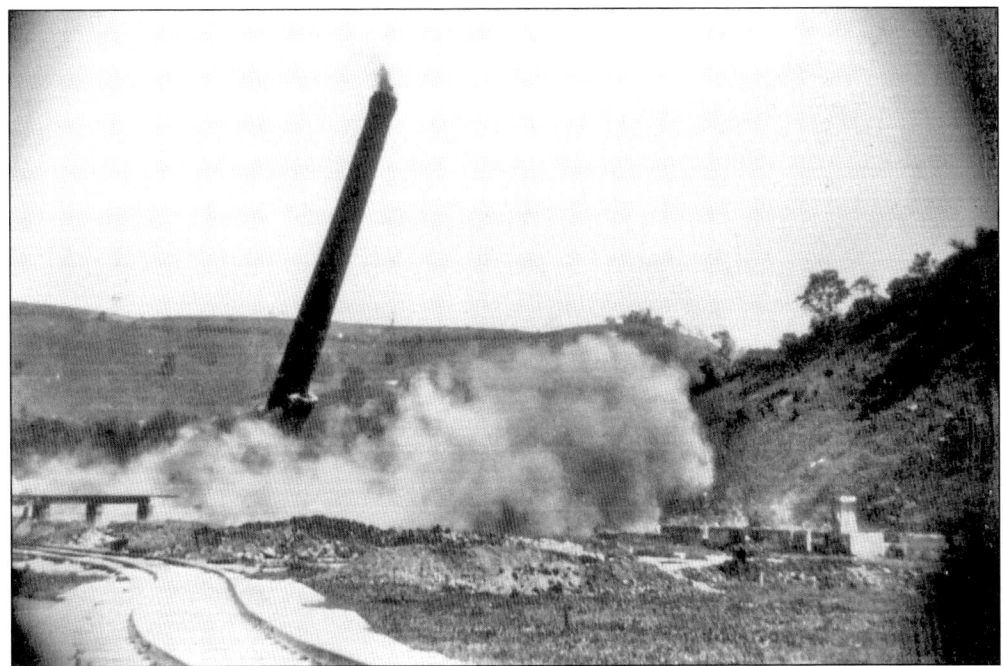

BLOWING UP A SMOKE STACK. This image shows the demolition of the ice plant in 1935. Facilities and buildings were constantly updated at Mathieson. Sometimes the processes were so obsolete that it was just cheaper to demolish something and start over.

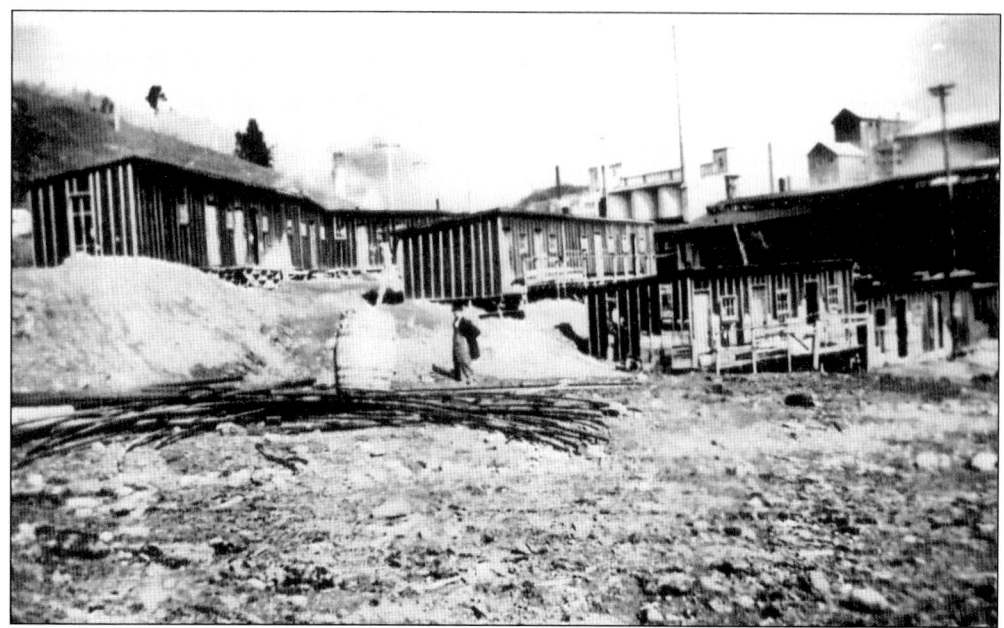

SHANTY TOWN. While not absolutely certain, this appears to be barracks built during the Depression for the single black men who worked for Mathieson Alkali Works. In those days, Jim Crow ruled the South and Virginia, and these men could not obtain lodging elsewhere. Mathieson's management was fair, but the housing was an unfortunate result of the segregation of the time. The appearance of the plant suggests a date of about 1930 for this photograph.

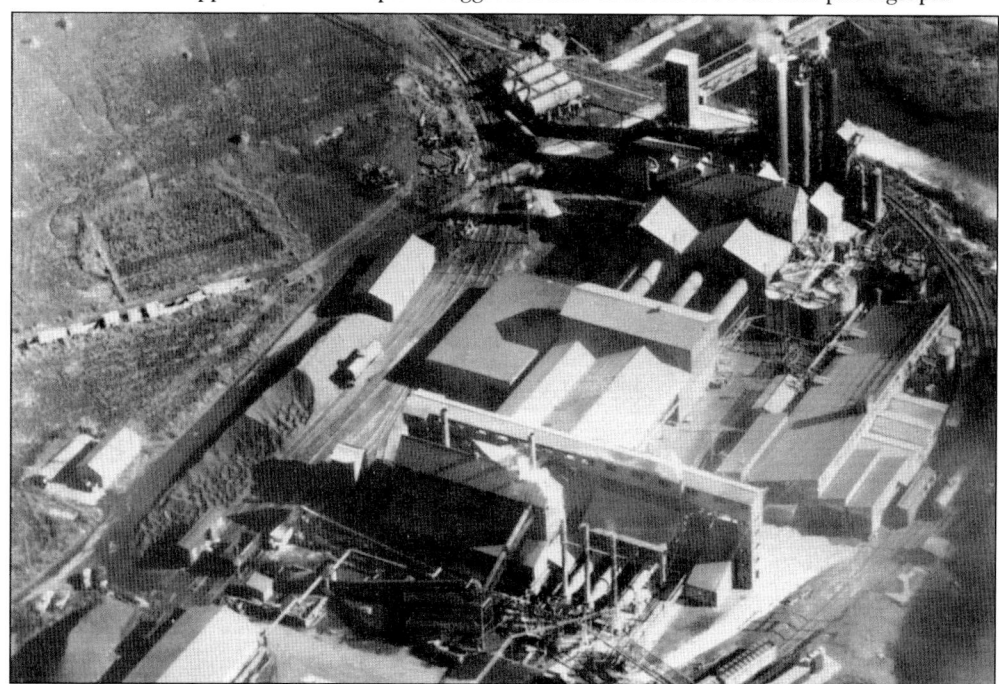

DRY ICE PLANT. One of the by-products of the chemical work done at Mathieson was a great deal of carbon dioxide. Mathieson produced dry ice in this facility, which was proclaimed to be "The World's Largest Facility" in this 1957 photograph. (Courtesy of Roger Allison.)

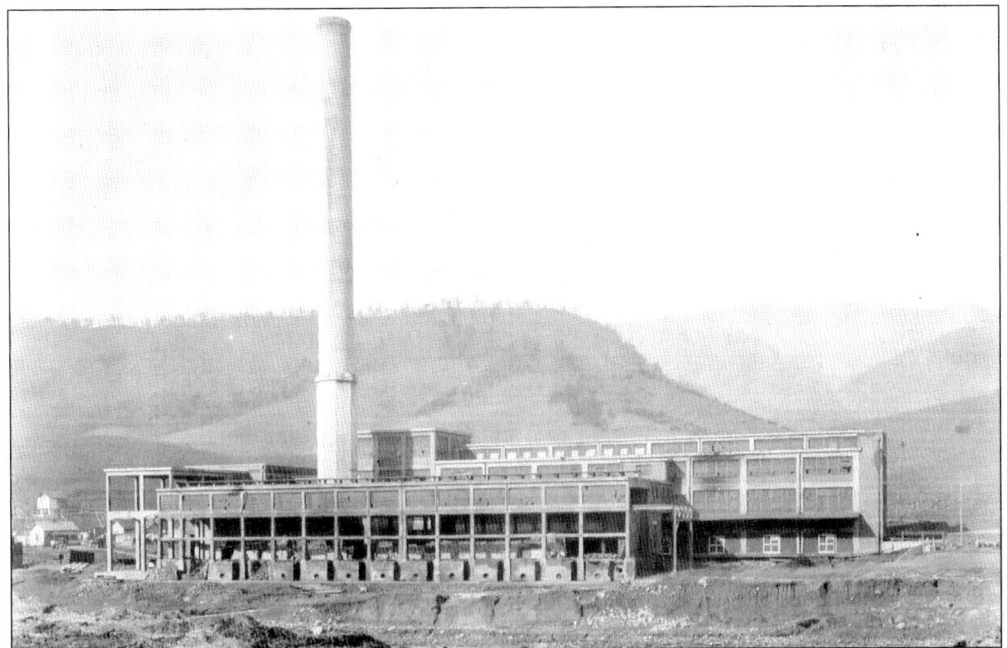

LABORATORY BUILDING. This building housed the chemists and engineers who developed new product lines for Mathieson. A chlorine facility was added to the laboratory. Mathieson conducted classes in the upper floor of this building to enable their employees to advance to more technically challenging jobs.

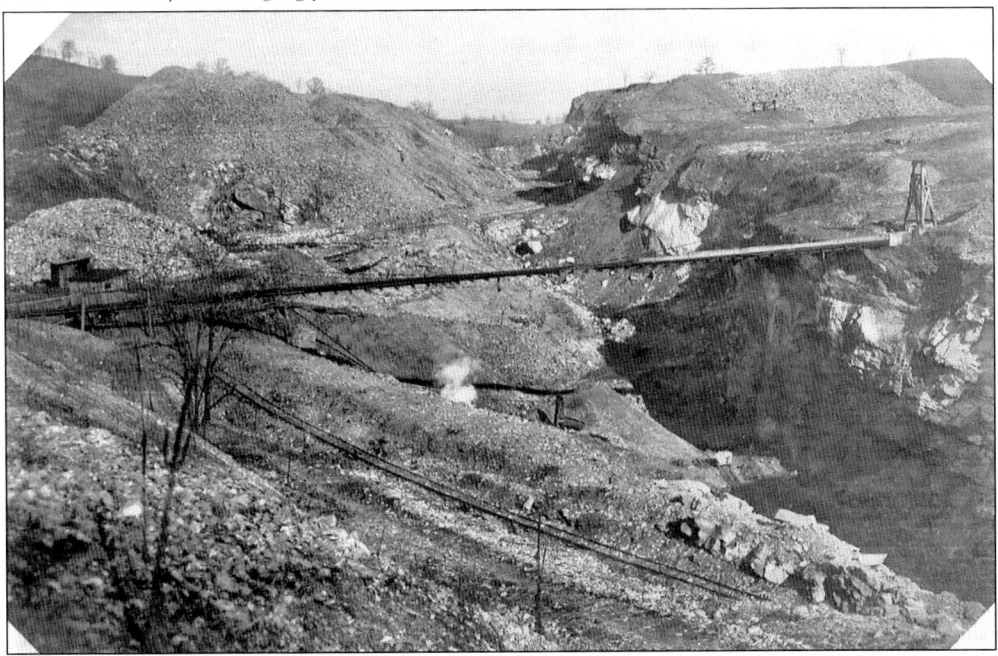

QUARRY. This image shows the "Lower Hole" of the quarry south of town. The line running through the center of the picture is a suspended culvert to carry water from the high side to the low side, so the pit would not fill in during operation. The white smoke in the center is from a steam shovel operating in the pit.

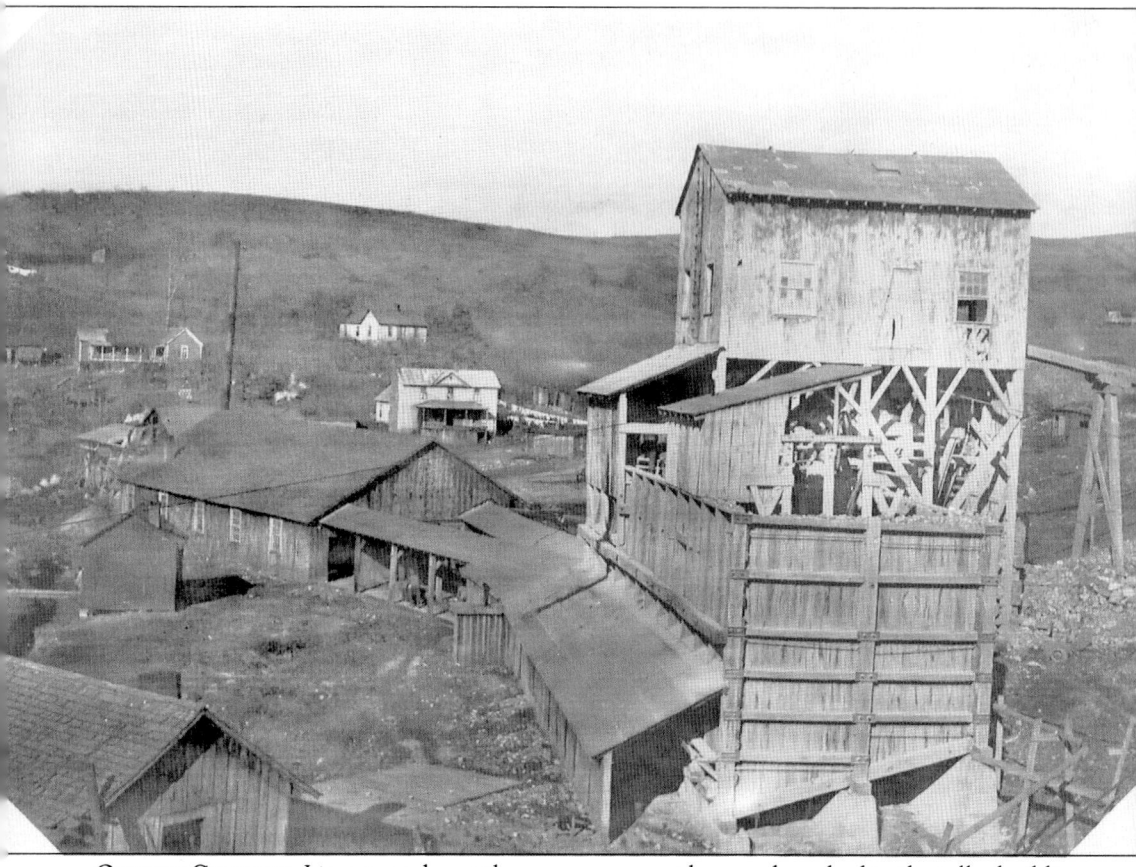

QUARRY CRUSHER. Limestone dug at the quarry was sent here and crushed in the taller building in the foreground. The lower building is where the crushed stone was loaded onto the aerial tramway (bucket line) for transport to the screening plant for further sizing.

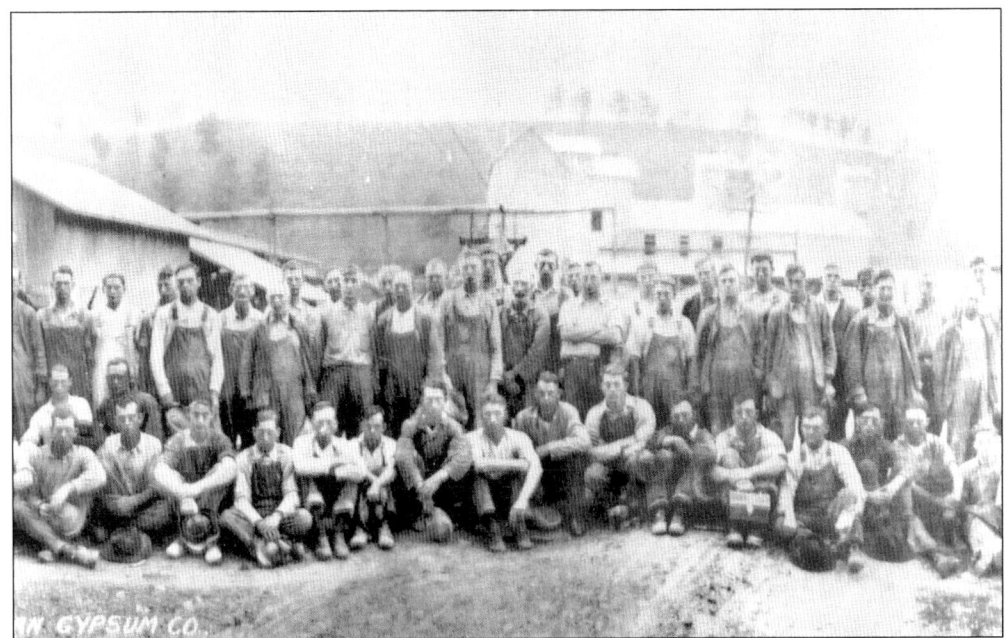

WORKERS AT NORTH HOLSTON. This 1930s-era photograph shows some of the employees of the Southern Gypsum Company at their North Holston facility, a few miles north of Saltville. Mathieson Alkali Works bought Southern Gypsum in 1933. The companies were managed separately and retained their respective names despite the acquisition.

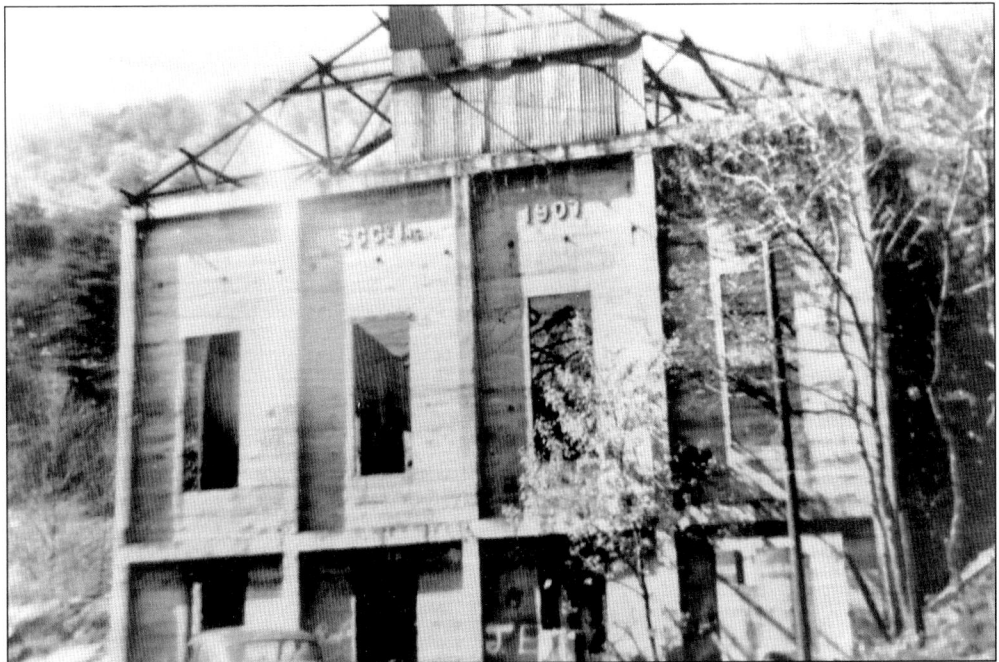

NORTH HOLSTON POWER HOUSE. This image taken in the 1950s shows the power station (built in 1907) at North Holston. This facility provided electricity to the Southern Gypsum operations at North Holston. This building appears to be in a state of disrepair when this photograph was made.

AERIAL TRAMWAY TOWER. Mathieson operated an aerial tramway to transport crushed limestone from outlying quarries to the main facilities in Saltville, Commonly called "the Bucket Line." This snow-covered tower was located at British Row in town. This tower was the tallest in the system, reaching 120 feet tall. This photograph was taken in 1962. (*Saltville Progress* photograph.)

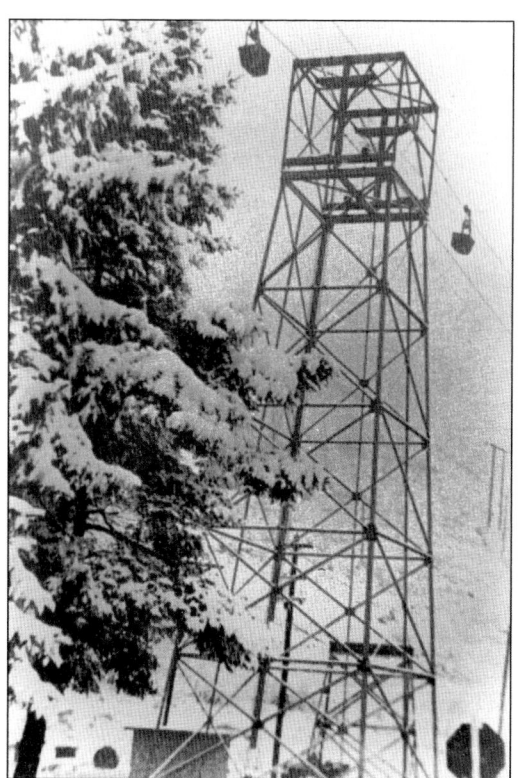

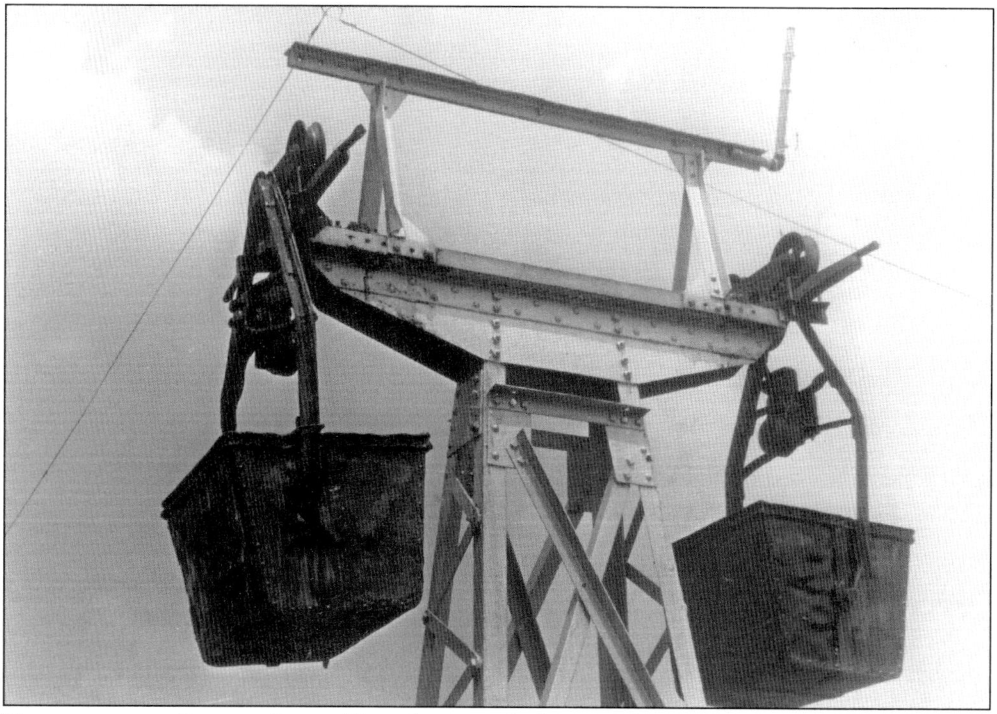

DETAIL OF THE BUCKET LINE. This photograph shows a close-up of the buckets and one of the towers. The equipment is on display in downtown Saltville. (Courtesy of Roger Allison.)

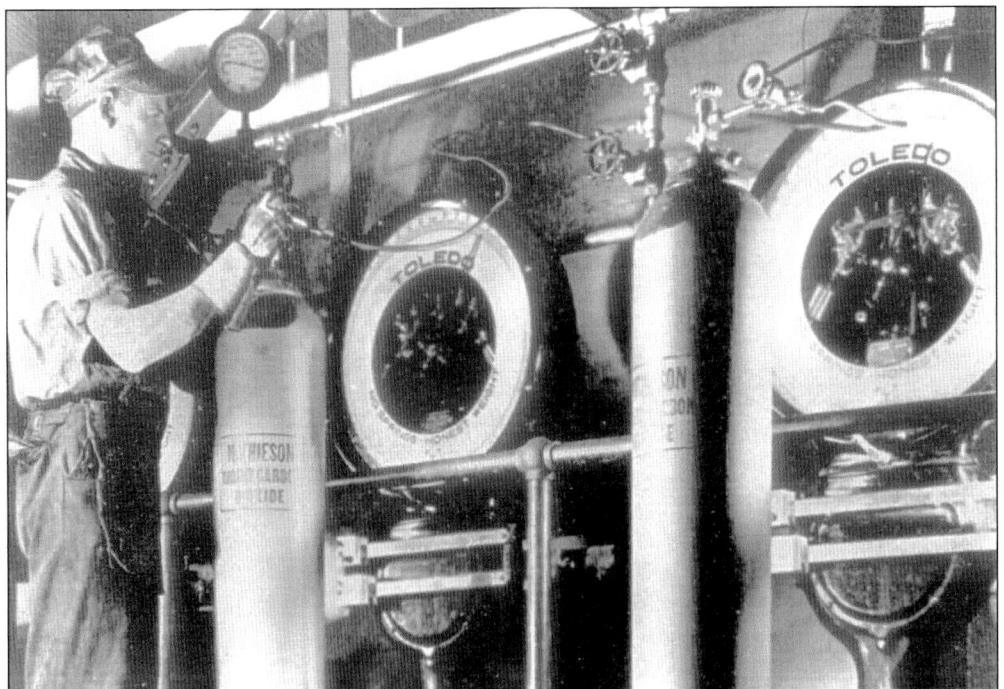

KEEPING CHECK. Much of the Mathieson equipment required constant monitoring. A plant employee here is refilling carbon dioxide cylinders necessary in some manufacturing processes. These tanks were weighed to see how full they were.

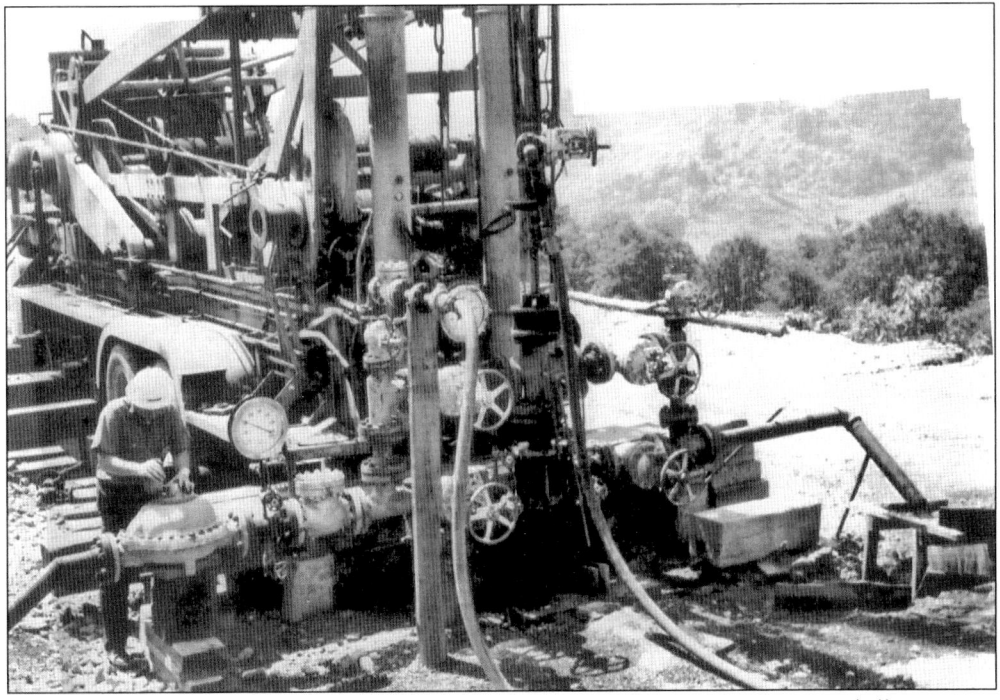

HIGH-PRESSURE DRILLING RIG. Olin operated some of the first high-pressure drilling rigs in America. This worker is checking a gauge during the drilling process.

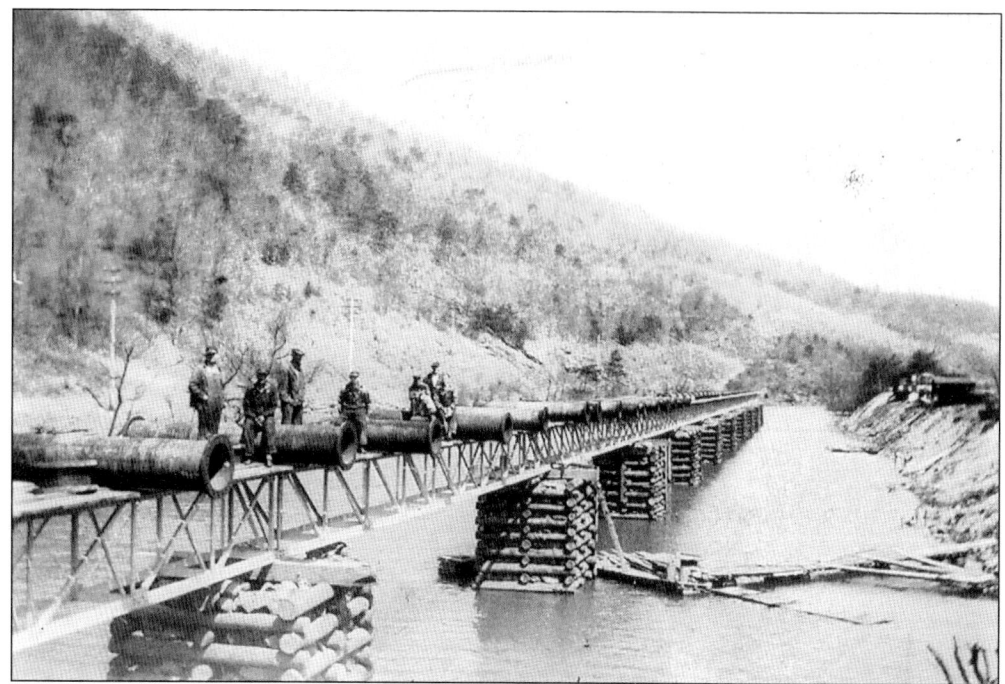

CONSTRUCTION OF WATER AERATOR. This image shows the construction of a water aerator to spray water into the river to cool it down. Considerable heat was generated by Mathieson's manufacturing processes, and it had to be dissipated.

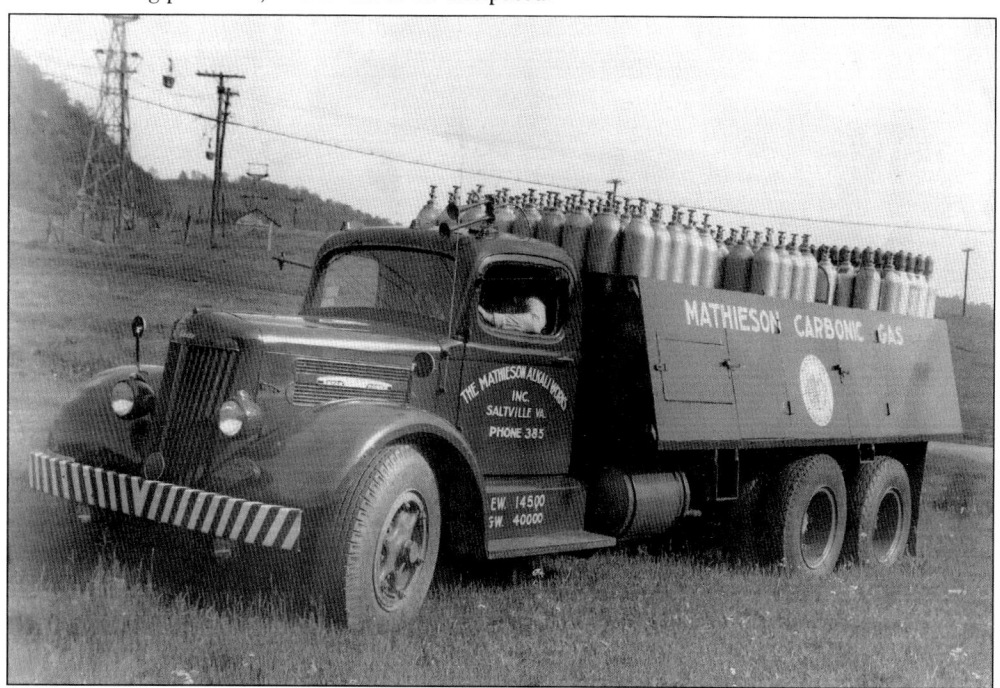

CARBONIC GAS DELIVERY. This Mathieson truck, driven by Lucien Walker, is loaded with carbonic gas headed for Marion, Virginia. Carbonic gas is also known as carbon dioxide gas. This was used to add the fizz to soda, and this load is headed to the Pepsi bottling plant in Marion.

Four
NEW SALTVILLE

When Mathieson came to Saltville in 1892, Saltville became one of the first "company towns" in the United States. The company became the benevolent despot over most aspects of life in the town. The company provided the company stores, where one could buy whatever was needed. The company provided housing for their workers and health coverage, and education was included as well. Some company towns were noted for abuse of their workers, reducing them to near serfdom. This system was not the Mathieson way of doing business, and this did not happen in Saltville. The vast majority of Mathieson's employees enjoyed their life in Saltville. Mathieson workers were paid above-average wages for their time and work. A job at the plant was coveted. There was no Great Depression in Saltville. During that national economic catastrophe, work slowed at Mathieson, but layoffs were avoided by scaling back work hours and staggering shifts. Workers at the plant coped by fishing in the river and hunting in the mountains—a mountaineer birthright. Gardens were planted in the backyards of many homes in Saltville during this period.

Most of the images in this section relate to the amenities of the town in the Mathieson era. Not all of these were directly related or owned by the company, but all benefited by the prosperity and security the company offered.

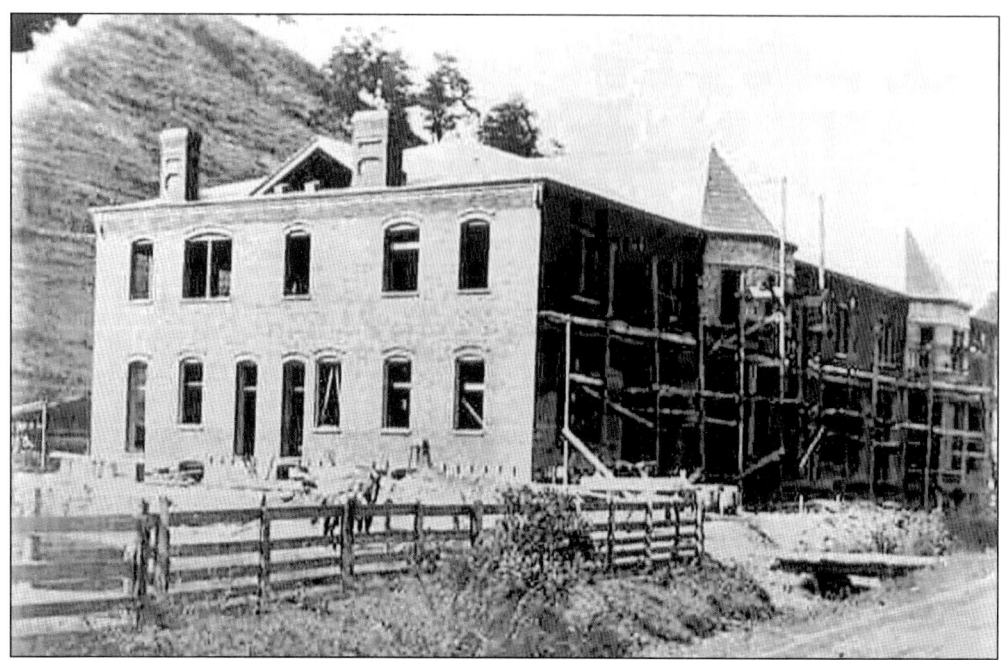

CONSTRUCTION OF THE COMPANY STORE. This 1894 image shows the Mathieson Company Store under construction. It was the largest department store for at least 100 miles in any direction. Clothing, household goods, hardware, and groceries were offered for sale. The company store's pharmacy could supply one's medical needs.

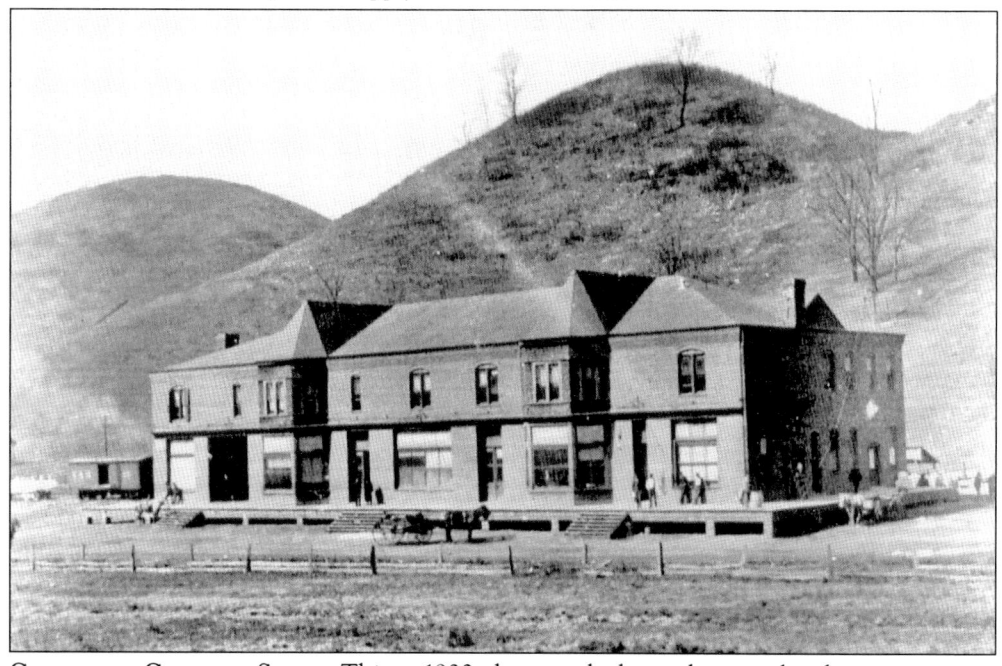

COMPLETED COMPANY STORE. This c. 1900 photograph shows the completed company store. Note the horse and wagon to the right and the boxcar to the left of the building. This site is at the intersection of present-day Palmer Avenue and Main Street. A Rite Aid drug store occupies part of this site today.

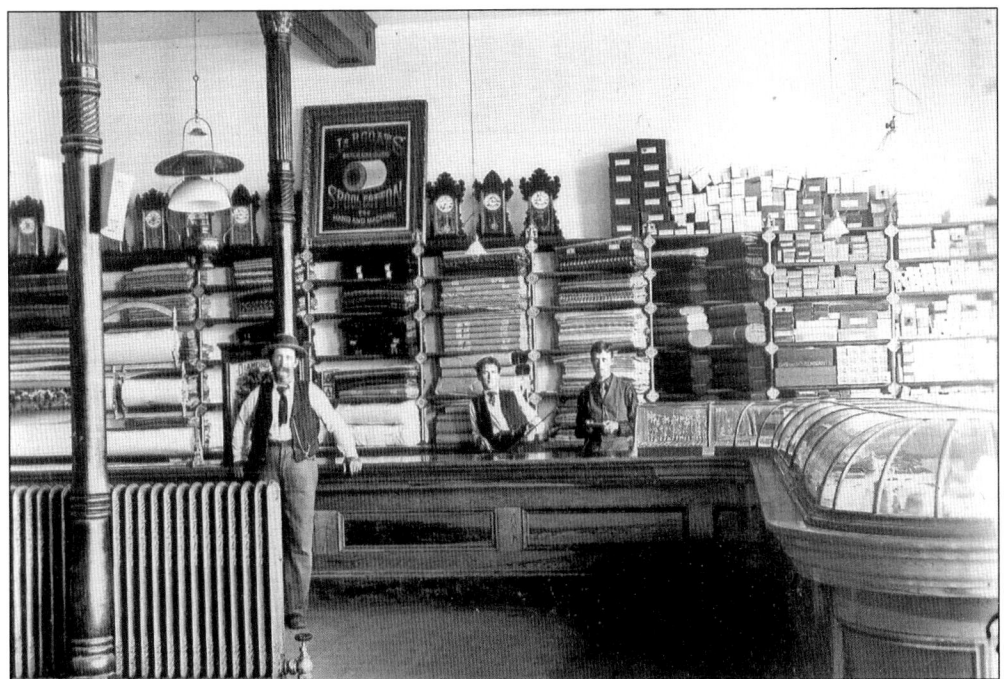

NOTIONS DEPARTMENT. This c. 1900 image shows the clerks in the general merchandise department. Items offered for sale here include bolts of cloth and other sewing needs, clocks, wallpaper, and other trinkets. (Courtesy of Roger Allison.)

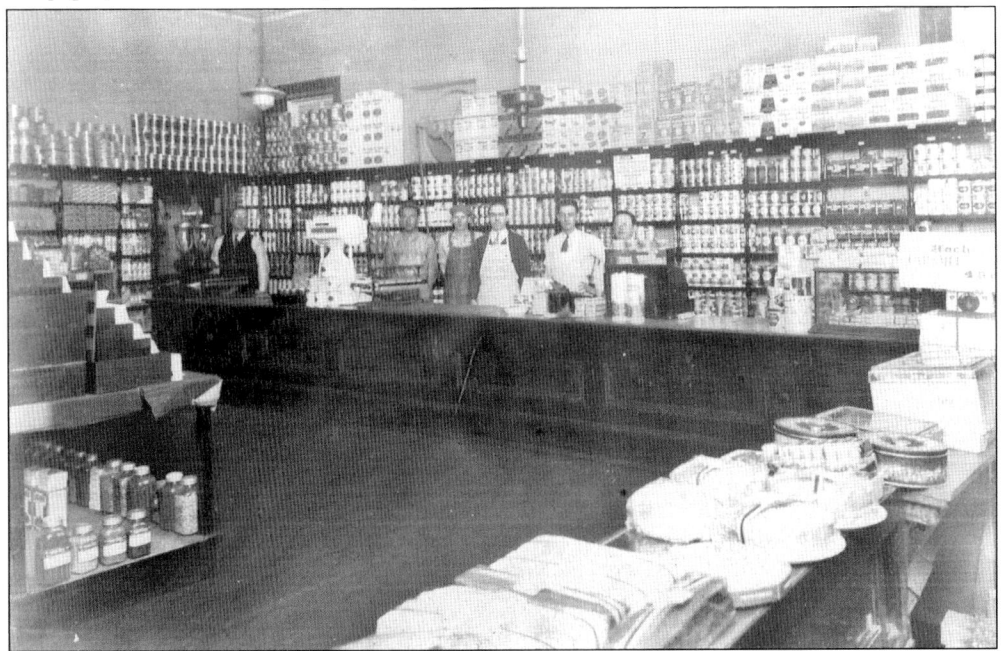

GROCERY DEPARTMENT. This 1930s photograph shows the grocery department of the company store. One could call in an order and have it delivered. If you were not home, the delivery boys would leave your order on the back porch or kitchen table and put perishables in the icebox. There was no extra charge for home delivery.

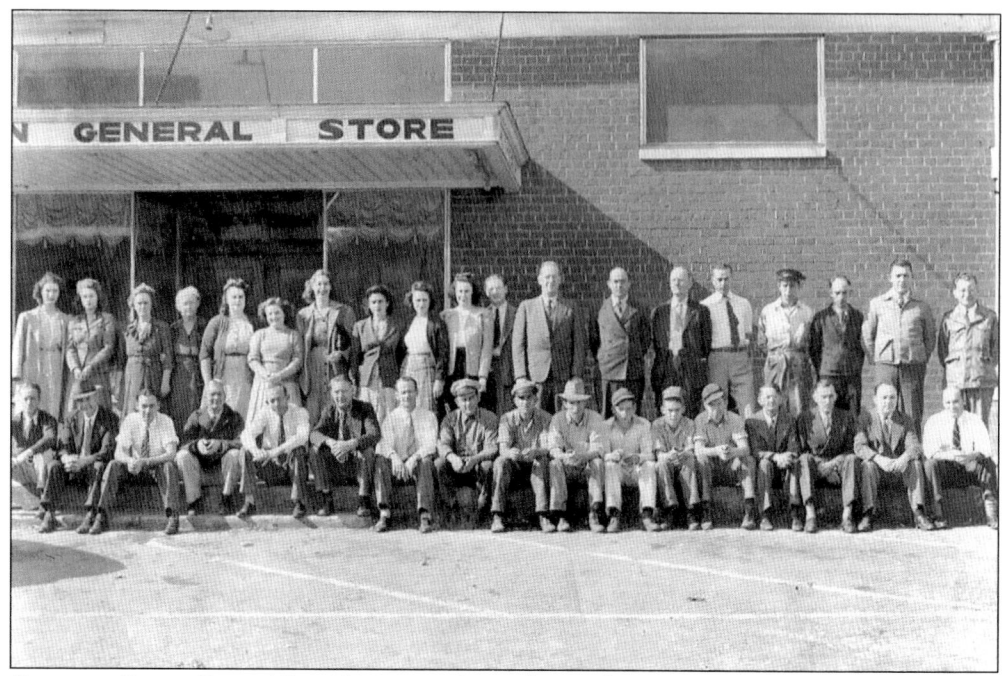

COMPANY STORE STAFF. This 1944 image shows the employees of the company store posing for a group photograph. There are 36 workers shown here. By the time the company store closed in 1968, the staff was reduced to seven employees.

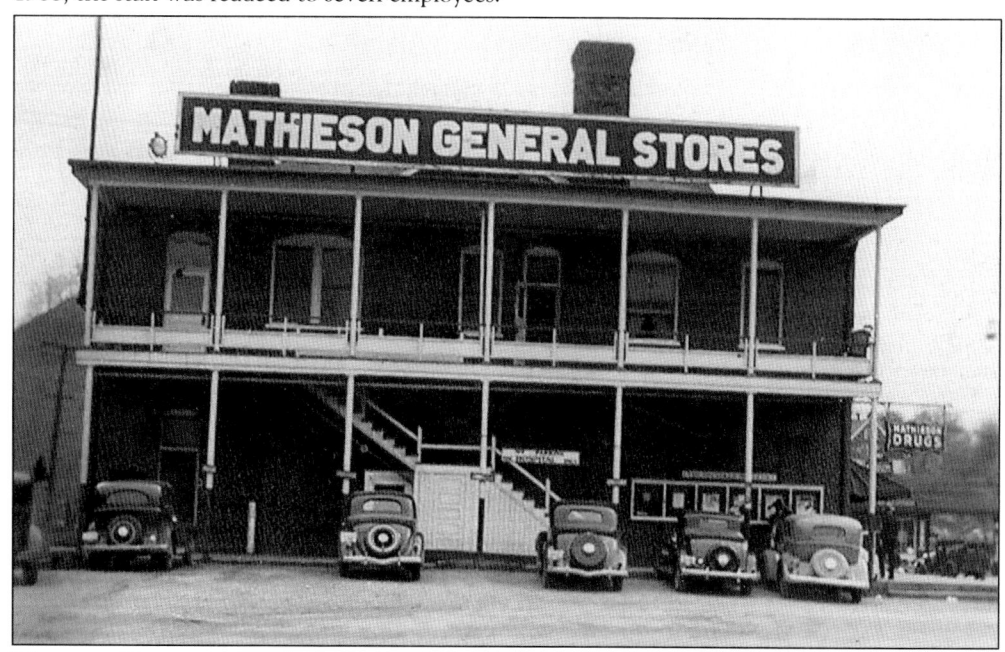

MEDICAL DEPARTMENT. Before construction of McKee Hospital, Mathieson Alkali Works operated a hospital over the company store from 1925 until 1950. This is the hospital entrance. Company employees were covered for all medical needs without cost to the patient or their family. Prior to the opening of these medical facilities, the company maintained an "accident house" between British Row and the main plant.

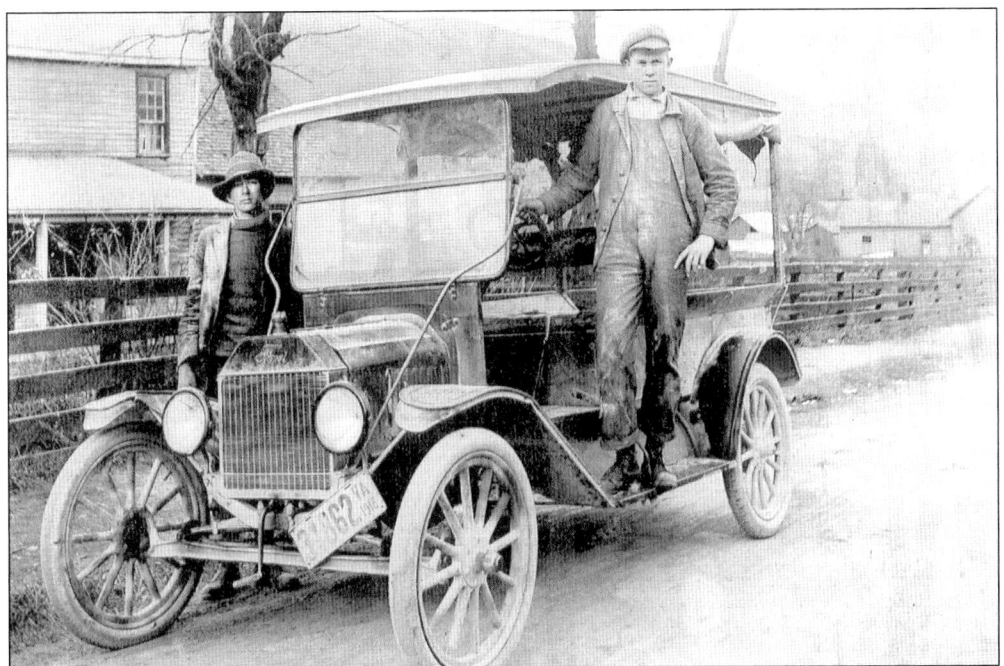

DELIVERY TRUCK. This 1918 photograph shows the delivery truck for Mathieson General Stores. Locally this was called the company store dray. Before this Ford Model T came along, the deliveries were made by horse-drawn drays or wagons. The chap on the left is Arthur Price, and the fellow at the steering wheel is Kent Lane.

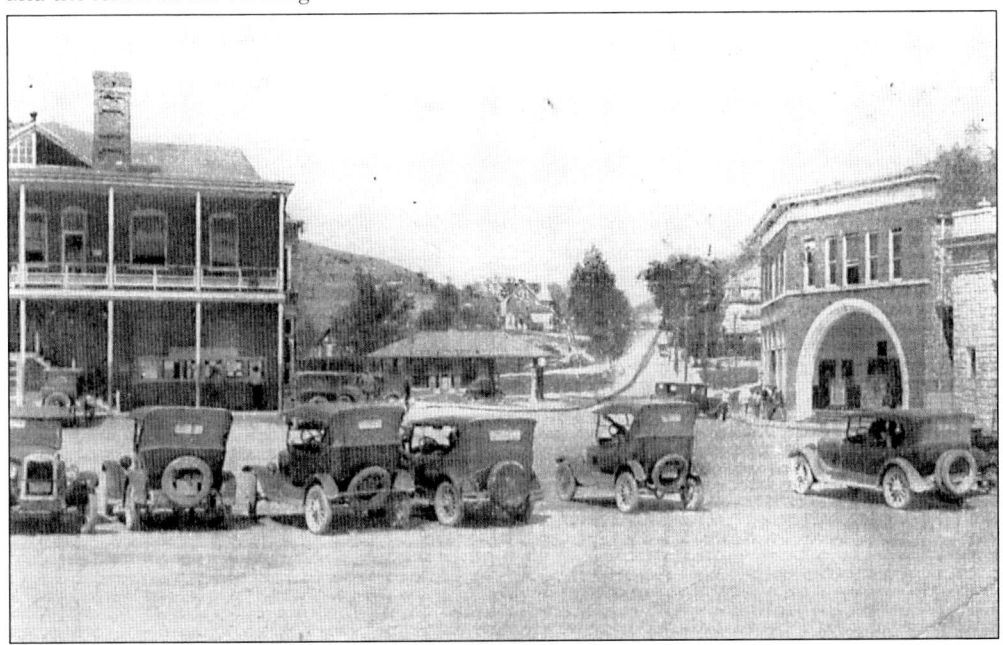

TAXI STAND. This late-1920s view shows the taxi stand located in front of the company store. The Victory Theater, Saltville's second movie house, is located to the right in the building with the arch. Billiards and bowling were available in the basement of this building. The company store's service station is the building in the center of the photograph.

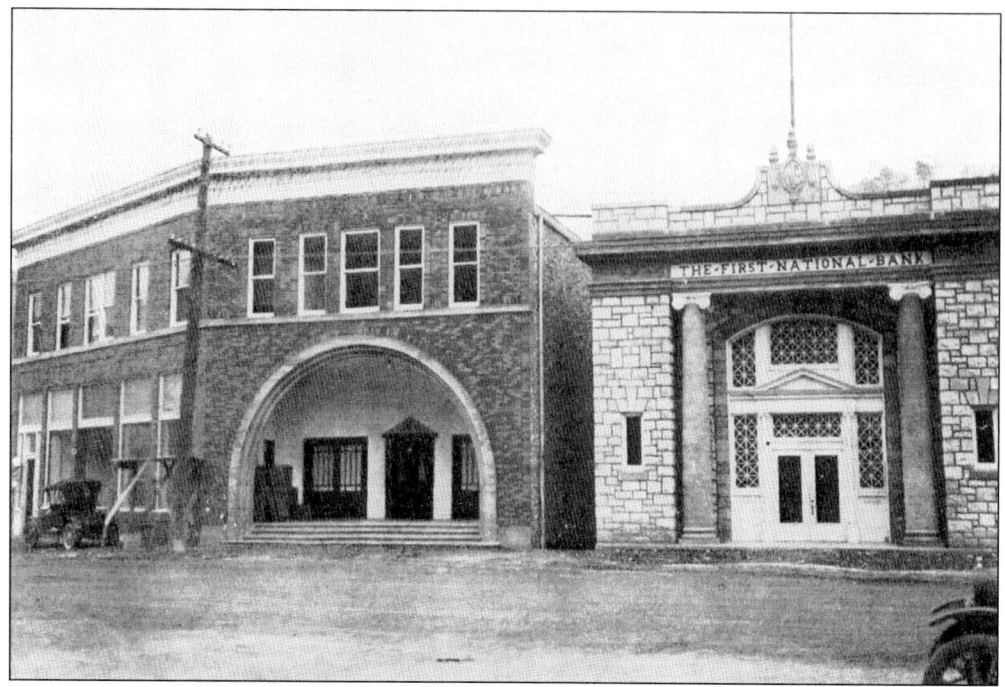

VICTORY THEATER AND BANK. This photograph made in the 1930s by Tom Totten shows the First National Bank of Saltville to the right and Victory Theater on the left. The Victory Theater was built in 1922. The theater has since been torn down, but the handsome bank building is now the home of Saltville's branch of BB&T Bank.

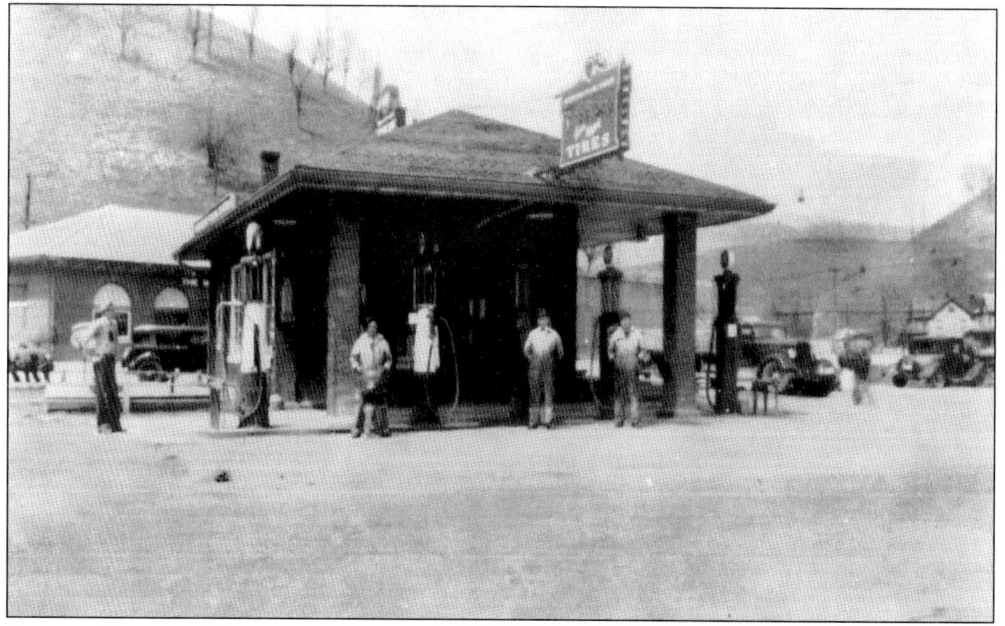

SERVICE STATION. The company operated a service station on Main Street near the intersection with Allison Gap Road. Those who had automobiles could buy gasoline and other products and have their vehicles repaired by the mechanics who worked here. This site is now occupied by the Rite Aid drug store parking lot. Chester Totten is the fellow standing on the right.

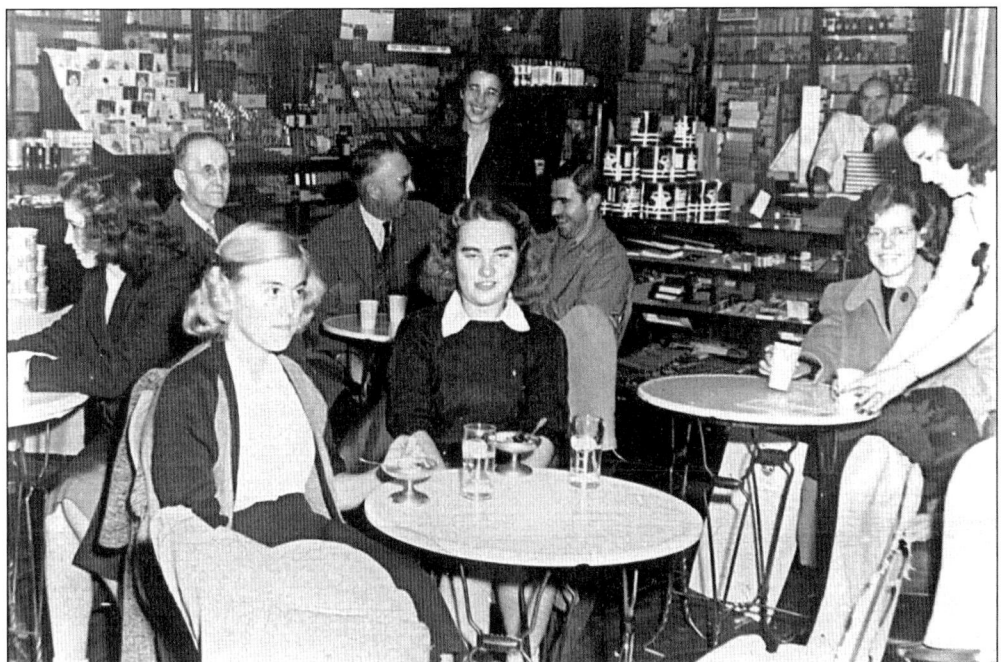

SODA FOUNTAIN. This 1949 image shows young and old enjoying treats offered at the company store's soda fountain. It was a popular gathering place for an after-school social rendezvous. In the 1960s, the parking lot was a popular place for local kids to hang out.

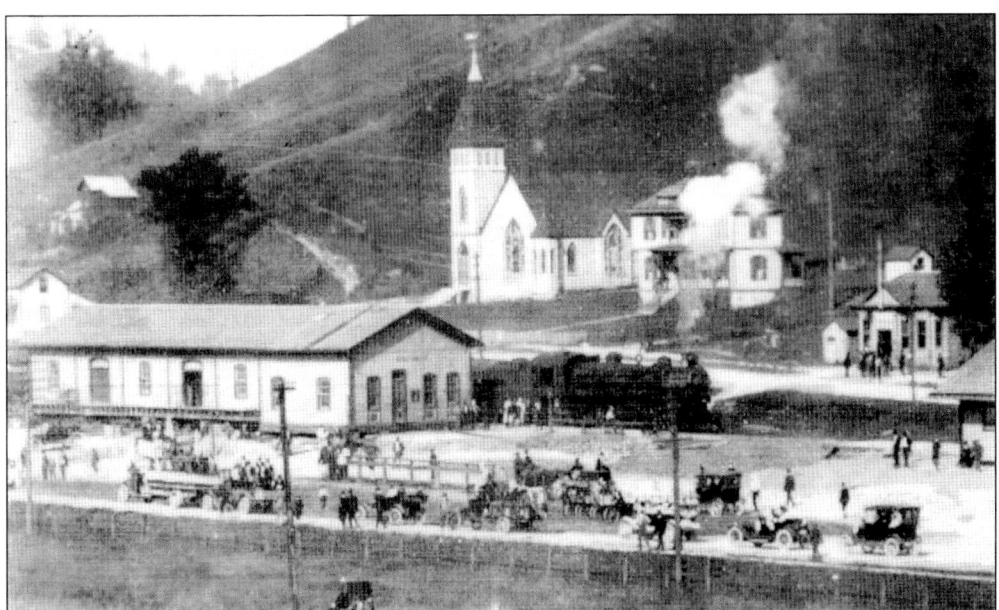

WORLD WAR I EVENT. The crowd at the Saltville Depot in this image indicates either the arrival or departure of Saltville's sons during World War I. Note the crowd gathering at the depot. Madam Russell Memorial Methodist Episcopal Church South and parsonage are in the center background. The street in the foreground was called Jockey Street, because it was a popular place in that era to trade horses.

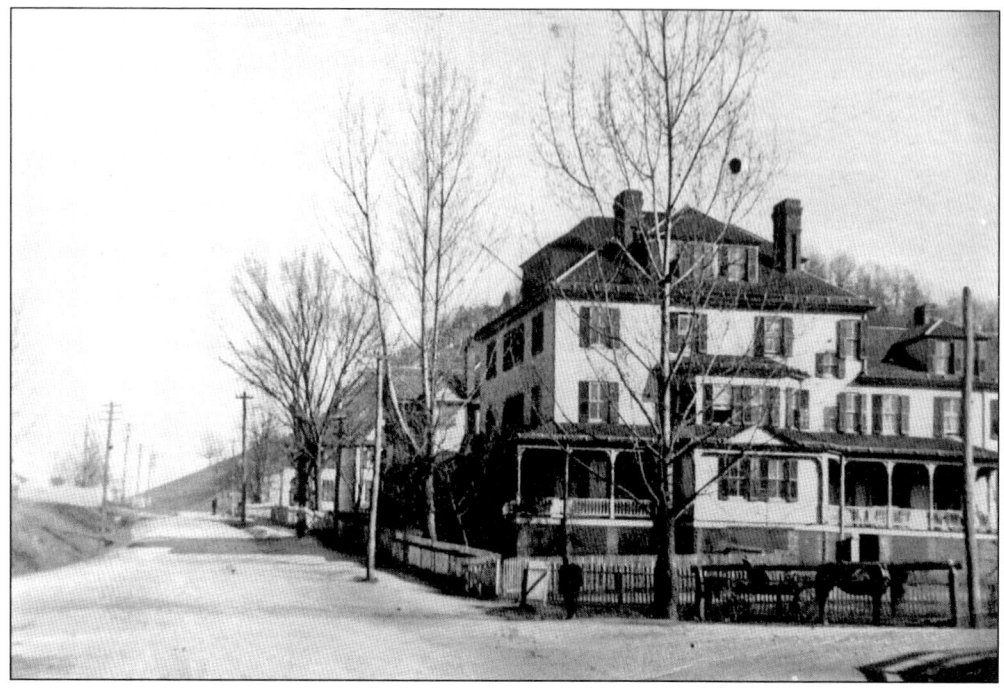

SALTVILLE HOTEL. The Saltville Hotel was a beautiful Victorian-era hotel located at the western end of East Main Street. This image was probably made about 1910. This hotel was demolished in the 1960s and was replaced with the Salina Motel and Restaurant.

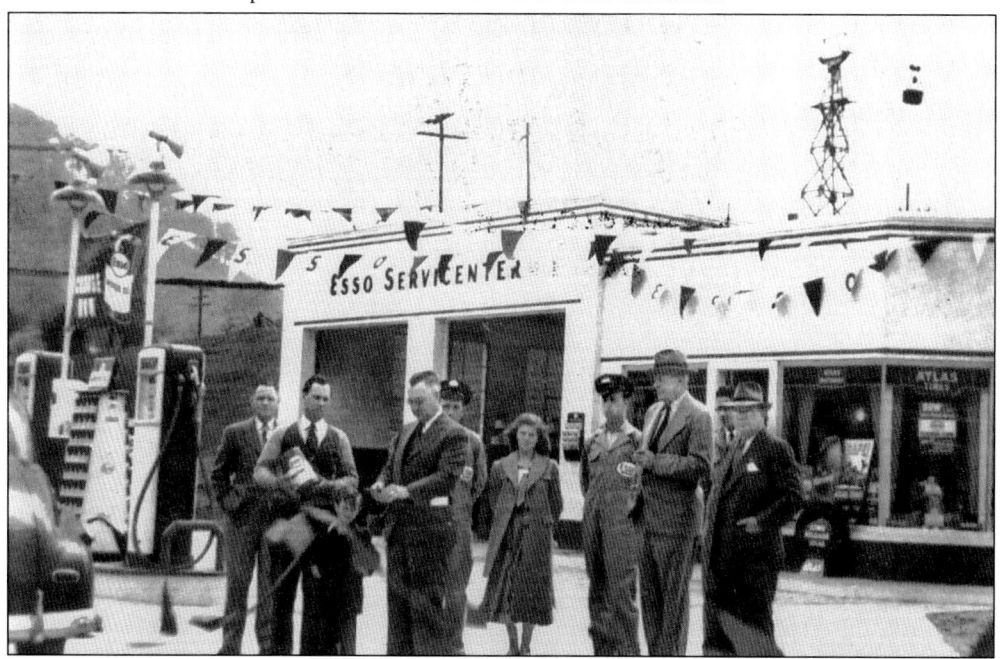

GRAND OPENING OF THE HAYDEN MOTOR COMPANY AND ESSO SERVICE STATION. An option to the company store's service station was made available about 1950 with the opening of the Esso Service Station. Hayden's also sold Chrysler products. This facility was located across the street from the company store. This building is now Taylor's Home and Garden Center.

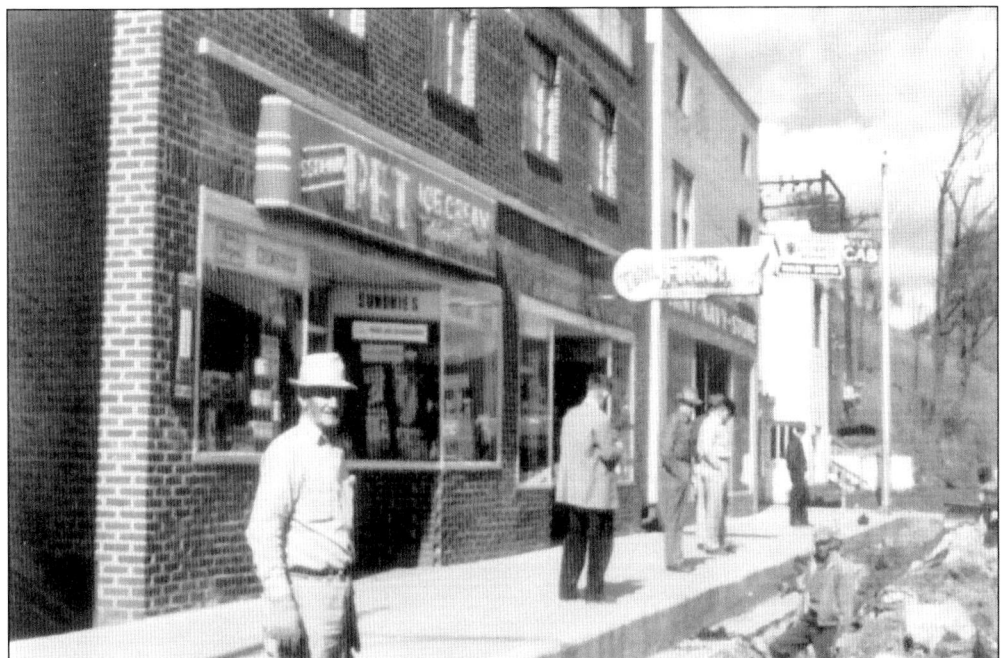

WEST MAIN STREET BUSINESS. Totten's City Store and a furniture store are shown here in the late 1940s. They were two of the non-Mathieson businesses in Saltville at that time. The workers in the lower right of the photograph are apparently extending the water line to the newly constructed buildings farther down the street.

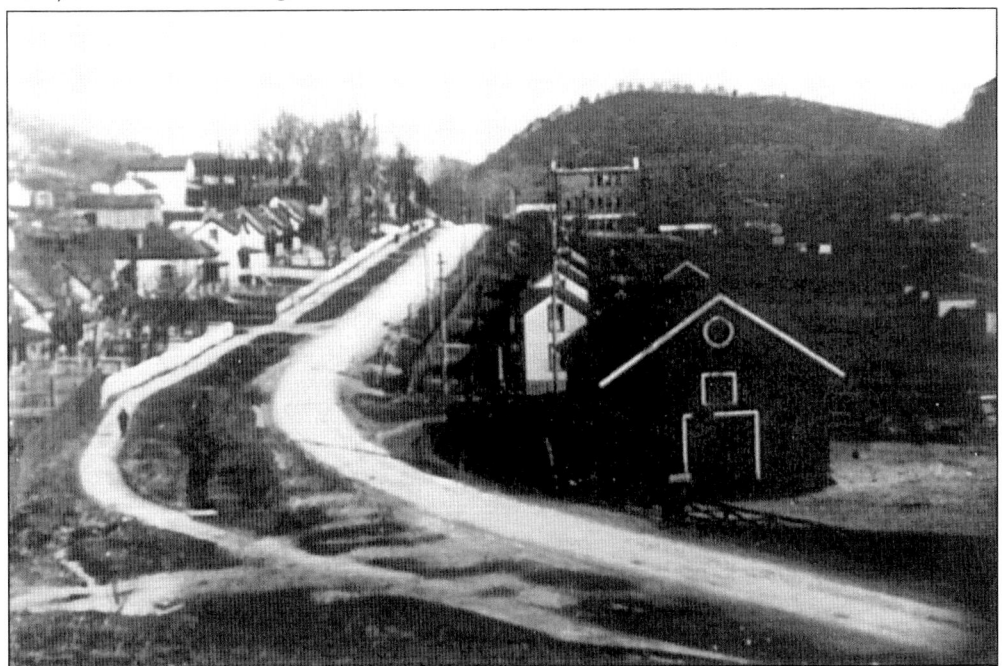

WEST MAIN STREET. This shot, taken about 1906, shows the Saltville High School in the right rear. The street had also been recently widened, and several houses have been added on the left.

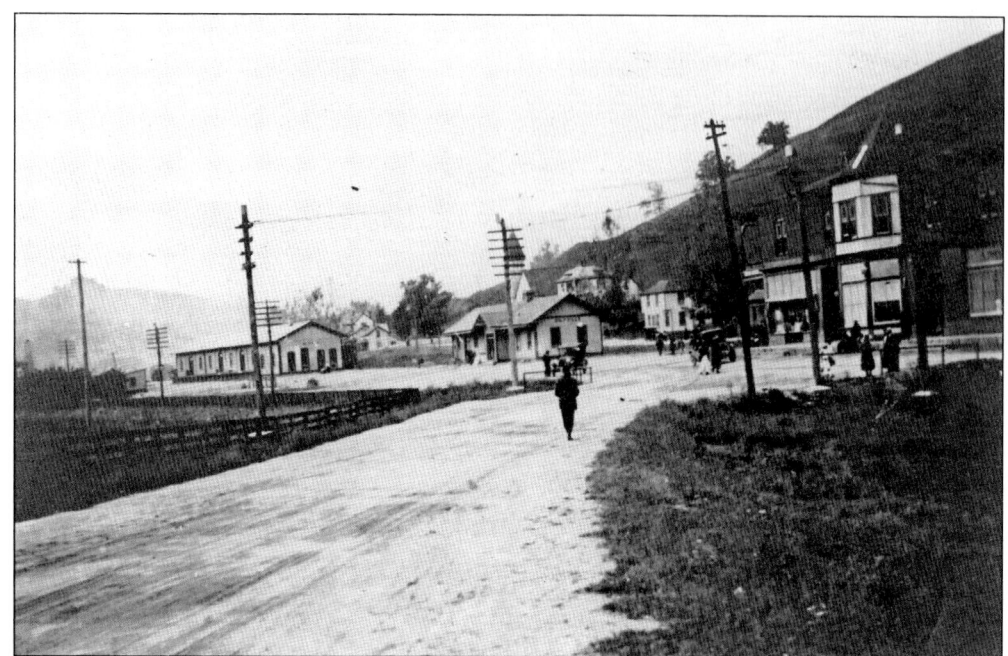

MAIN STREET C. 1915. This is a view of the center of "New" Saltville c. 1915. The building in the center left of the image is the freight depot. The building in the center is the passenger depot. The company store is shown on the right, with Madam Russell Methodist Church and parsonage in the background.

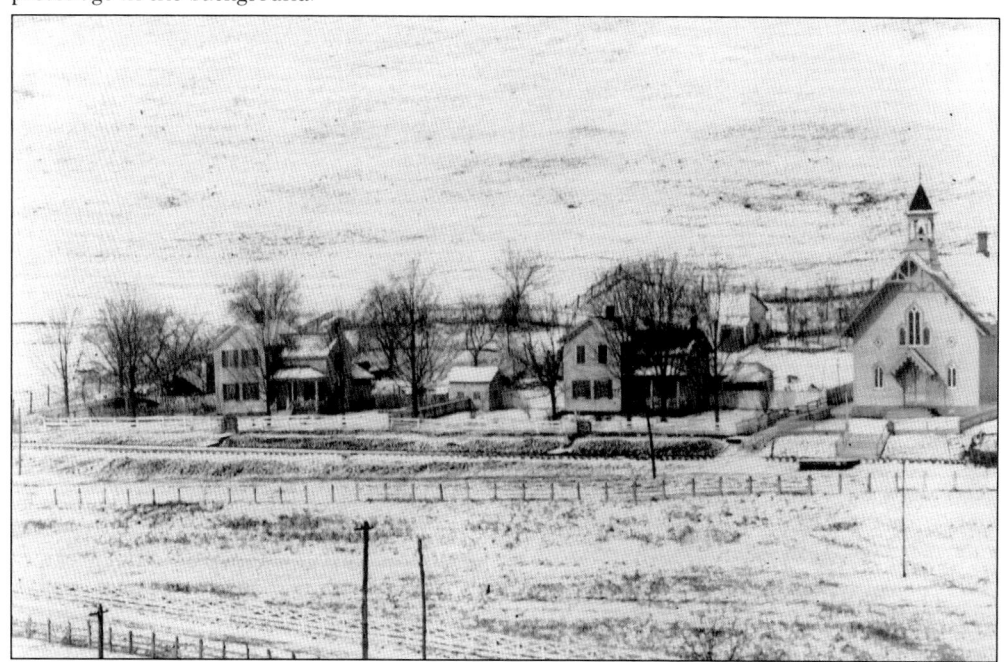

EARLY WINTER SCENE. This snowy scene shows a couple of the early homes and the Union Church, built in 1873. This photograph was probably made in the second decade of the 20th century and shows much of the detail of Victorian Union Church. Note the gingerbread fretwork over the door of the church and the truss work at the apex of the roof.

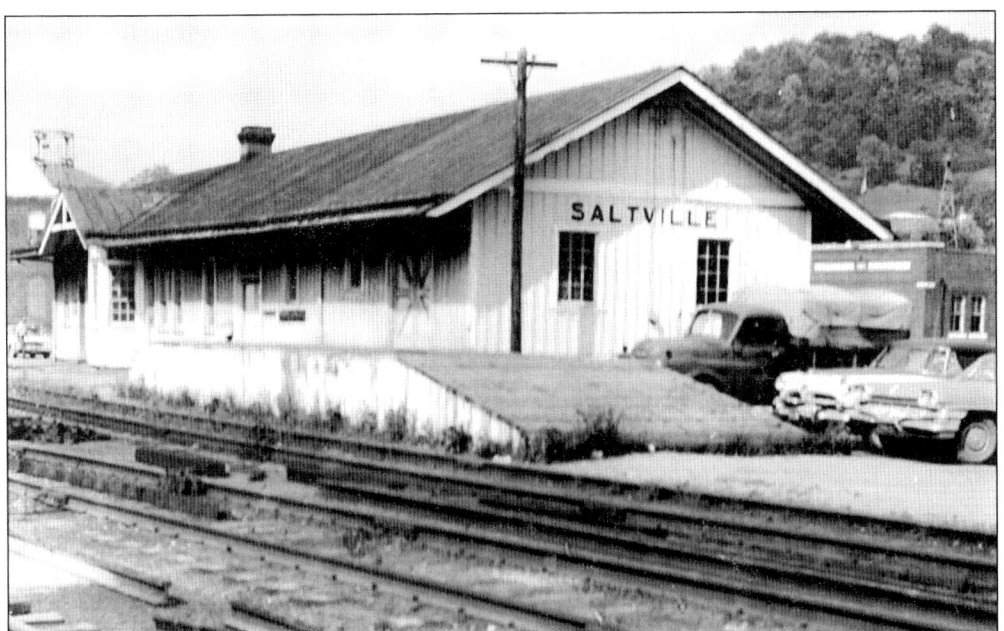

SALTVILLE PASSENGER DEPOT. This is a close-up view made in the early 1960s of the Saltville Railroad Depot. Each village in Southwest Virginia served by the Norfolk and Western Railroad had similar depots.

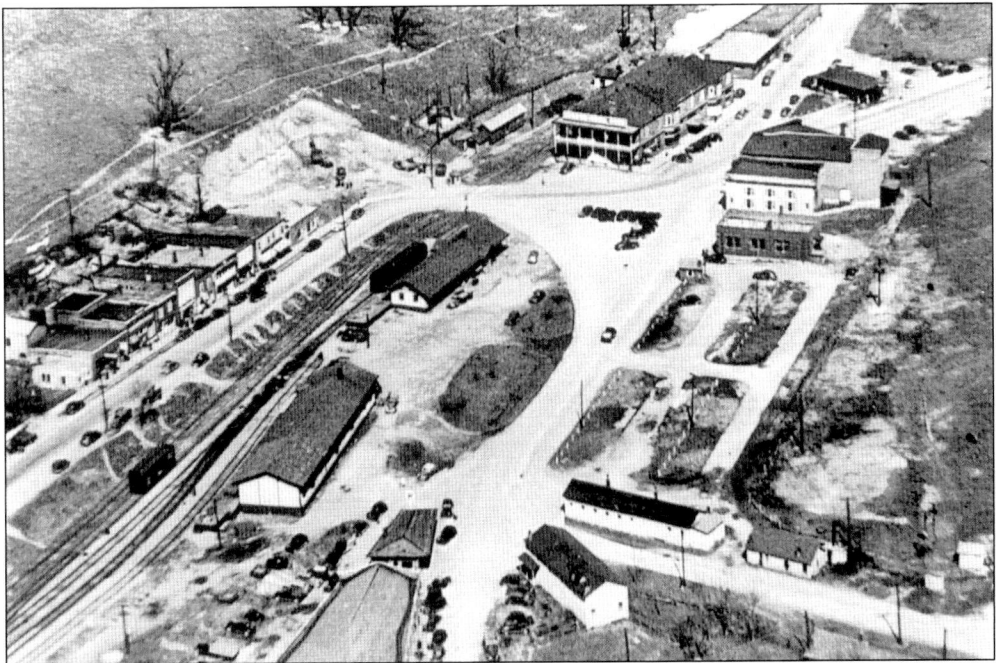

AERIAL VIEW OF SALTVILLE IN 1946. This early aerial shot graphically depicts the shops of West Main Street on the left. The railroad tracks and depots are in the center. The company store is shown in the upper center of the image. To the upper right, the old Saltville Post Office, bank, and Victory Theater can been seen. The grading at the upper left is for a barbershop. Longtime residents will observe the changes in the streets in front of the company store.

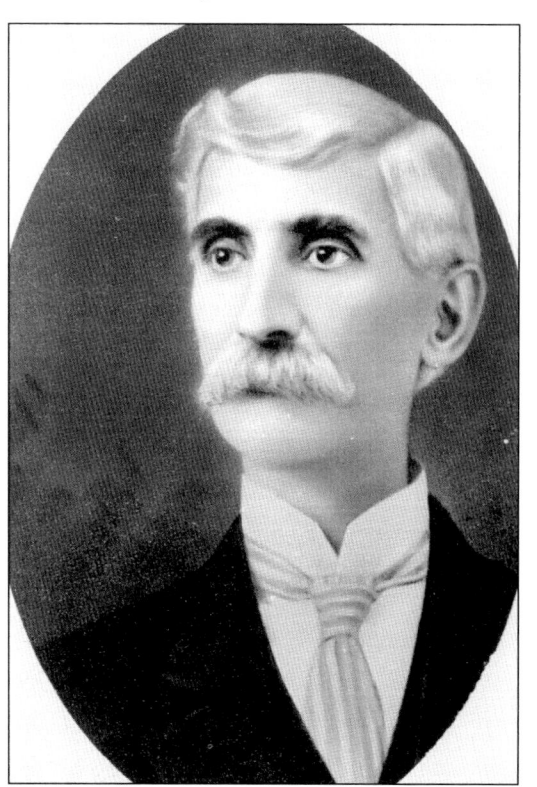

Joseph Crockett Kent. Kent was an early leader of Madam Russell Methodist Church and served as the first superintendent of Sunday schools from the organization of the church until his death in 1923.

Emile Lowe, Chemist. Lowe was the brain of the Mathieson Operation in Saltville. He developed many of the processes that made the Mathieson operation a successful business for many years.

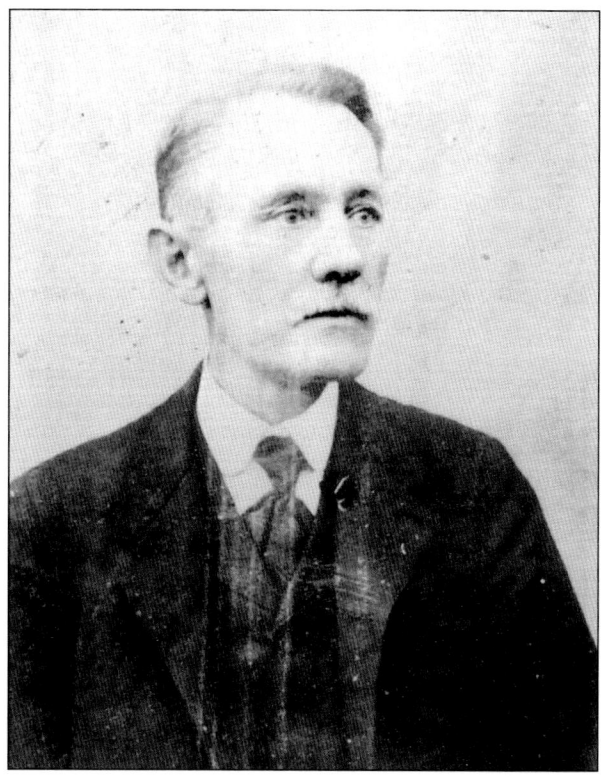

W. A. STUART. William Alexander Stuart was involved with the firm that produced most of the salt for the South during the American Civil War. Saltville has proclaimed itself "the Salt Capital of the Confederacy."

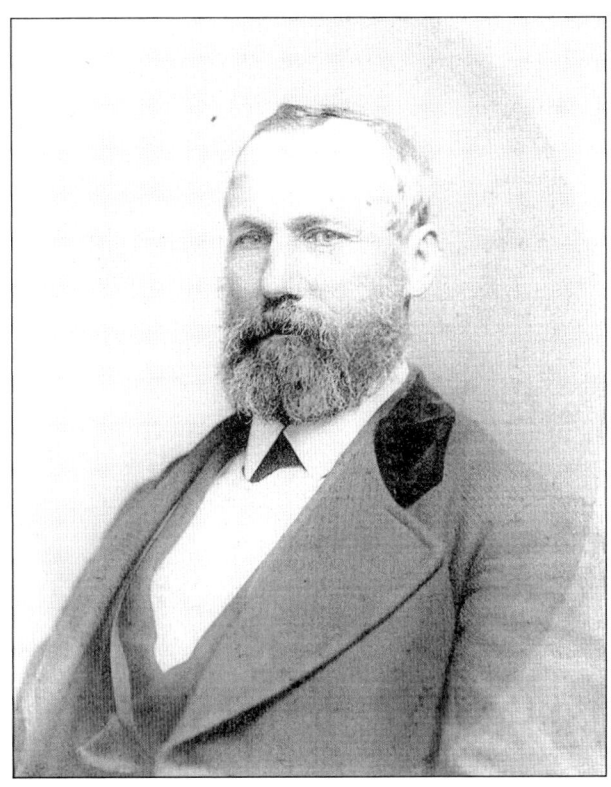

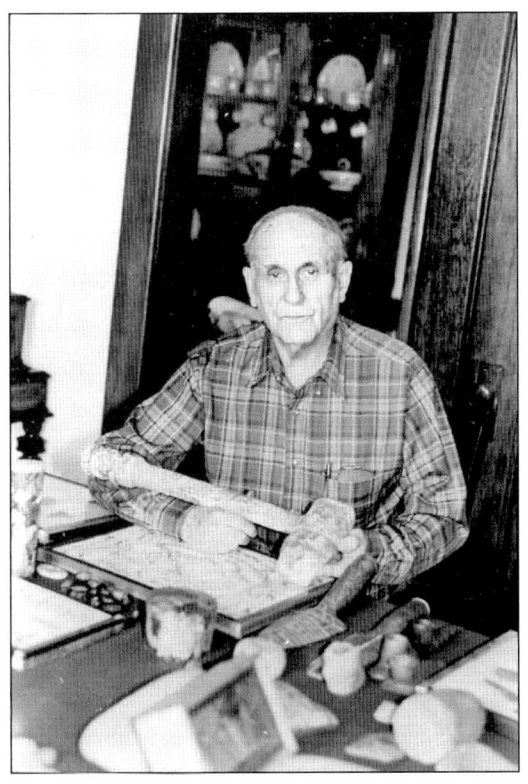

CECIL CURTIS HATFIELD, M.D. Dr. Hatfield is displaying some of his collection of Native American relics found near Saltville. Dr. Hatfield was also instrumental in the development of the town's rescue service.

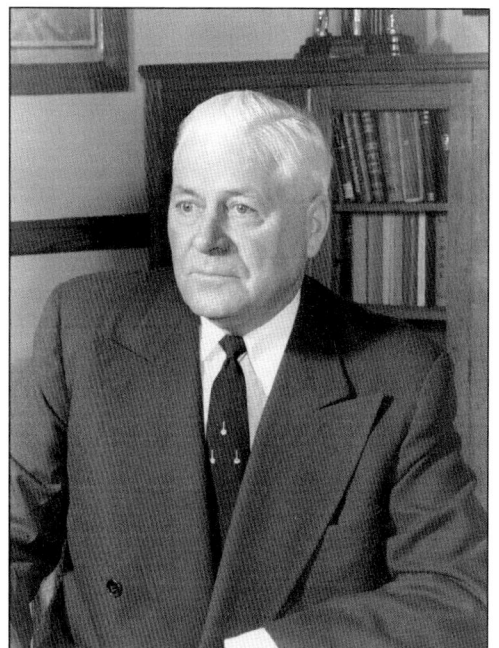 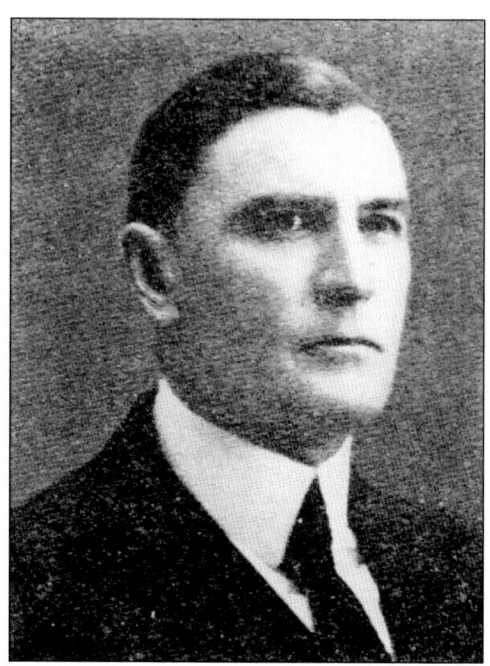

(LEFT) RAY BONNER WORTHY. Worthy was an engineer who came to Saltville in the 1920s to help find a way to dispose of the chemical by-products created by the Mathieson processes. He remained until his death in 1958 and was universally loved. The local high school, R. B. Worthy High School, was named in his honor.

(RIGHT) WILLIAM B. PORTERFIELD. Porterfield was manager of Mathieson's farm operations, beginning his employment in 1909. Mathieson owned several thousand acres in the Saltville area, and large numbers of cattle and sheep were grazed on these lands. Porterfield was the father of Robert Porterfield, founder of the Barter Theater.

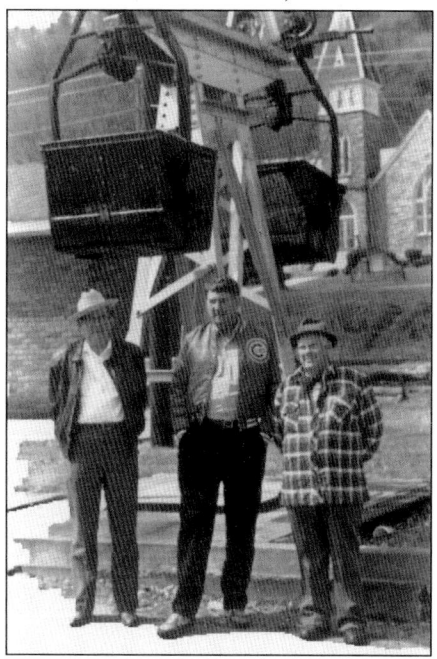

FRED SINGLETON. Singleton (far left in the photograph), a native of Dickenson County, Virginia, came to Saltville in the mid-20th century. He operated Singleton's department stores for several years and later ran a carpet business in the old Salt Theater building. He donated this building to the Museum of the Middle Appalachians. He currently operates three convenience stores in town.

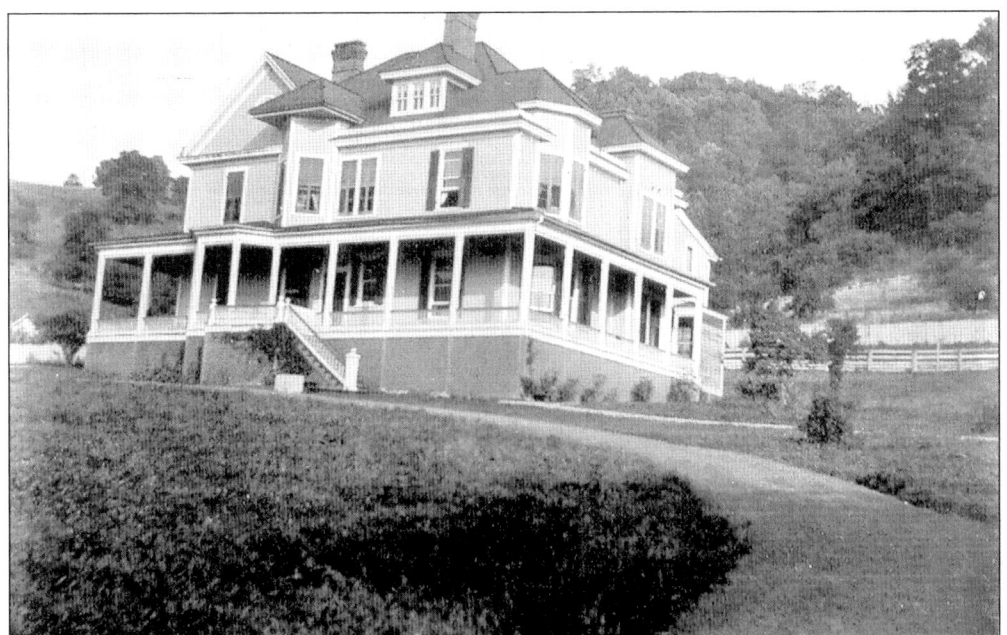

CHARLIE PALMER HOUSE. This house was the home to several of Saltville's leading citizens. It was built in the late 19th century for Charlie Palmer. Dr. James Louis Early moved into this house in 1921, and he remained here until he retired. R. B. Worthy lived here until his death in 1958. It sat on the edge of Saltville's municipal golf course, but it has been torn down, much to the detriment of the community.

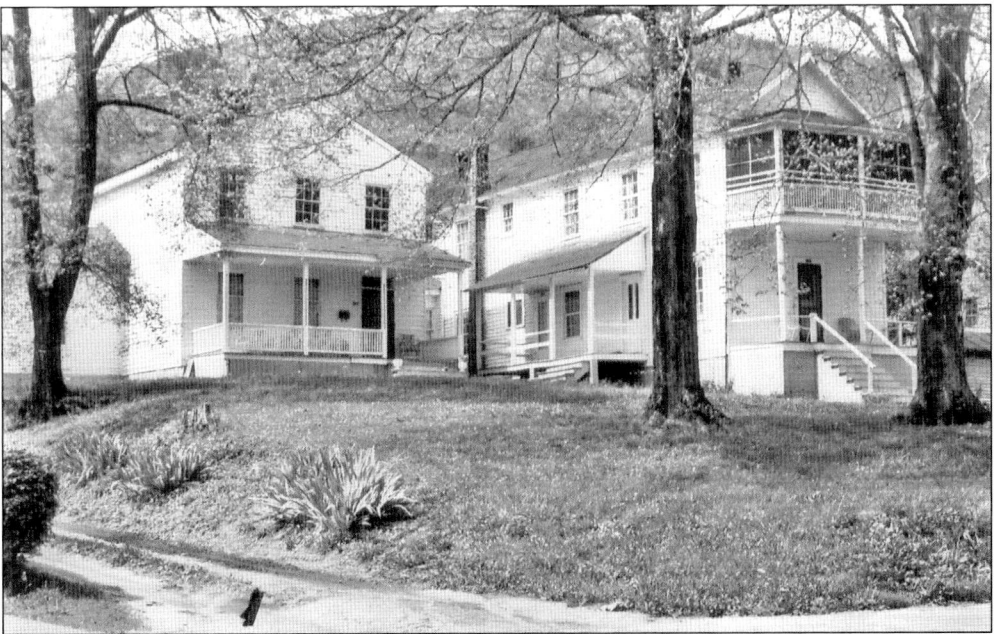

KENT HOUSE. The house in the left of this snapshot was known as the Kent House. It was built around 1800 and served as Saltville's hotel prior to 1871. This house was damaged during the December 1864 battle. The building to the right served as an annex to the 1925 Saltville High School. Home economics and other classes were taught here.

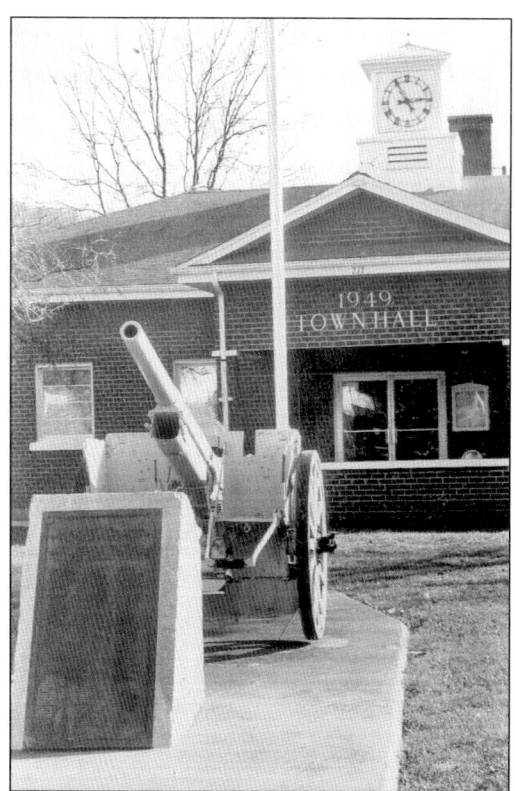

TOWN HALL. Saltville's Town Hall was constructed in 1949. This facility houses the council chambers, the town clerk, and the police department. A World War I memorial is located in front of Town Hall with a captured German 77-mm howitzer and bronze plaque containing the names of the town's citizens who served "over there." (Courtesy of Roger Allison.)

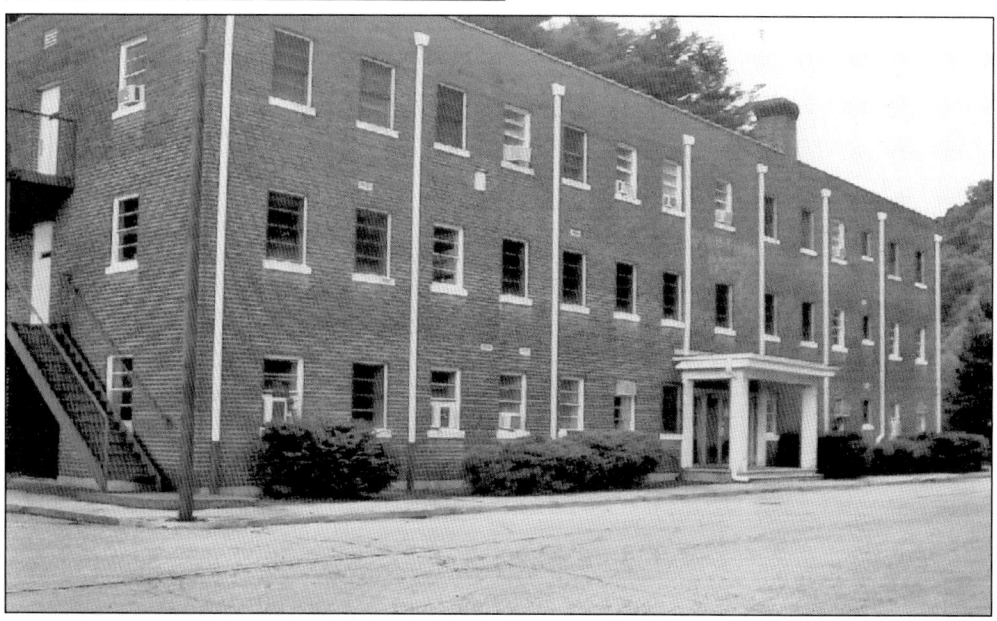

T. K. MCKEE HOSPITAL. In the late 1940s, Mathieson built a separate hospital facility, moving the medical department from the company store building. This facility, which opened to the public in 1950, offered a full range of medical procedures, including surgery and obstetrics. The company deeded the hospital to Smyth County Community Hospital in 1967 with an agreement that it was to be kept open for 25 years. It was closed in 1974. (Photograph by J. Weaver.)

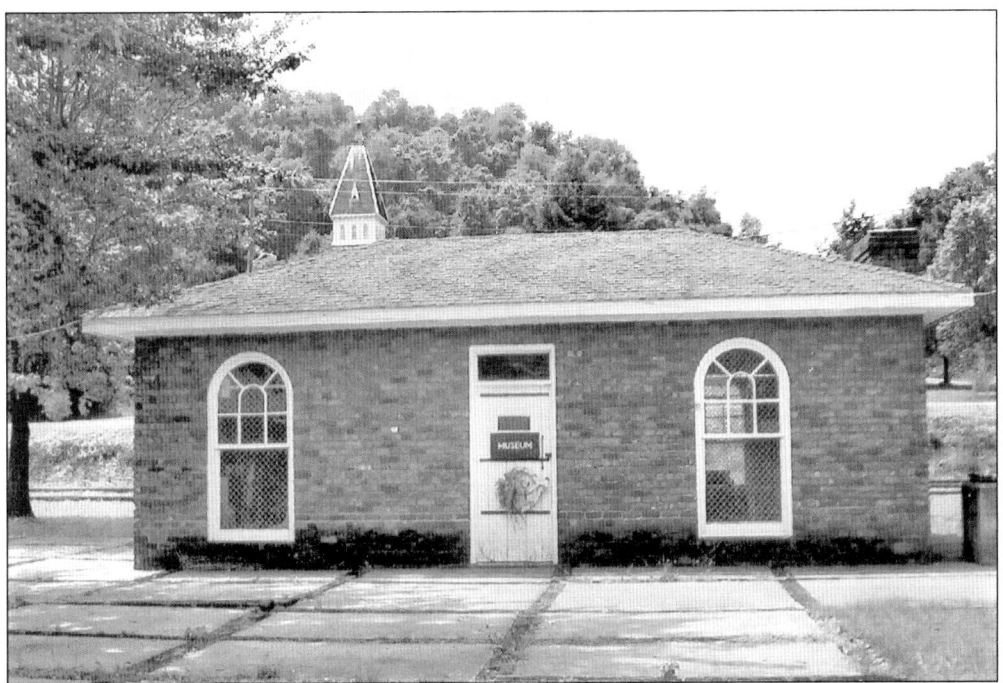

OLD SALTWORKS OFFICE. This building, located across the street from Madam Russell Church, has been relocated from its original site but has been faithfully reconstructed at its current site. It was the saltworks office from the George W. Palmer era. The bricks were made in Saltville by slave labor. (Photograph by J. Weaver.)

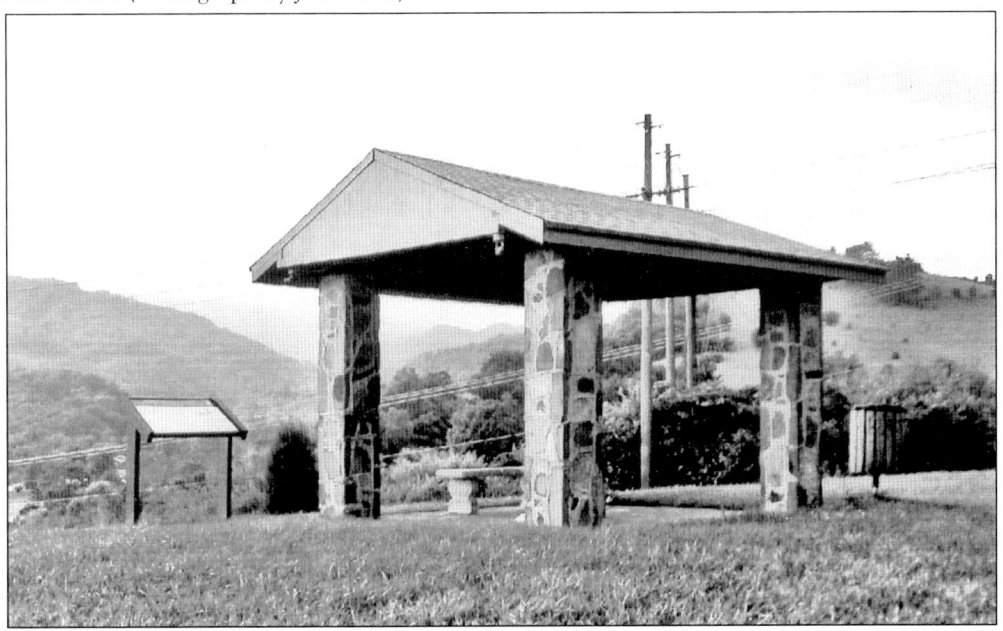

BATTLEFIELD OVERLOOK. This pavilion was constructed for those who would like to get a good visual idea of the October 2, 1864, battle of Saltville. The display to the left of the pavilion has a description and map of the battlefield. Confederate trenches are still visible just below this open structure. This is a Virginia Civil War Trails site. (Photograph by J. Weaver.)

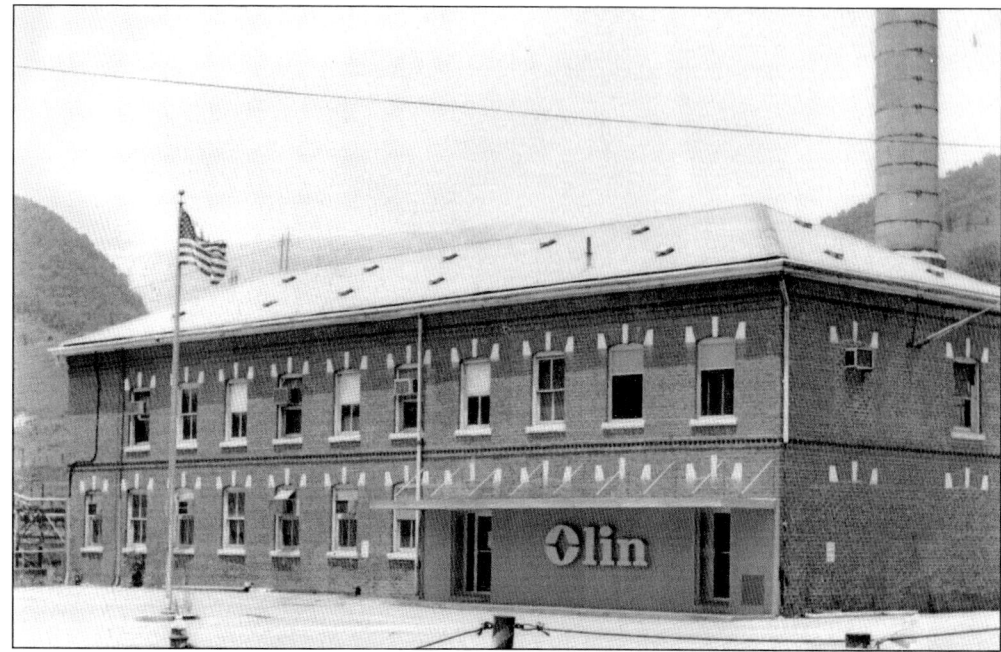

OLIN OFFICE BUILDING. This 1972 image was taken of the Olin offices in Saltville after the closure of the manufacturing facilities in town. Olin and its antecedent companies released mercury into the North Fork of Holston River over the years. Saltville was placed on the EPA's superfund list of polluted sites, but has recently been taken off, and most of the pollution created over the years has abated.

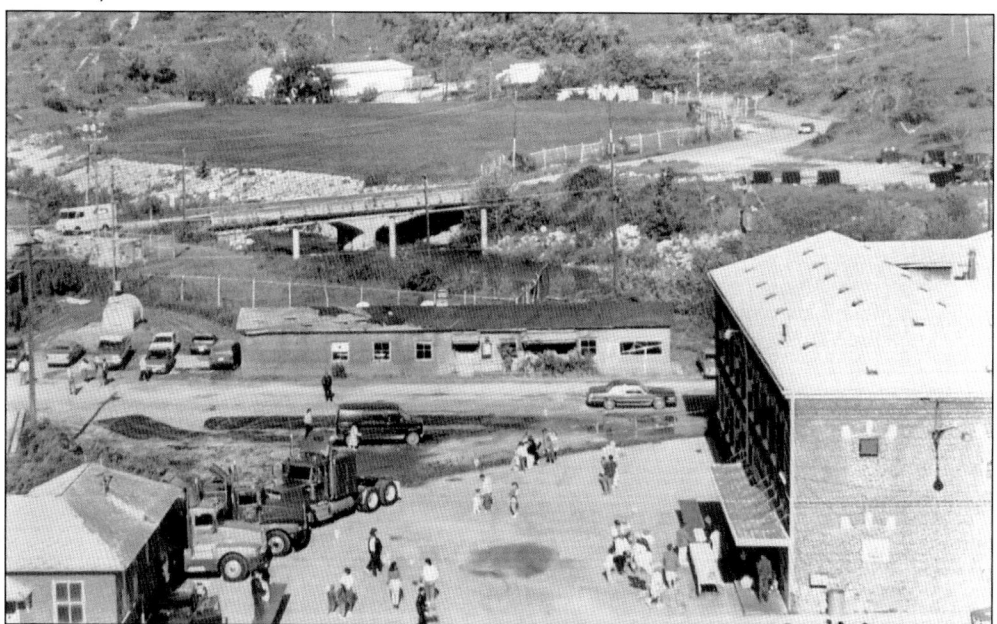

GRAND OPENING OF TITAN WHEEL. After Olin withdrew from Saltville, the town suffered about 70-percent unemployment. The town was able to attract some businesses, but all were considerably smaller than the Olin operation. This is the 1980 grand opening of Titan Wheel, located on the site of the old Olin plant and offices.

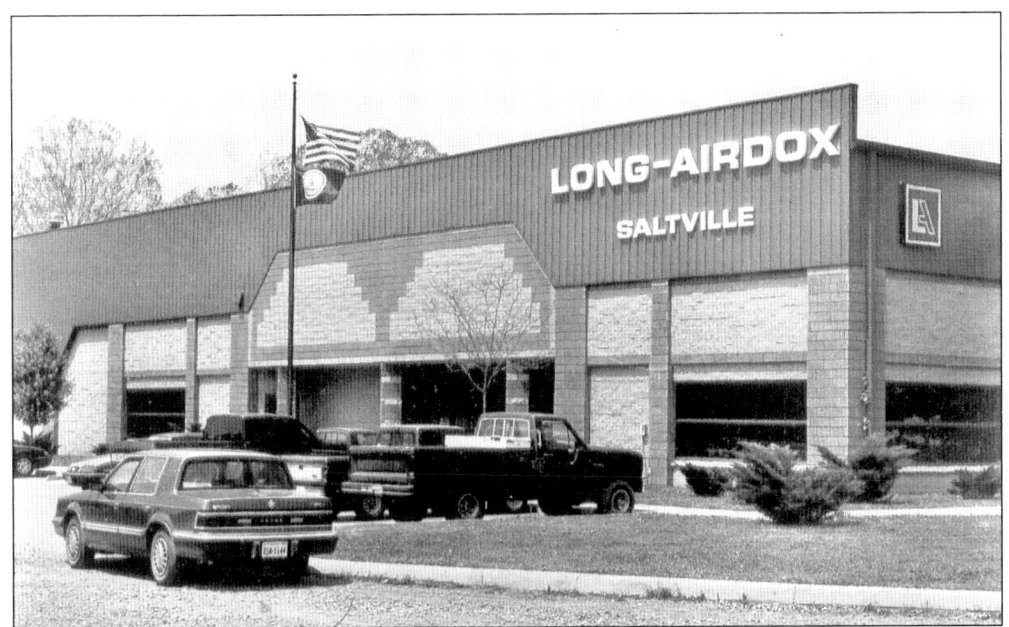

LONG-AIRDOX SALTVILLE. Long-Airdox was another company that came to Saltville after the closure of Olin. This company manufactured mining equipment in Saltville for a few years. This photograph was made in the mid-1990s. Many of the businesses that have come to Saltville after 1972 have not maintained a long-term relationship with the town. (Courtesy of Roger Allison.)

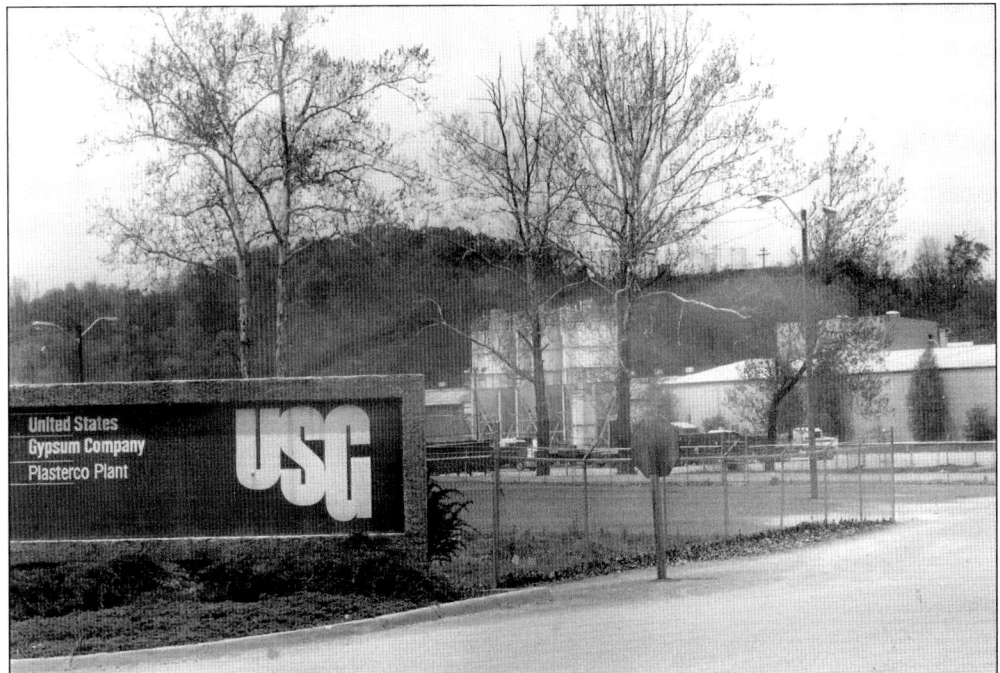

U.S. GYPSUM. U.S. Gypsum held out in Saltville for a few years after Olin. This mid-1980s photograph shows part of their facilities at Plasterco. This company too has closed, leaving additional residents out of work. (Courtesy of Roger Allison.)

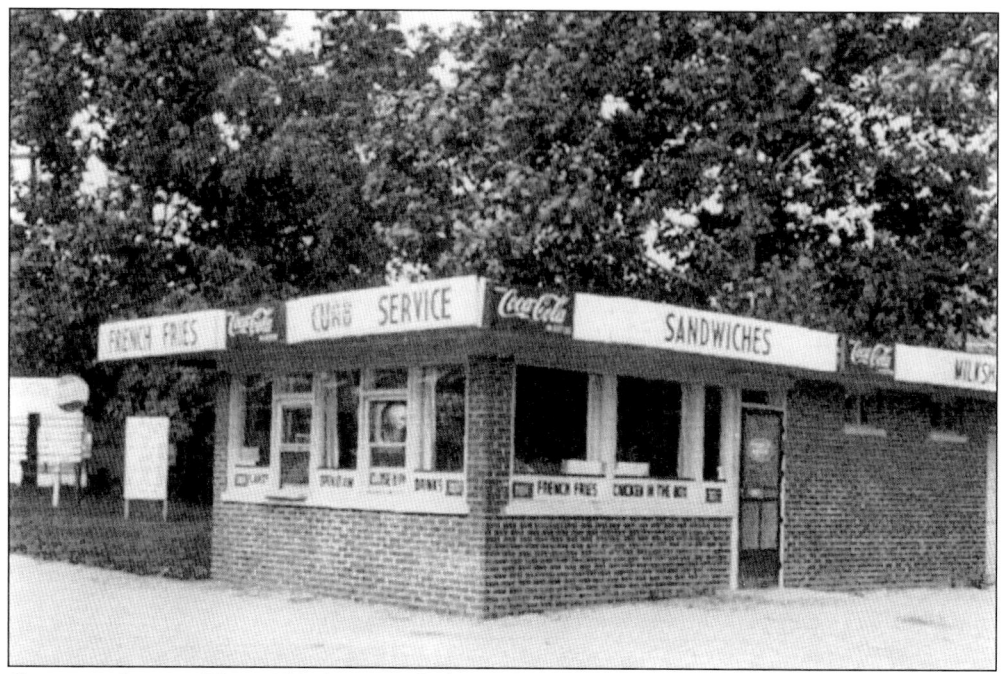

CUSTARD STAND. This 1958 photograph shows the Custard Stand in downtown Saltville. This building now houses T. J.'s Restaurant. You can get one of the best burgers in Virginia here. (Courtesy of Roger Allison.)

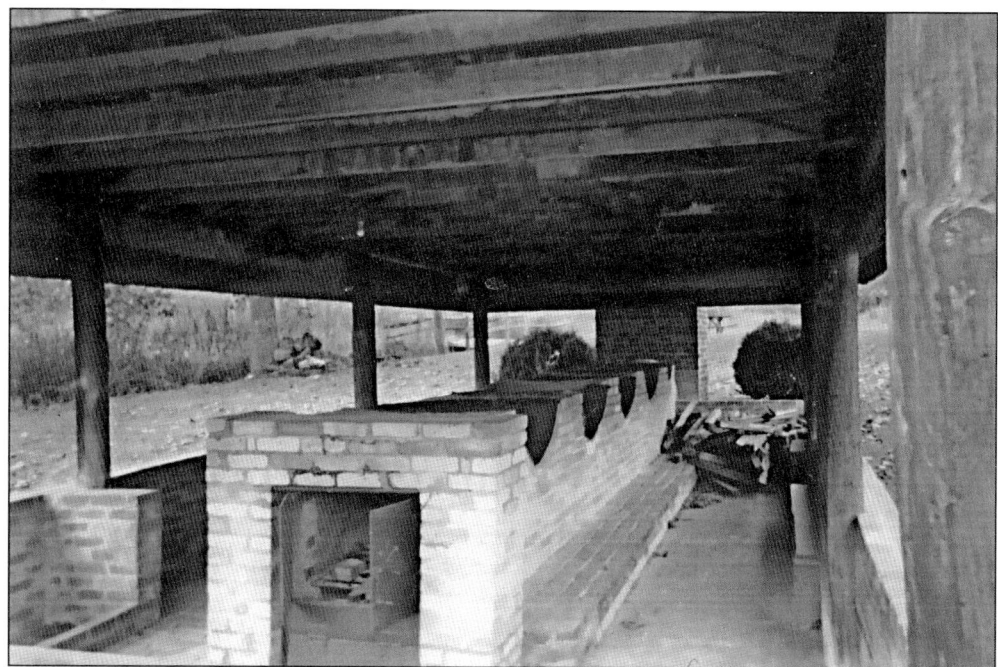

SALT PARK. This is one of the buildings at the Salt Park, located on West Main Street. Perhaps the future of the town is tied to tourism. The Civil War battlefield was acquired by the Civil War Preservation Trust in 2004, and a rails-to-trails program is underway. The history and natural beauty of the place are apt to be the town's economic salvation. (Photograph by J. Weaver.)

Five
SALTVILLE SUBURBS

In the days before easy transportation, many communities grew up around a central place, usually a church or store. These very small communities were often granted a post office and a unique name. Southwest Virginia had a profusion of these small post offices and communities. There are several surrounding Saltville, and they are now served by the amenities in the town. Some of these hamlets antedate Mathieson, and some were ancillary to the work of the company.

The more notable communities that are a part of greater Saltville include Allison Gap, about a mile northwest of the center of town; McCready's Gap, about two miles northeast of town; Quarry, about two miles south of town; Plasterco, formerly Buena Vista, which abuts the western end of town; and North Holston, about five miles northeast. Neighboring communities are Clinchburg, Glade Spring, and Emory in Washington County; Chilhowie, Broadford, and Rich Valley in Smyth County; and Tannersville in Tazewell County.

Mathieson and U.S. Gypsum provided company stores for their workers in Plasterco, Quarry, North Holston, and Allison Gap, as well as in downtown Saltville.

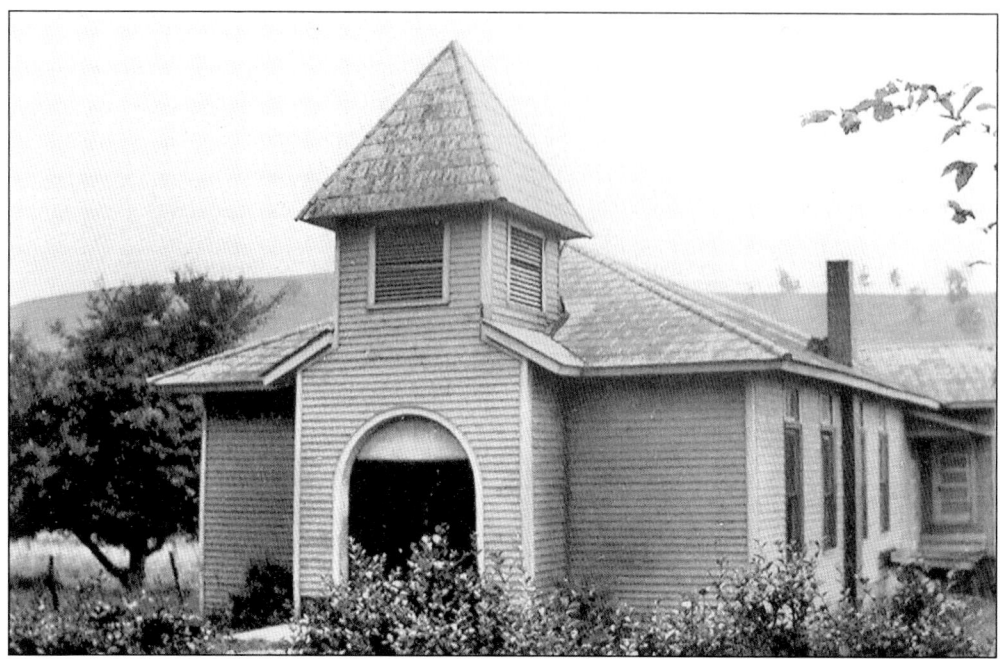

NORTH HOLSTON COMMUNITY CENTER. Southern Gypsum and Mathieson Alkali Works and their management usually contributed heavily to community facilities. This is one of those facilities, the North Holston Community Center.

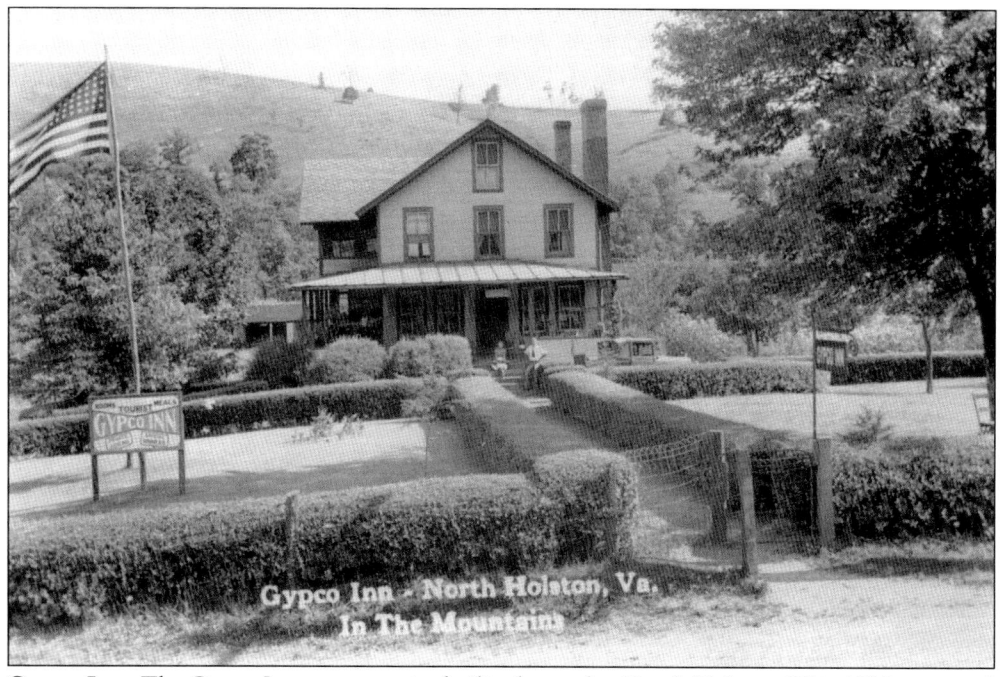

GYPCO INN. The Gypco Inn was a tourist facility located at North Holston. This 1930s postcard shows a neat, well-maintained lodging house. They offered tourists rooms, meals, and private dining. This inn is presently a private residence.

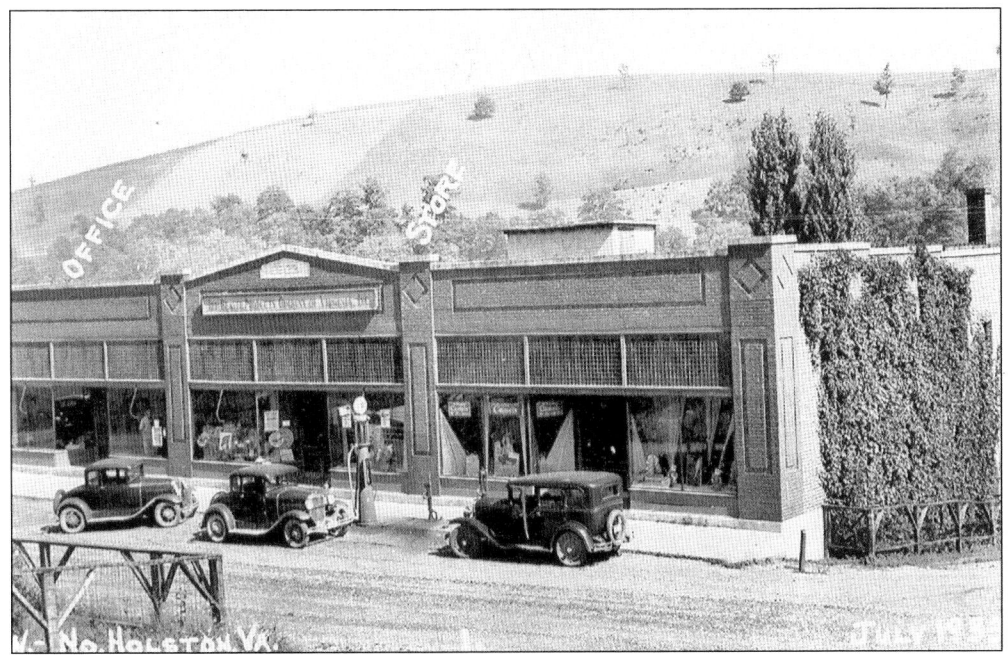

NORTH HOLSTON COMPANY STORE. Built in 1922, the North Holston company store offered many of the same goods and services to workers in this section as could be obtained in the Saltville company store. This building also housed offices of the Southern Gypsum Company, a subsidiary of Beaver Products Company of Virginia. This photograph was taken in July 1933, when Southern Gypsum was acquired by Mathieson Alkali Works.

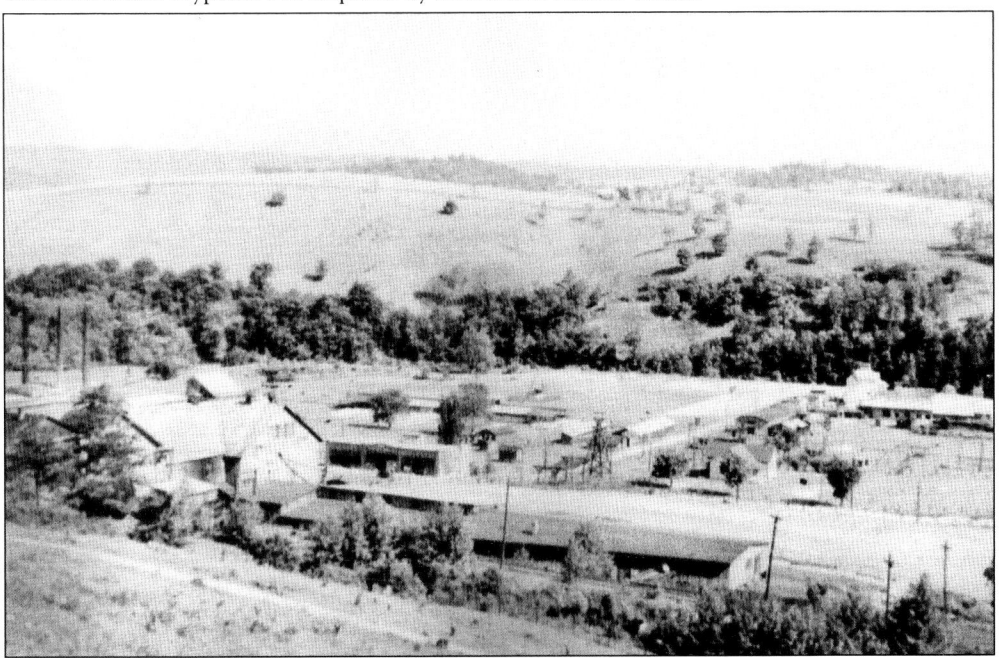

NORTH HOLSTON. This is a general view taken in the mid-20th century of the main facilities at North Holston. These operations included the Southern Gypsum mine, a mill to grind the stone into a usable powder, and the company store.

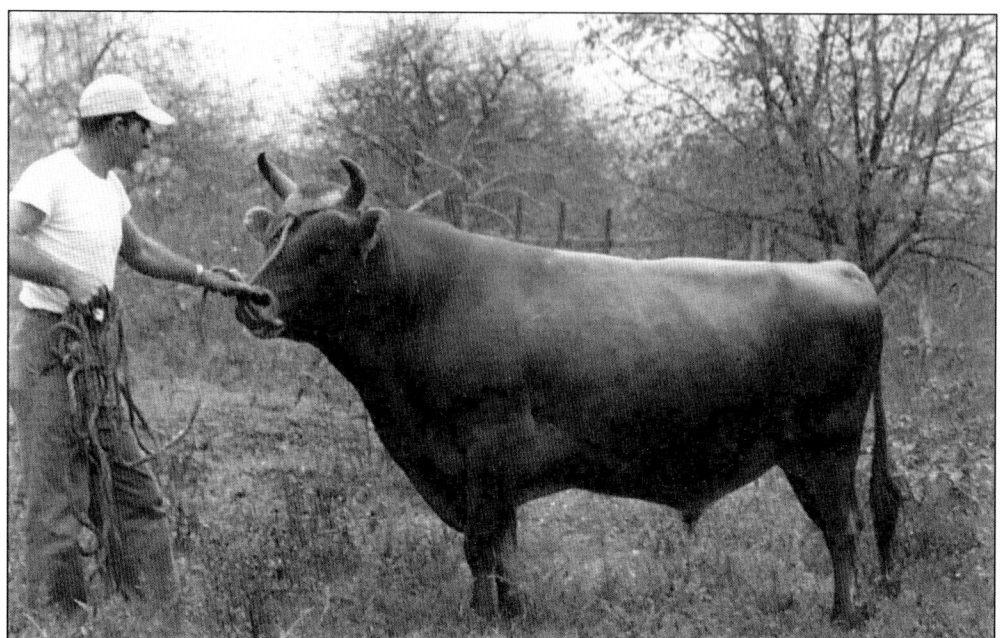

GREEN HILL JERSEY FARM. The Green Hill Jersey Farm at North Holston has long been noted for its fine cattle. This 1958 image shows a gentle brown Swiss bull. There are many fine farms in the countryside surrounding Saltville. (Courtesy of Roger Allison.)

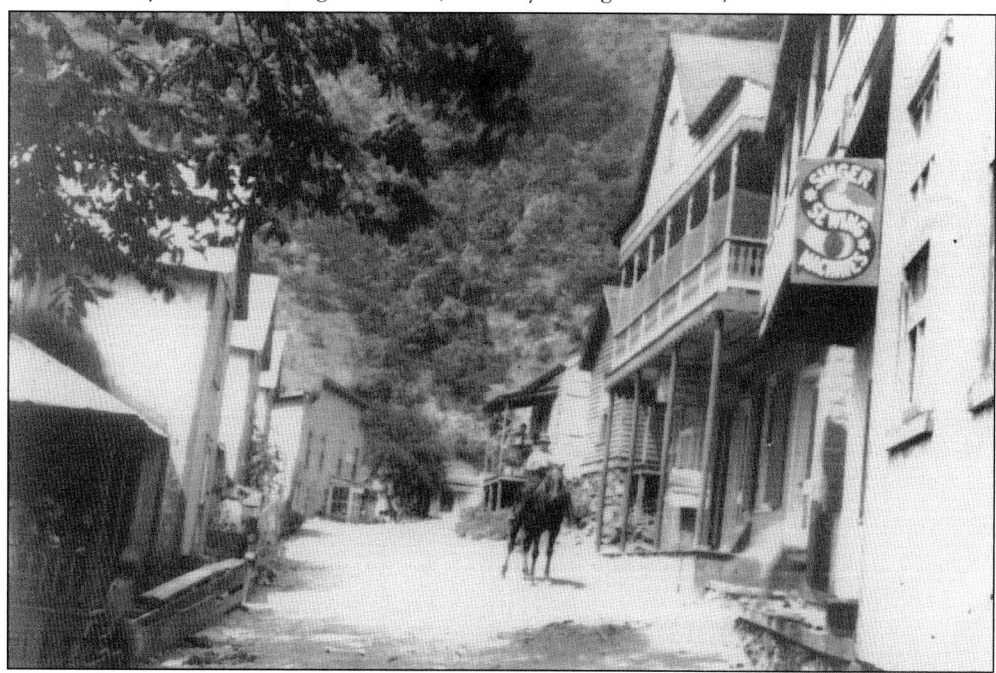

MAIN STREET ALLISON GAP. This is perhaps the most famous view of the main street of Allison Gap. The narrow street with shops on either side is reminiscent of the Old West. A building just out of this frame to the lower left is believed to have housed a brothel about the time this image was made, c. 1915. D. R. Henderson ran a store out of frame to the upper right. He operated one of the area's first funeral homes in the upstairs portion of this store.

DAVID ALLISON. David Allison, born in 1815 in Ashe County, North Carolina, moved to the Saltville area in 1836 and established the Allison Gap community just north of the town. Allison served in Company D, 4th Virginia Infantry, during the Civil War despite his age. This unit was part of the famous Stonewall Brigade, which made their reputation at the Battle of First Manassas. He died in 1888. (Courtesy of Roger Allison.)

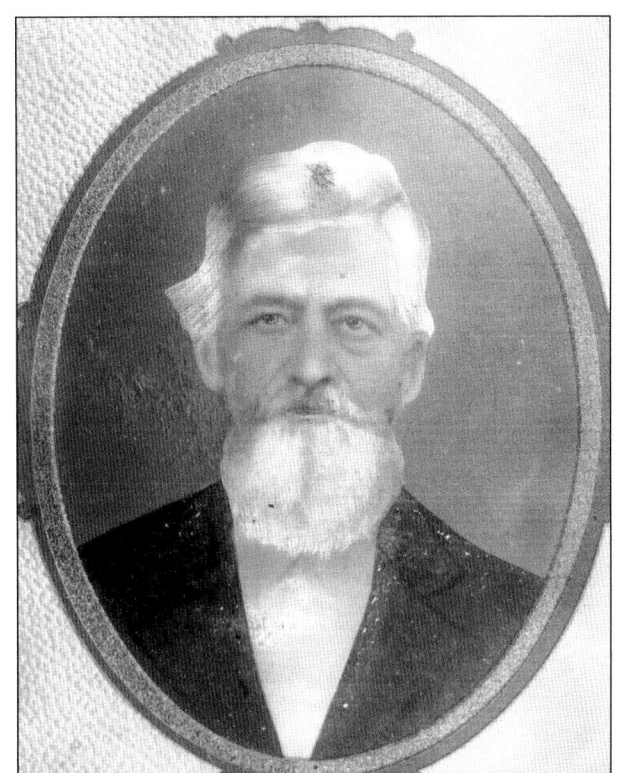

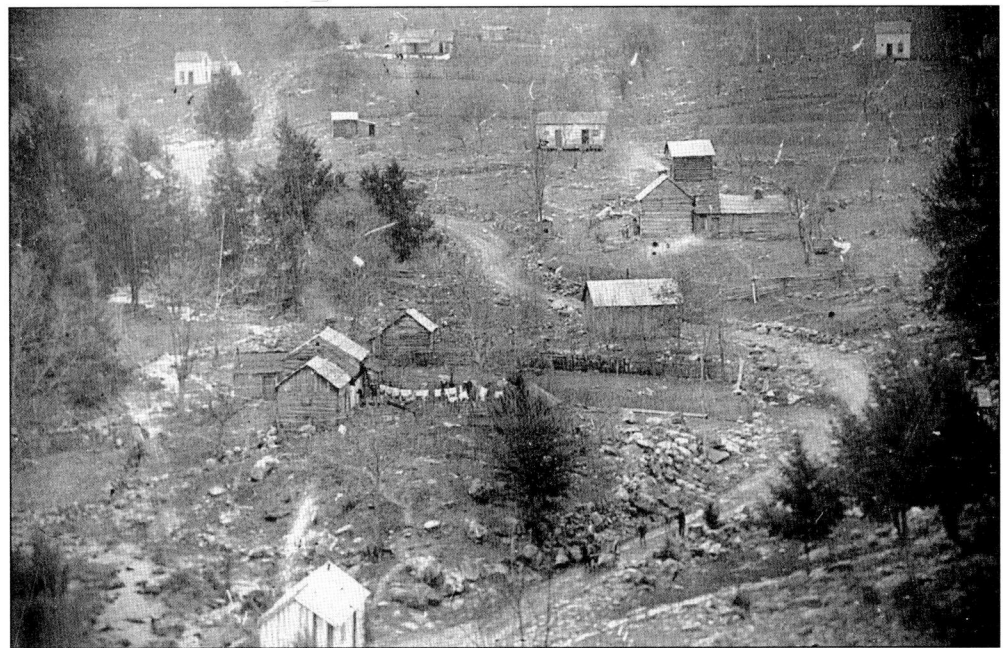

ALLISON GAP COMMUNITY. This is a general view of the Allison Gap community in the late 19th century. Allison Gap is a narrow passage in the mountains leading from Saltville to Poor Valley. The house in the upper right corner of the photograph was a slave cabin. Three other slave cabins to the right of this one are out of this shot.

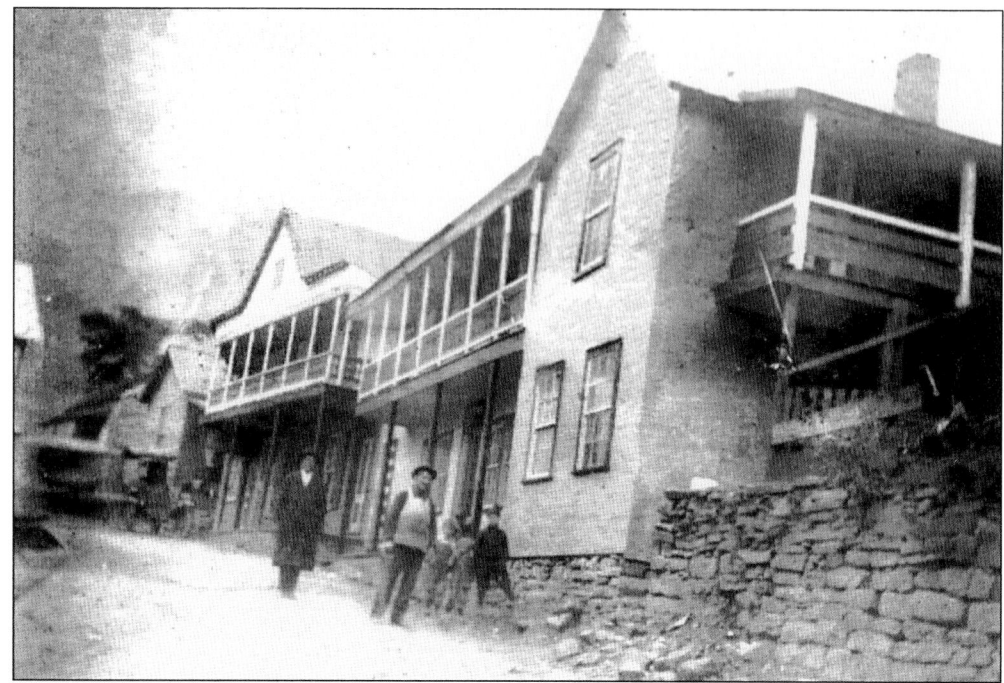

MAIN STREET, ALLISON GAP. This image shows the narrowness of the main street in Allison Gap, with the houses directly abutting the street. The photographer apparently had his session interrupted by a rare automobile. Note the shadow of the car as it comes down the street, denoting a long exposure for the camera. The car is probably a 1908 Maxwell. (Courtesy of Roger Allison.)

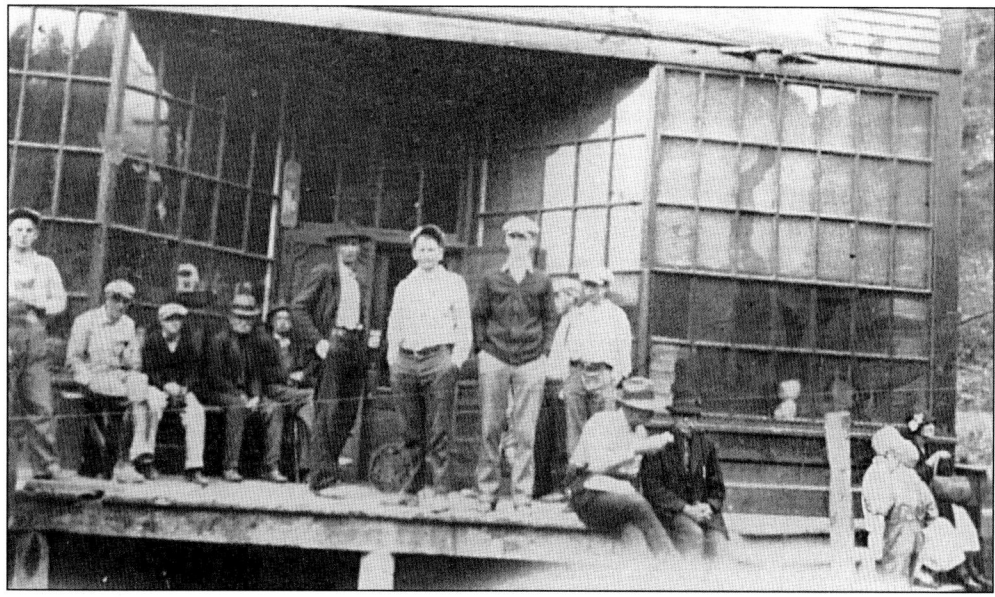

ALLISON GAP COMPANY STORE. This 1930s image shows a group of neighborhood boys and men sitting on the front porch of the company store at Allison Gap. In rural communities, this was the principal means of learning the news of the day or plain old gossip before television or other modern means of communication.

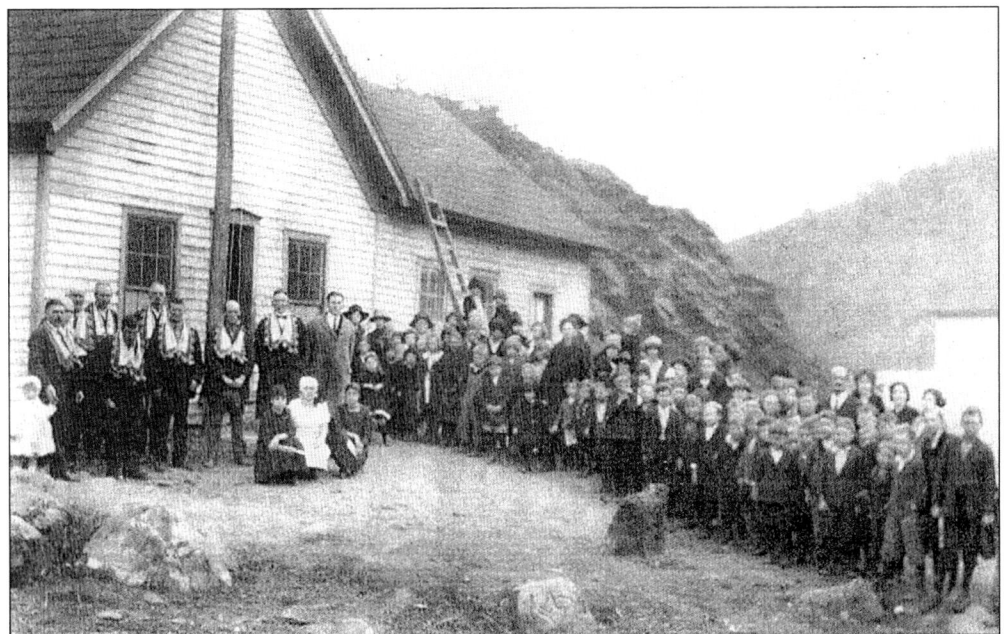

ALLISON GAP SCHOOL, 1925. One- or two-room schoolhouses were common in rural Appalachia in the 1920s; this school had five rooms. As school bus transportation was added in the 1930s, many of these "old field schools" were closed or consolidated to more modern facilities. Note the men in the left of the images wearing Junior Order of United American Mechanics regalia. This school site is now occupied by Fred's Trading Post in Allison Gap. (Courtesy of Roger Allison.)

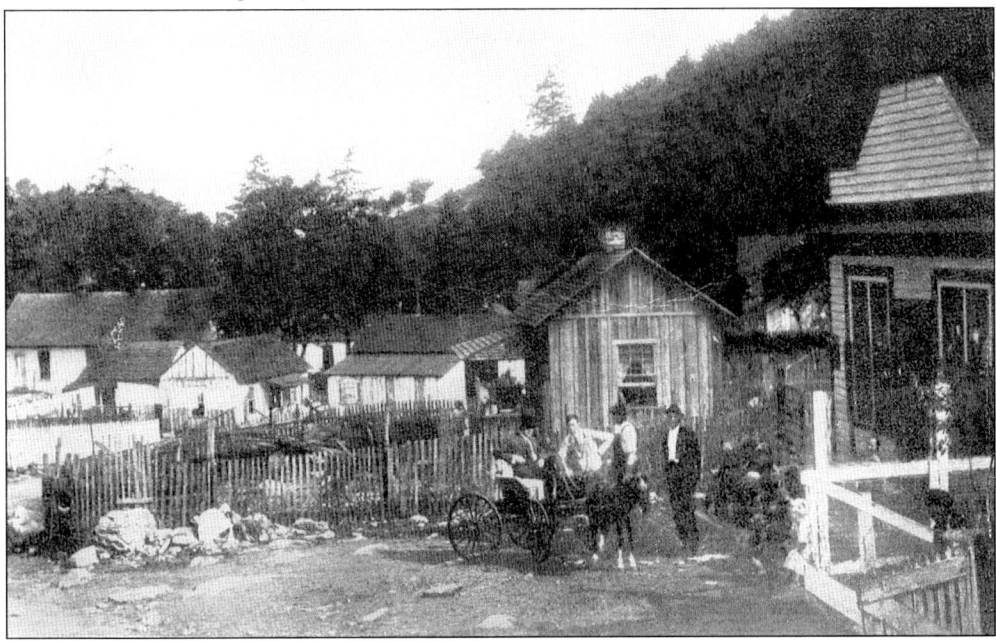

ALLISON GAP. This early colored postcard of Allison Gap shows some of the density of the houses in this neighborhood. Note the colt hitched to the buggy in the center of the photograph. Perhaps the purpose was to introduce the colt to the feel of the buggy, but the animal is clearly too small to do much work. (Courtesy of Roger Allison.)

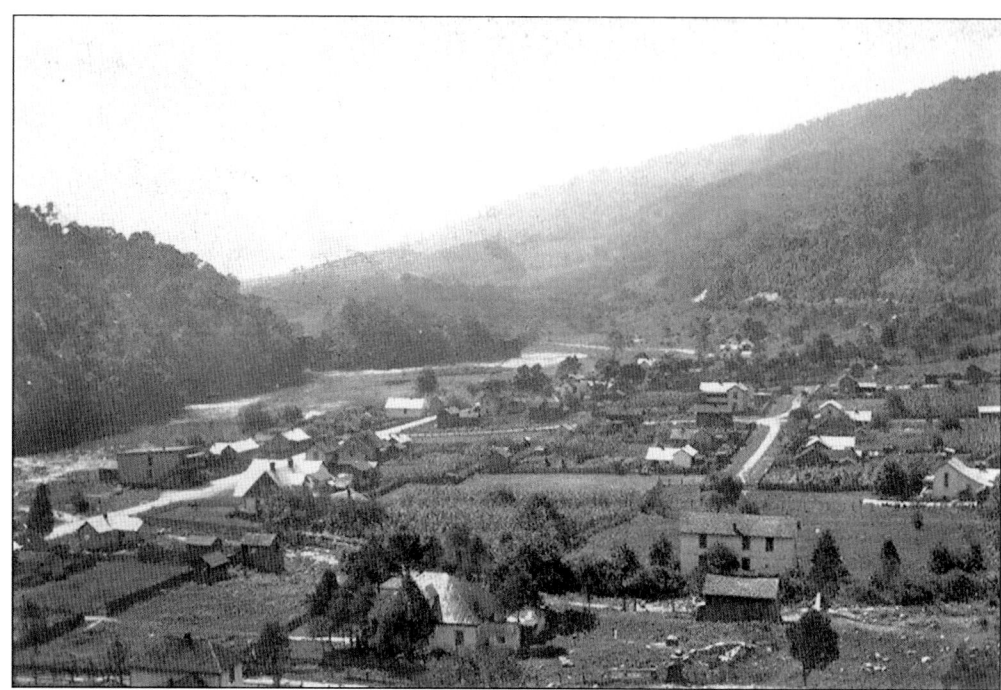

McCready's Gap Community. This general view is of the attractive McCready's Gap community, about two miles northeast of Saltville. This image was created in the early 20th century and shows neat houses, gardens, and streets. This hamlet is not much changed today.

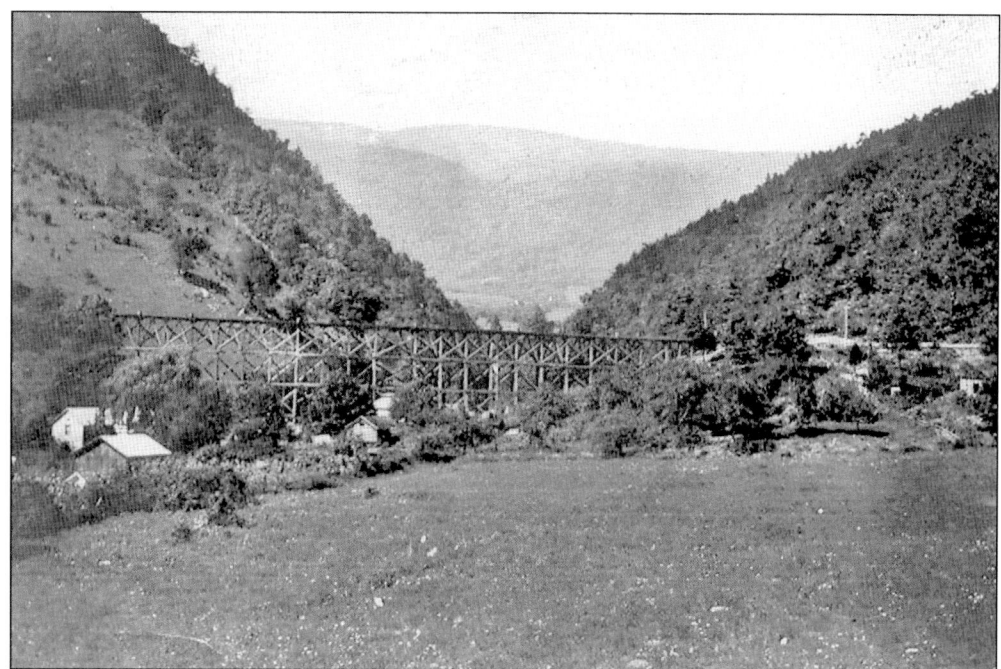

The Trestle at McCready's Gap. This scene is one of the more famous images of the area. This wooden trestle carried the steam locomotives from Saltville to the Southern Gypsum operations at North Holston.

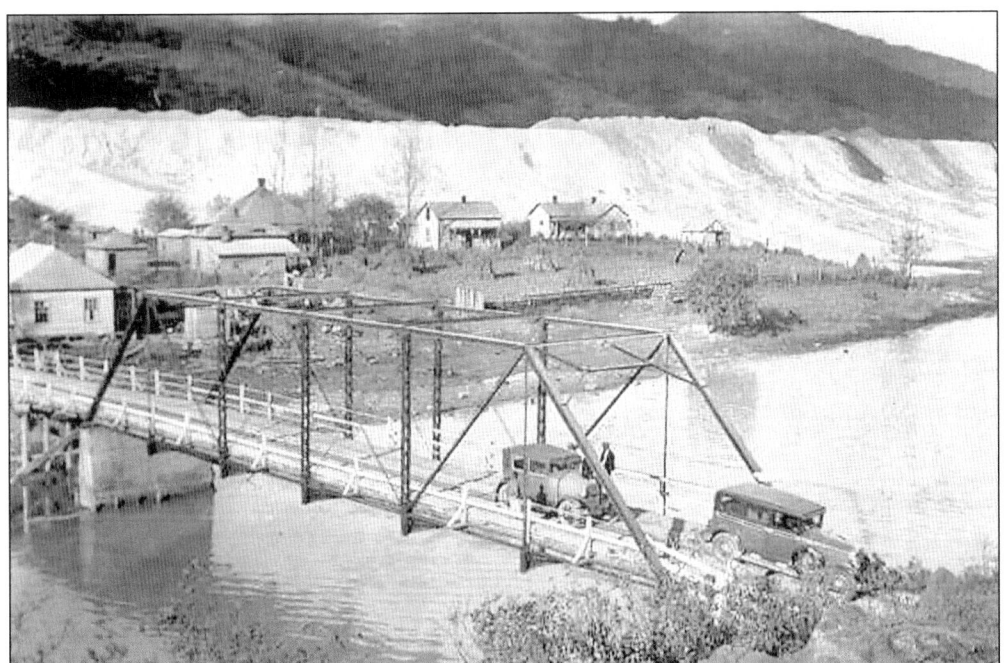

HENRYTOWN BRIDGE. This early-1930s shot shows the bridge over the North Fork of Holston River at Henrytown. The white wall in the background is a limestone sludge dam similar to the one that caused the Palmertown Tragedy in 1924.

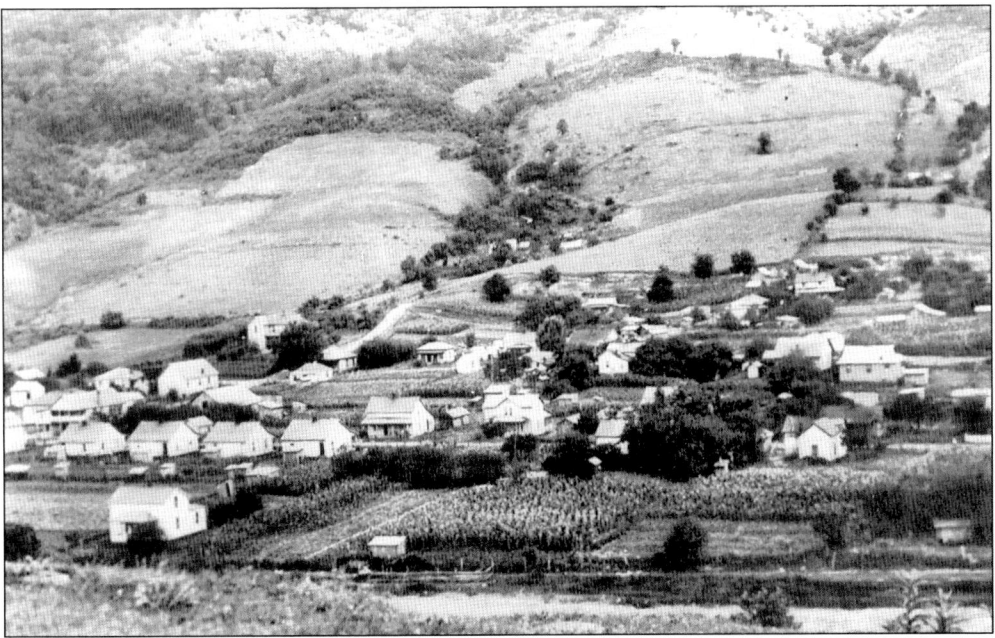

HENRYTOWN. This was another company-owned neighborhood for workers at the plant. Henrytown lay outside the corporate limits of Saltville. In the early days, no one was quite sure who was responsible for it. This community developed without policing and was the place to get into trouble if one was so inclined. This idyllic scene was taken in the first third of the 20th century.

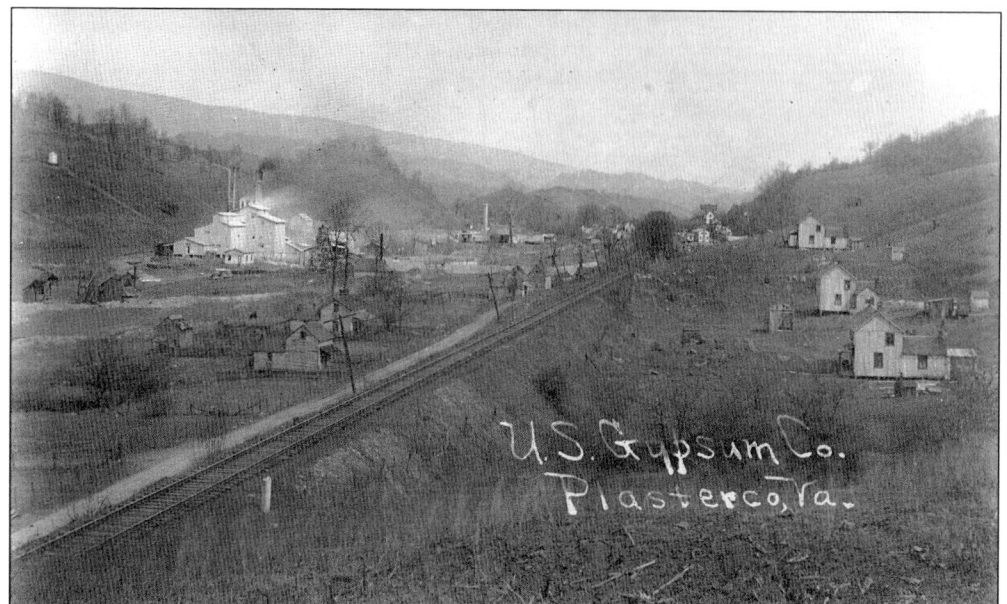

U.S. GYPSUM COMPANY. The first commercial exploitation of gypsum in the area dates from 1808. This 1917 image shows the main processing plant on the left and some company housing on the right. Nearly 200 years of mining has made much of this area geologically unstable.

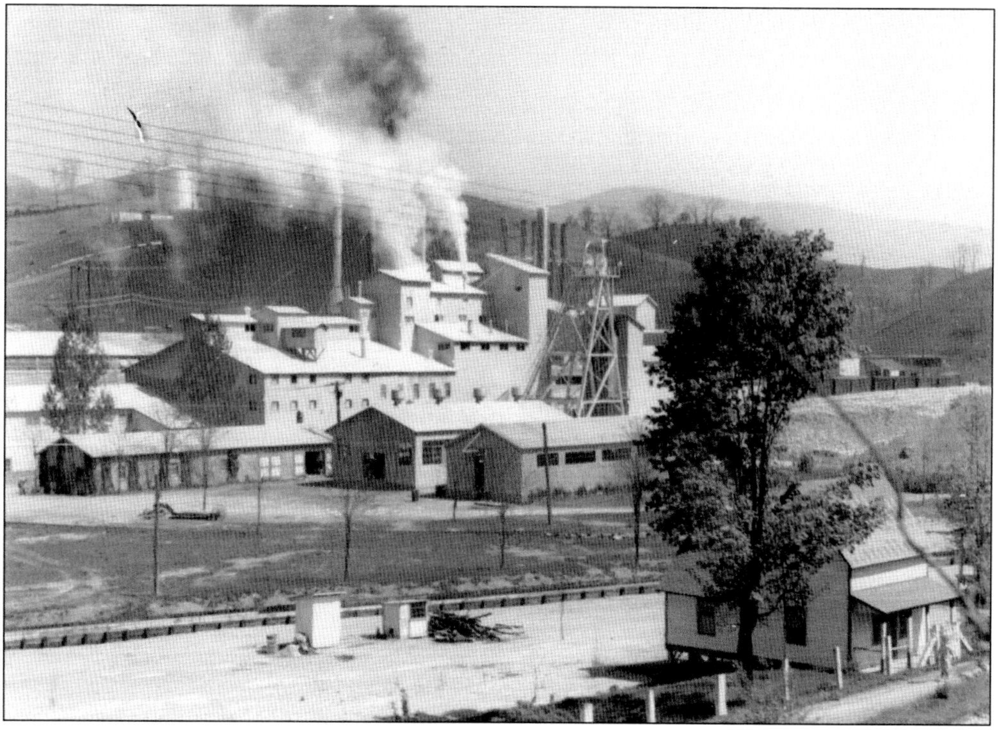

U.S. GYPSUM. This snapshot shows the main facilities at U.S. Gypsum at Plasterco. The belching smoke from this facility and those at Saltville degraded the environment for years, but jobs were scarce outside the Saltville Valley, and there was little complaint about the pollution. Workers' houses were situated very close to the plant. (Courtesy of Roger Allison.)

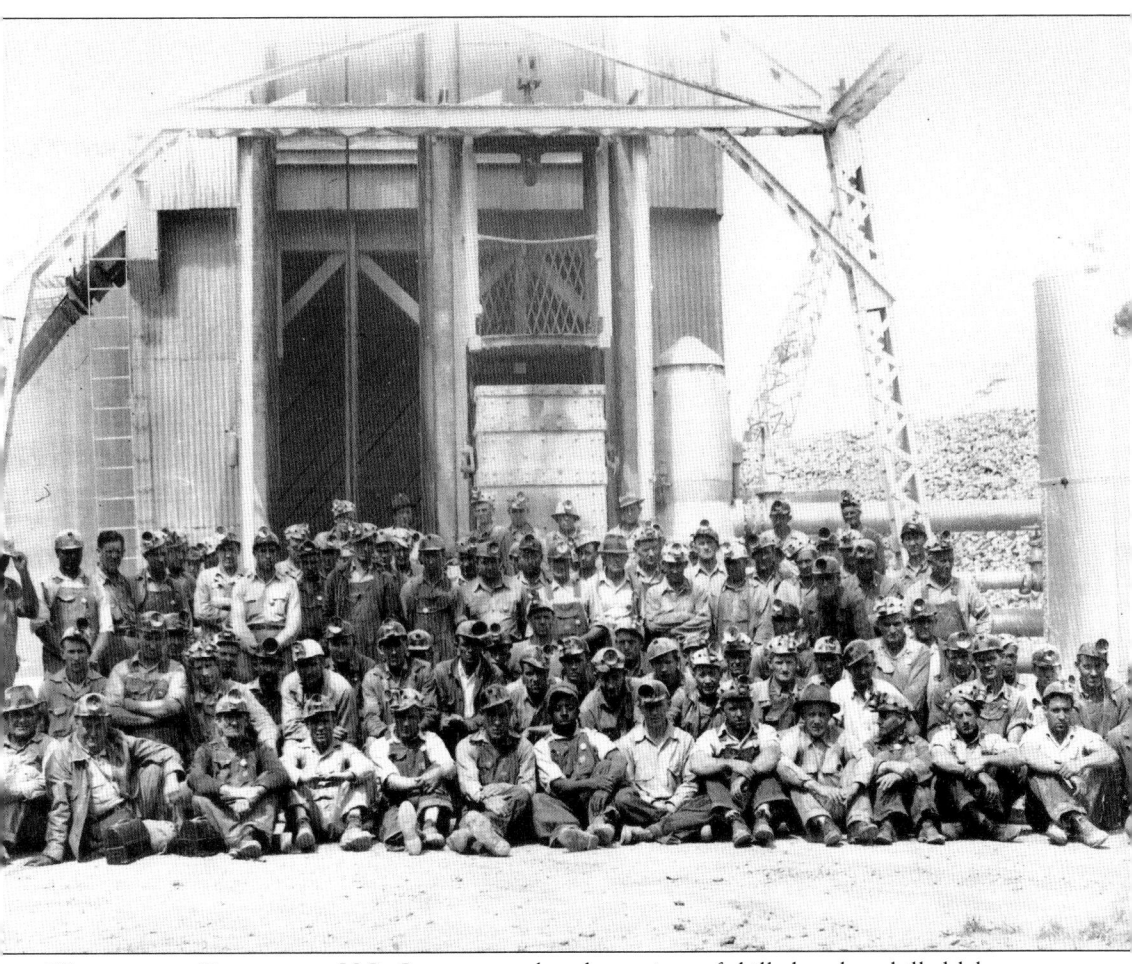

WORKERS AT PLASTERCO. U.S. Gypsum employed a variety of skilled and unskilled labor at their Plasterco facility. This 1930s shot shows some mechanics, fabricators, and miners. Gypsum underlies the valley in boulders. Unlike the salt, it had to be extracted in the old-fashioned way—by hand and underground. (Courtesy of Roger Allison.)

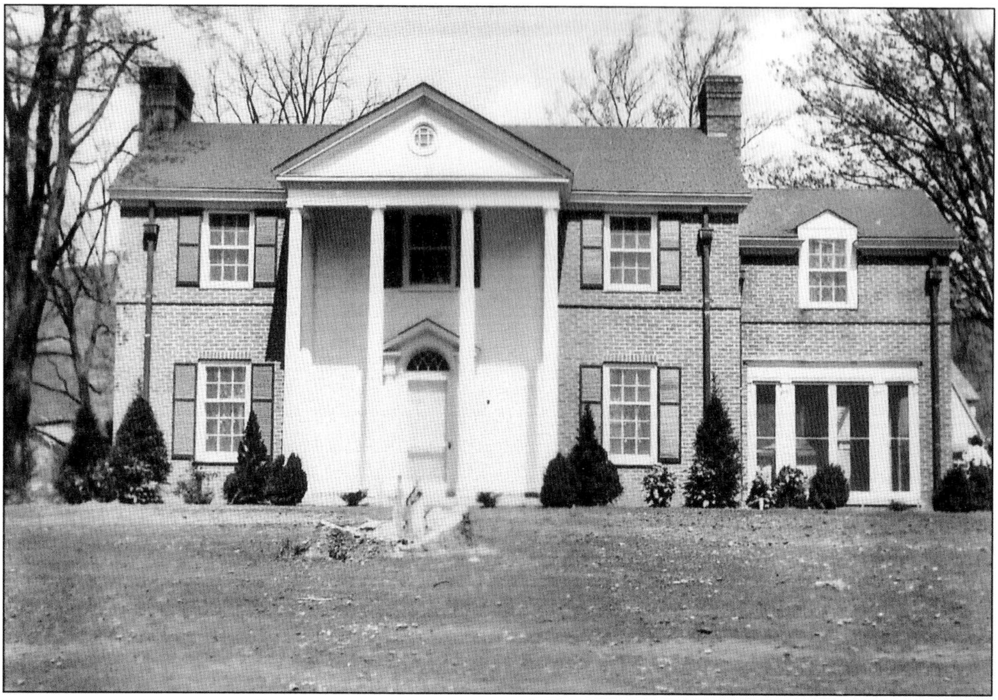

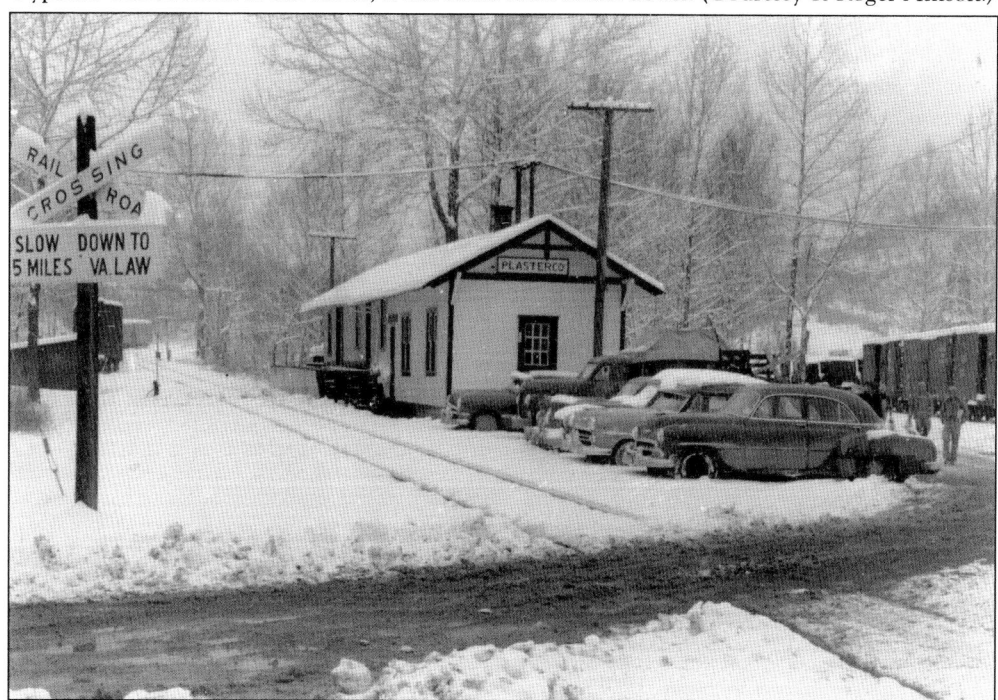

MANAGER'S HOUSE AT PLASTERCO. This elegant home was the house of the manager of U.S. Gypsum. Constructed in the 1930s, it has since been taken down. (Courtesy of Roger Allison.)

PLASTERCO STATION. This wintry 1950s scene shows the Plasterco Station. The snow did little to slow down work in these facilities. Two members of the yard crew can be seen between the rail cars and automobiles on the right side of the photograph. (Courtesy of Roger Allison.)

Six
DISASTERS

Most communities have had disasters that have held the memories of the citizens long after the events took place. Saltville is no different. There were several minor calamities that are still remembered: a mudslide above British Row, mine collapses in the Plasterco area, a train wreck, industrial accidents at "the Plant," and the 1917 tornado. Many men were killed in accidents in the gypsum mines and around the heavy equipment used at Mathieson. Saltvillians' minds quickly turn to the Palmertown Tragedy, also known as the "Muck Dam Disaster," when disasters are discussed.

On Christmas Eve 1924, the dam that was built to hold back lime sludge gave way. A wall of debris 100 feet high and 300 feet wide swept down the North Fork of Holston River, taking everything in its path. The community of Palmertown was in its path. Nineteen people died during this event. It might have been worse had it not been Christmas Eve. Many of the residents of Palmertown were in Saltville finishing up their Christmas shopping. A few reported being at the Victory Theater taking in a show. There are still elderly residents of Saltville who can remember the event vividly.

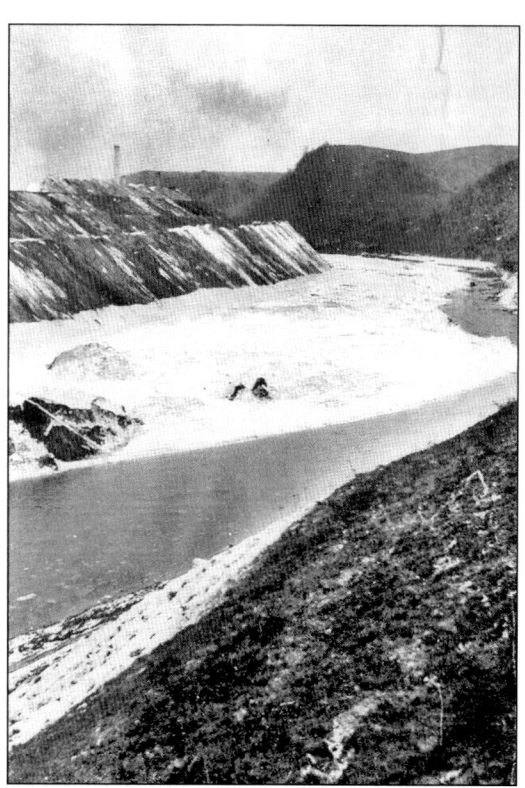

NORTH FORK OF HOLSTON RIVER. This December 1924 image shows the level the sludge reached on the riverbank when the muck dam holding the sludge back failed. Most accounts place the height of the wall of muck and debris at about 100 feet.

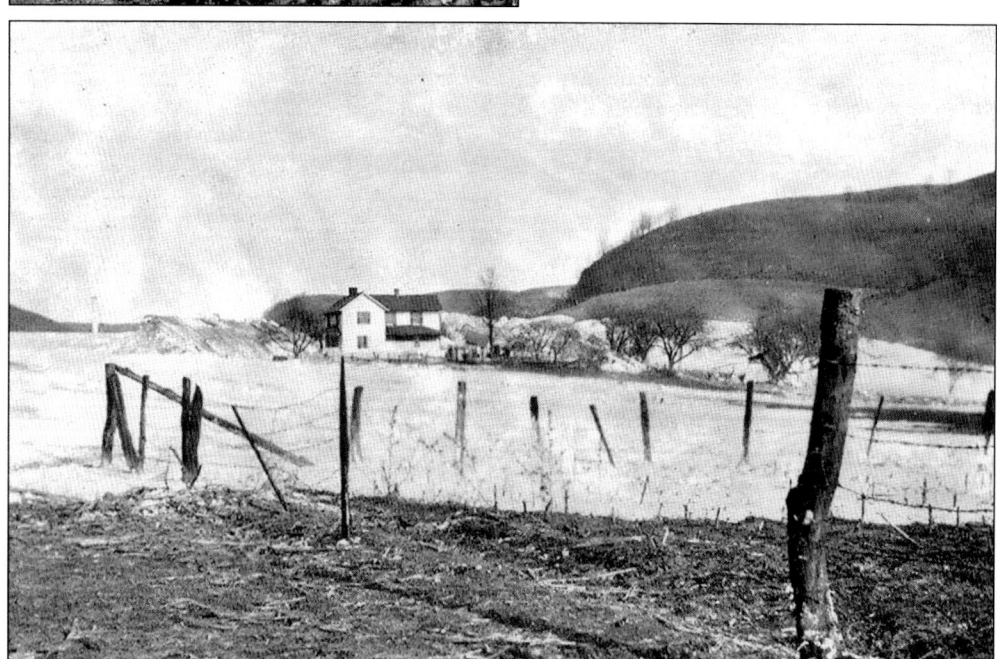

ANOTHER RIVER VIEW. This is another general view of the river immediately after the collapse of the muck dam on Wednesday, December 24, 1924. The river has returned to its natural course in this shot, but the white material on the left shows the width of the wall that crashed down the valley that fateful night.

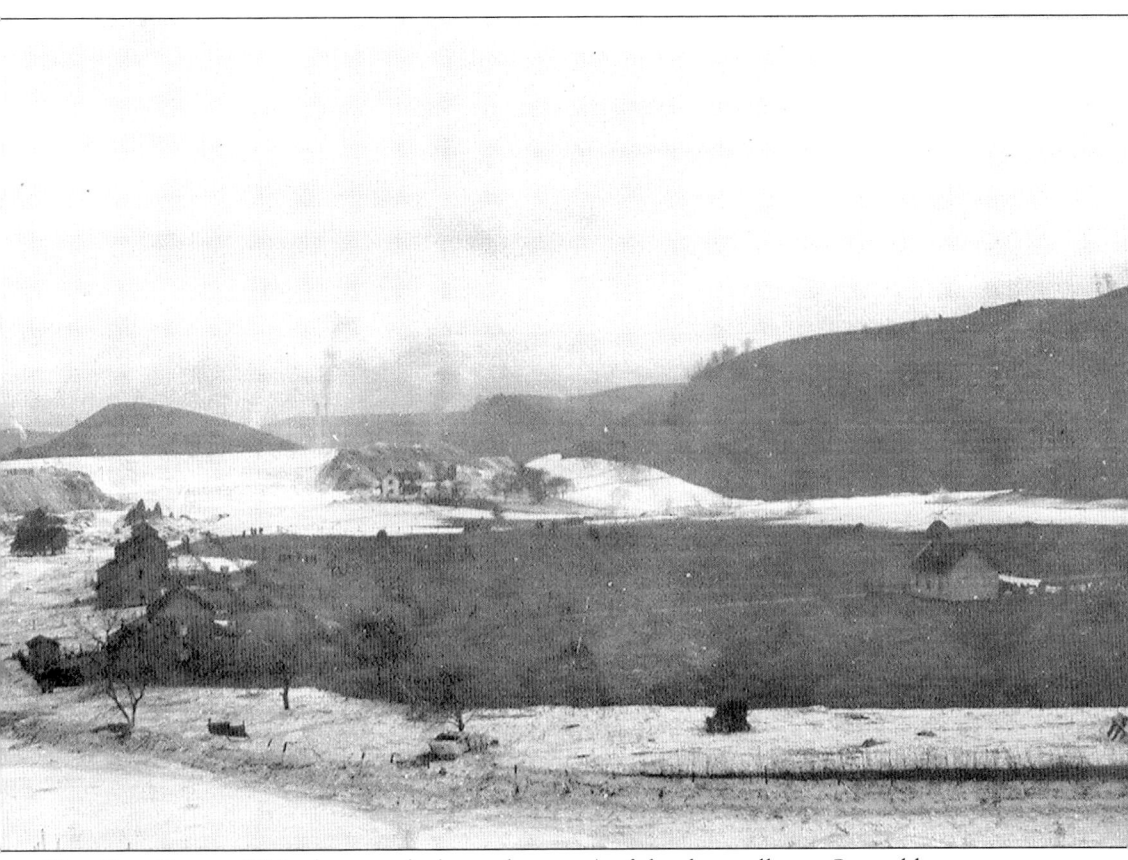

THE DAM BREAK. This photograph shows the extent of the dam collapse. Several houses were immediately in front of the dam, which contributed to the loss of life. The Palmertown Church is shown in the right of this photograph. Some of those left homeless by the disaster camped out in this house of worship. Note the wash hanging out on the line to the right of the church.

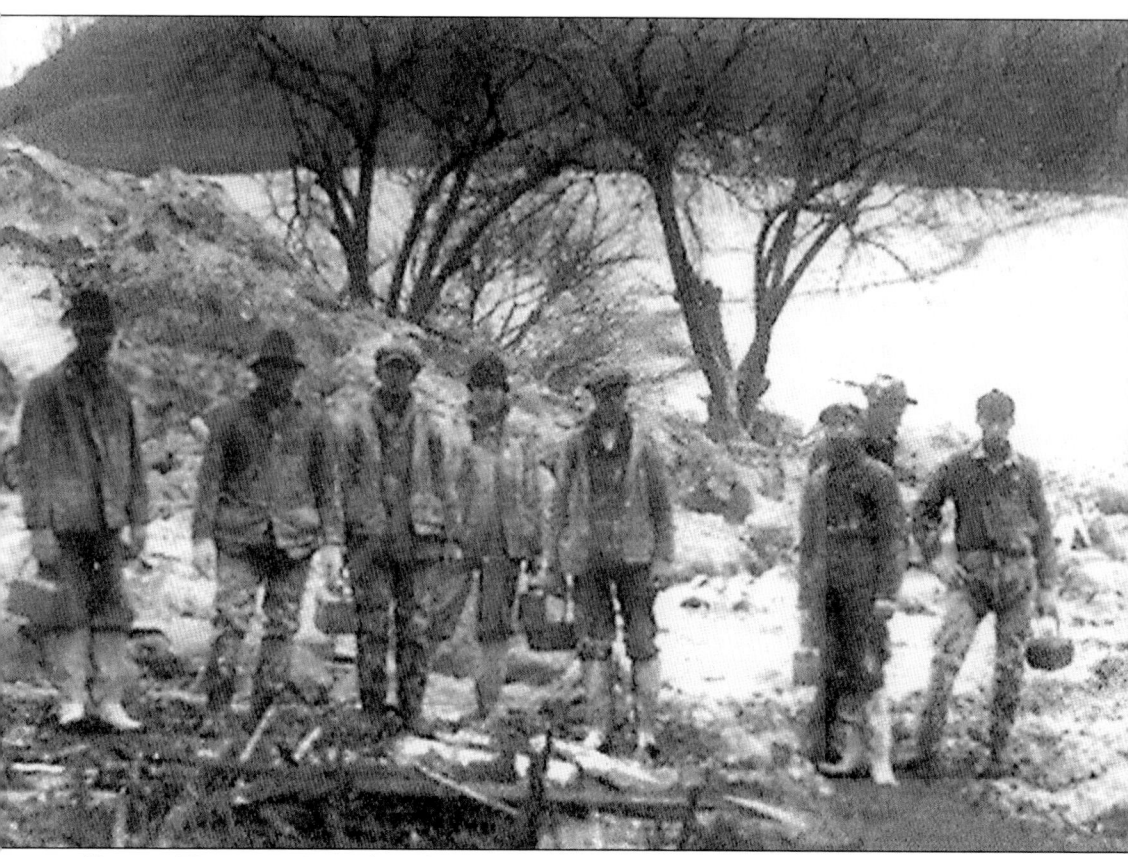

RESCUE WORKERS. Several residents of Palmertown escaped when the dam collapsed because they were in Saltville shopping in anticipation of Christmas the next day. Others were at home, and dozens of men turned out to search for those who might be trapped. This is a rescue crew of eight men after a hard day of searching for survivors. Some were found alive and were rescued.

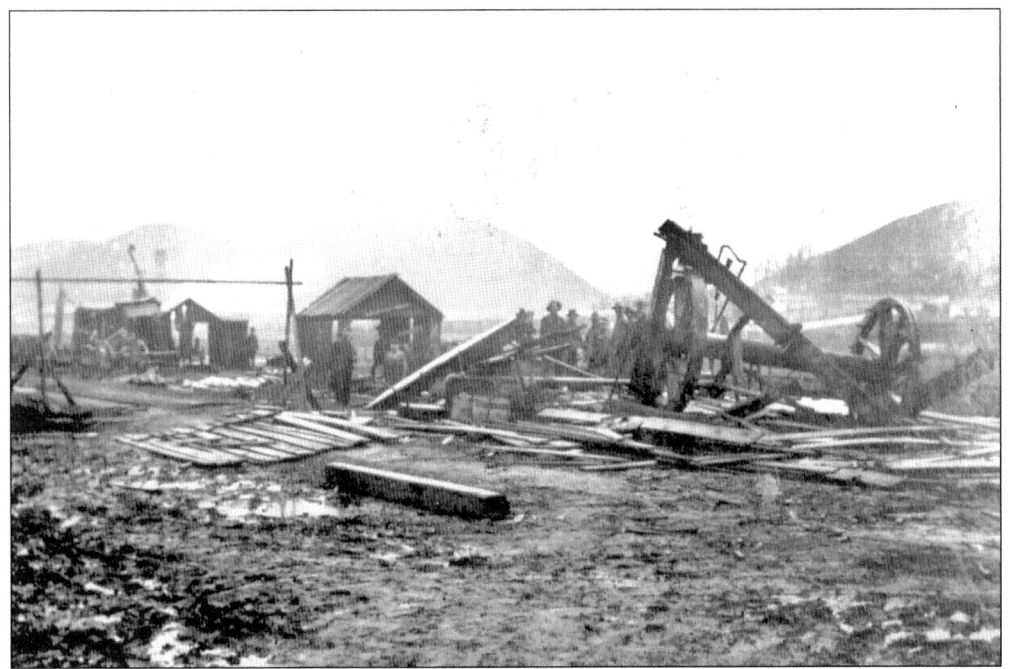

THE 1917 TORNADO. This image shows some of the wreckage from the 1917 tornado that came through town. Tornadoes are a relatively rare event in Appalachia; the mountains tend to break up the circular storms before they can do much damage.

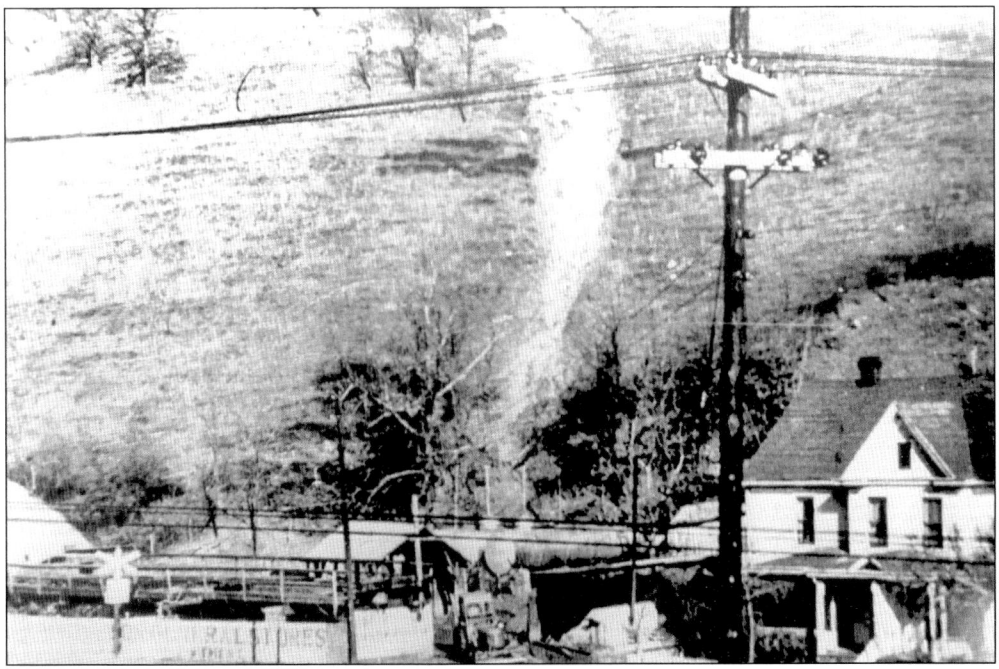

BRITISH ROW MUD SLIDE. This image from the 1940s shows a mudslide behind British Row. Mathieson, for reasons that are not clear, kept the hills around town cleared of trees. The grass was insufficient to hold the hill together after a heavy rain. The house in the lower right was one of the first built by Mathieson around 1892.

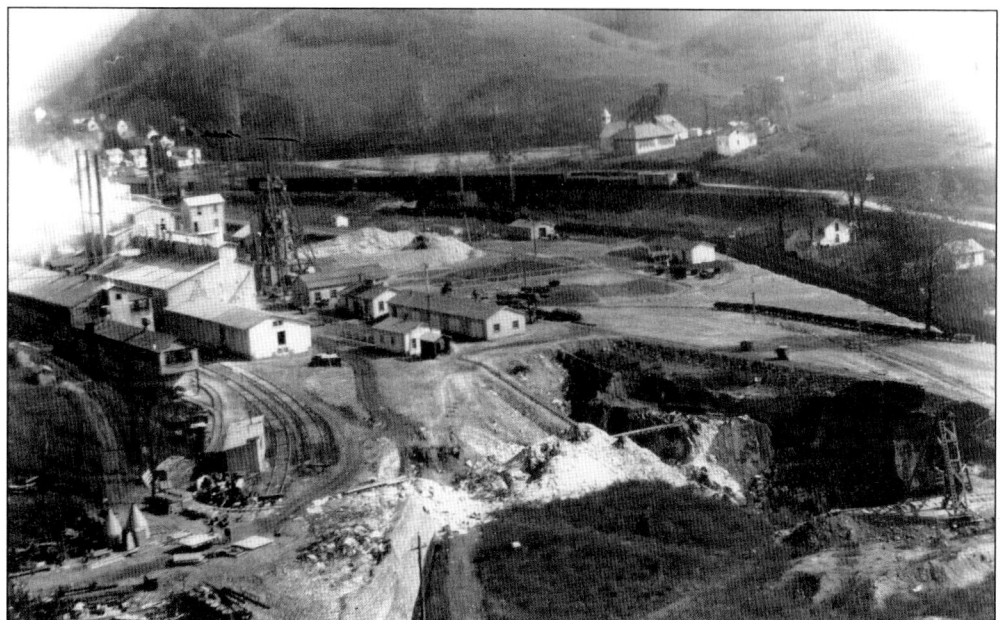

PLASTERCO MINE. The karst geology already has created voids throughout the area. Near the town, gypsum mining created further pockets, which are unable to support the weight of the materials on the surface. These mines were pumped dry for many years, but this has recently stopped. This is a view of an open-pit mine at Plasterco. (Courtesy of Roger Allison.)

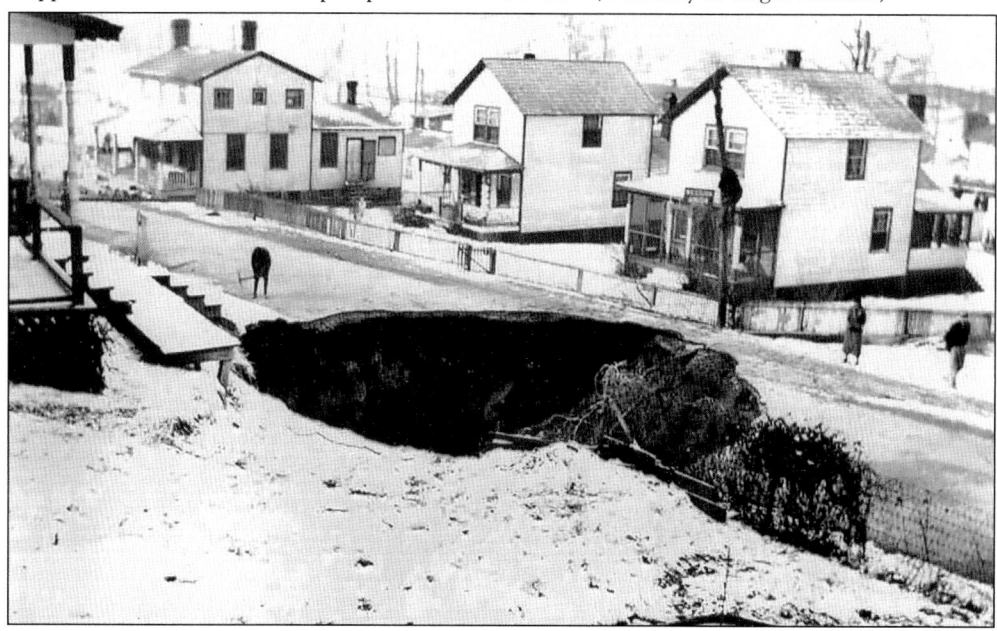

CAVE-IN AT PLASTERCO. Mining operations extended under many residential districts around Plasterco with some unfortunate results. This collapse necessitated the evacuation of several homes. These mining operations have also forced the abandonment of the rail line into Saltville. Some curious fellow has climbed a telegraph pole in front of the Western Union office on the right to get a better look into the hole. The man at the left with a pick seems to be exploring for additional weakness in the street.

Seven

TRANSPORTATION

Getting from here to there in the Appalachian Mountains has never been easy. Saltville is located in the North Fork of Holston River Valley. Clinch Mountain is on the west, and Big Walker Mountain is on the east. The first transportation routes followed the banks of the river. When manufacture of salt became a commercial reality, most of it was shipped by bateaux down river to King's Port in Sullivan County, Tennessee, until 1856, when the railroad came. In 1856, a nine-mile-long branch railroad called the Salt Branch Railroad reached the village. Salt was hauled to Glade Spring, where it joined the main line of the Virginia and East Tennessee Railroad. Trains provided most of the transportation in and out of Saltville for manufactured goods until the spur line was discontinued in 1984.

Gypsum mining around Plasterco had made the line unstable, and it was abandoned. Dean Adams, then an employee of Norfolk and Western Railroad, tells that he was making a routine visual inspection of the line near Plasterco and discovered a dangling piece of track. Olin had been the major customer of this spur line, but they had already left Saltville, so the economic necessity of the line was not much of a factor in its closing. This line is now under consideration for a rails-to-trails conversion in 2006.

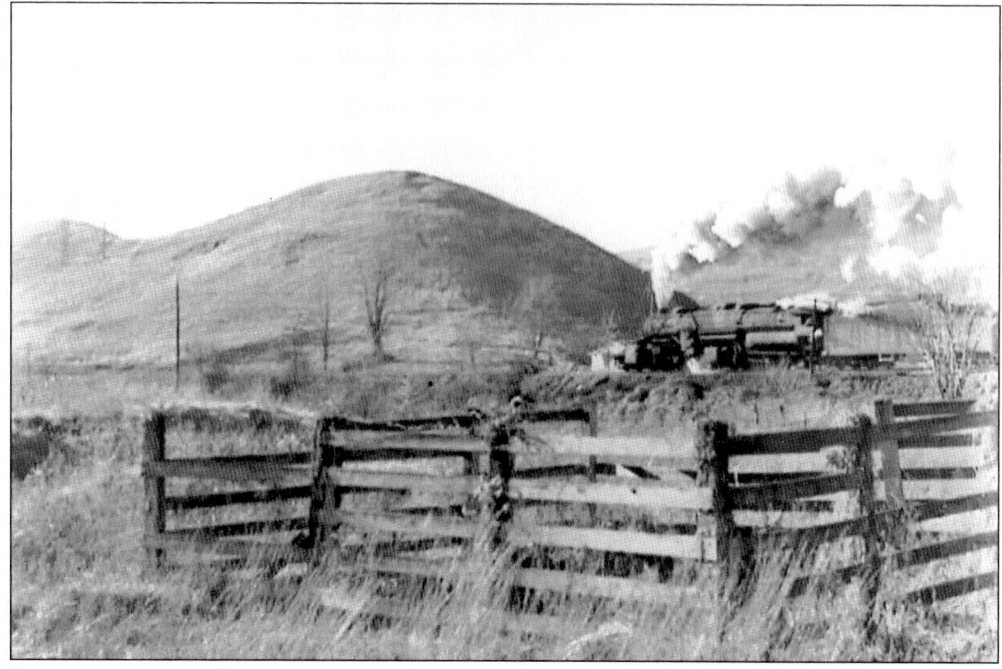

STEAMING OUT OF SALTVILLE. This great photograph shows a train crossing into Washington County from Saltville. The hills have been denuded of their trees. Trees were cut as fuel to fire the evaporators in the salt production process.

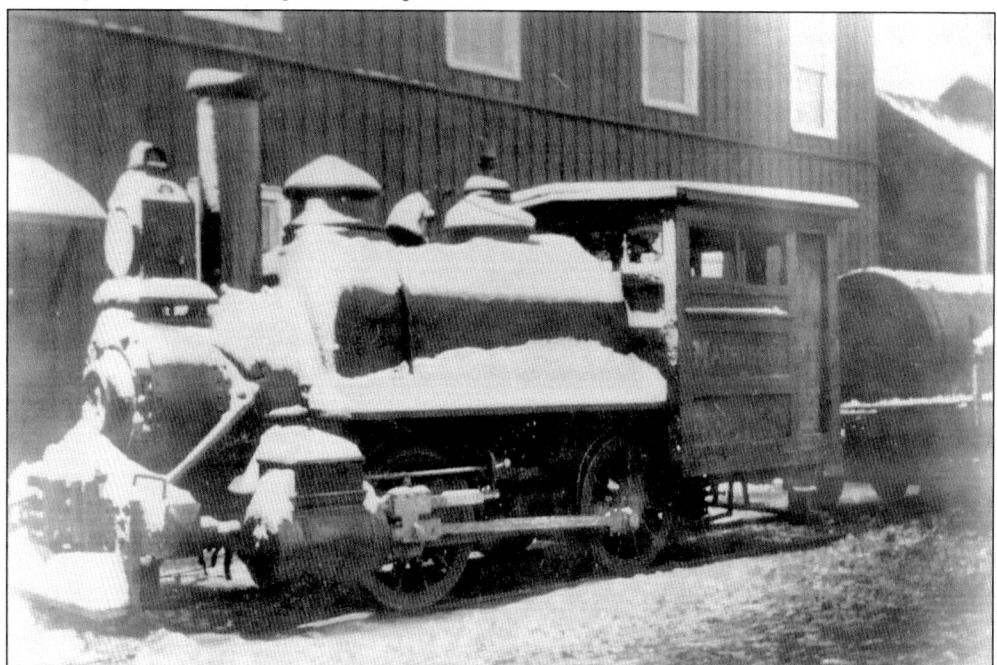

ENGINE IN THE SNOW. This is one of the first smaller engines bought by the Mathieson Alkali Works when they came to Saltville. The date of the photograph is uncertain, but it is probably from the late 19th century. This engine is sitting in the rail yard in Saltville. The company had extensive rail facilities for a community of Saltville's size, including a round house.

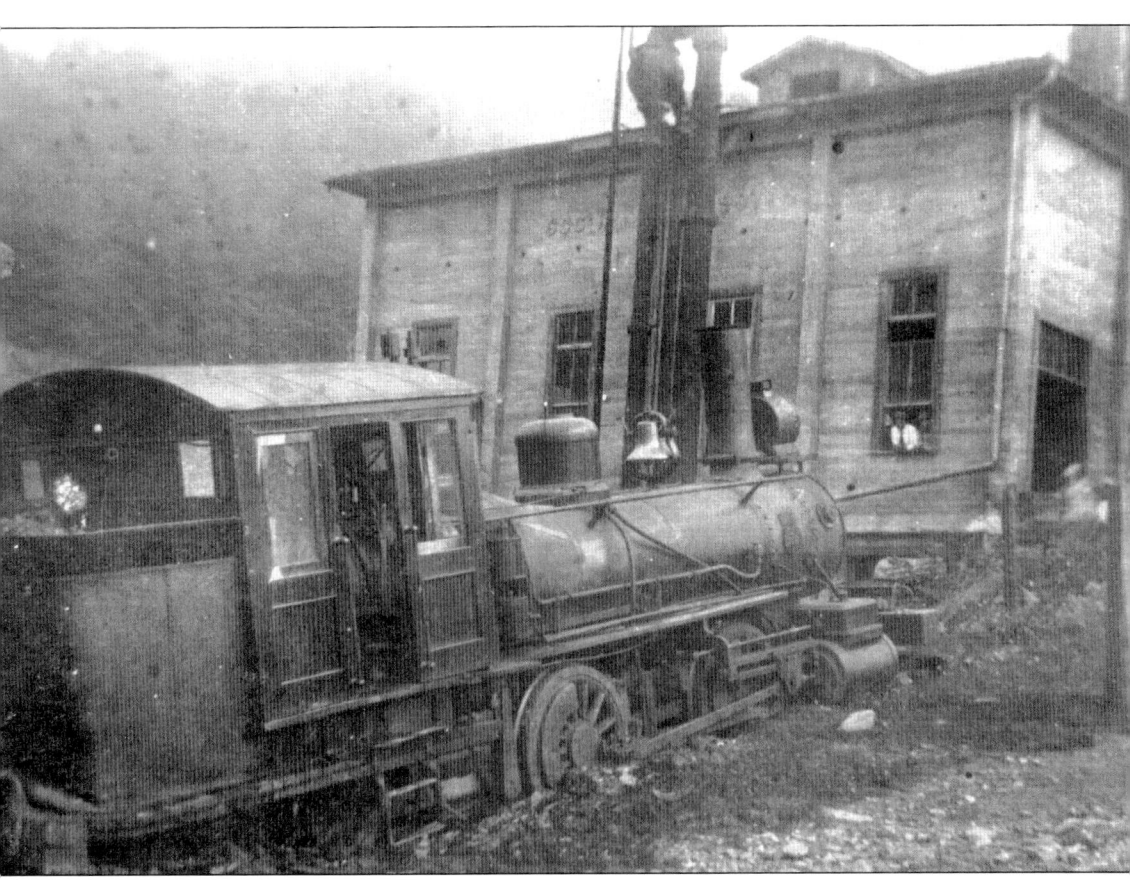

DERAILED AT NORTH HOLSTON. This shot shows one of Mathieson's steam engines derailed in front of the North Holston powerhouse. A crew put the engine back on the track by brute force. This photograph dates from after 1907.

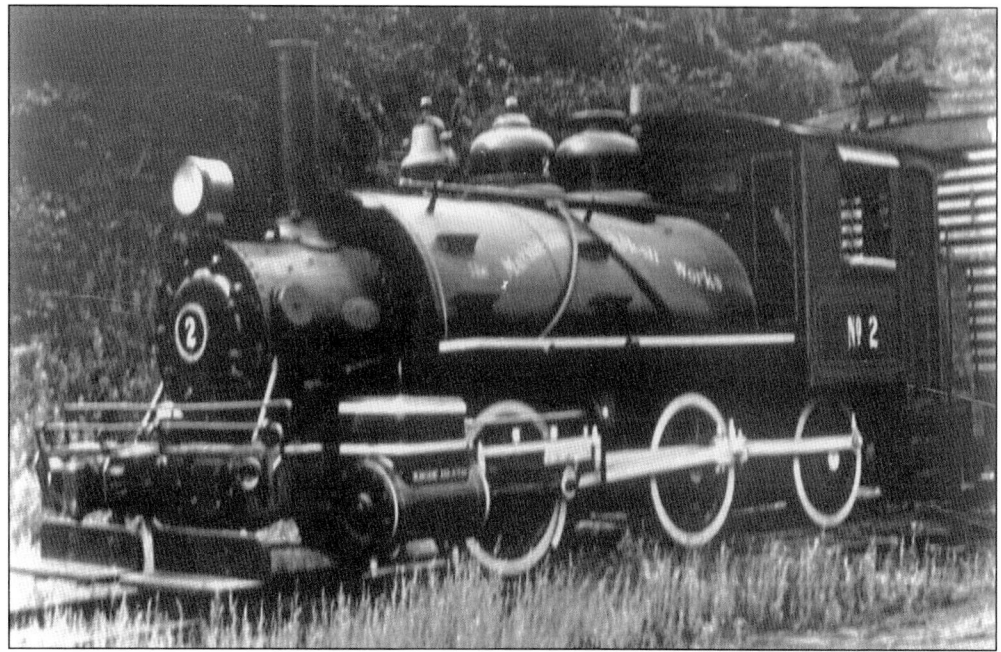

ENGINE NO. 2. Engine No. 2 has long been a familiar sight in Saltville. It was the smaller of two large engines bought by Mathieson in the 1890s. It ran on the Salt Branch Railroad from the 1890s until the mid-20th century. No. 2 is currently a museum piece and is on display in Saltville. This engine was built by the Rhode Island Locomotive Works in 1893.

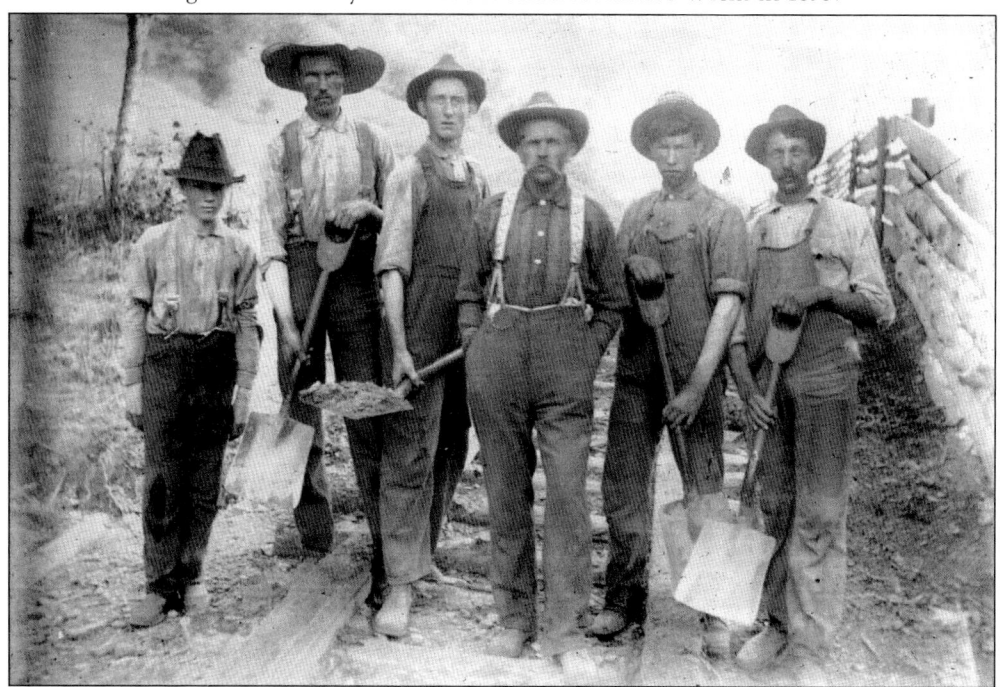

RAILROAD CONSTRUCTION CREW. This c. 1890 photograph, taken by C. L. Totten, shows a crew constructing a wooden-rail railroad in the Saltville Valley. These wooden-rail tracks were used for logging trains. (Courtesy of Rick Davidson.)

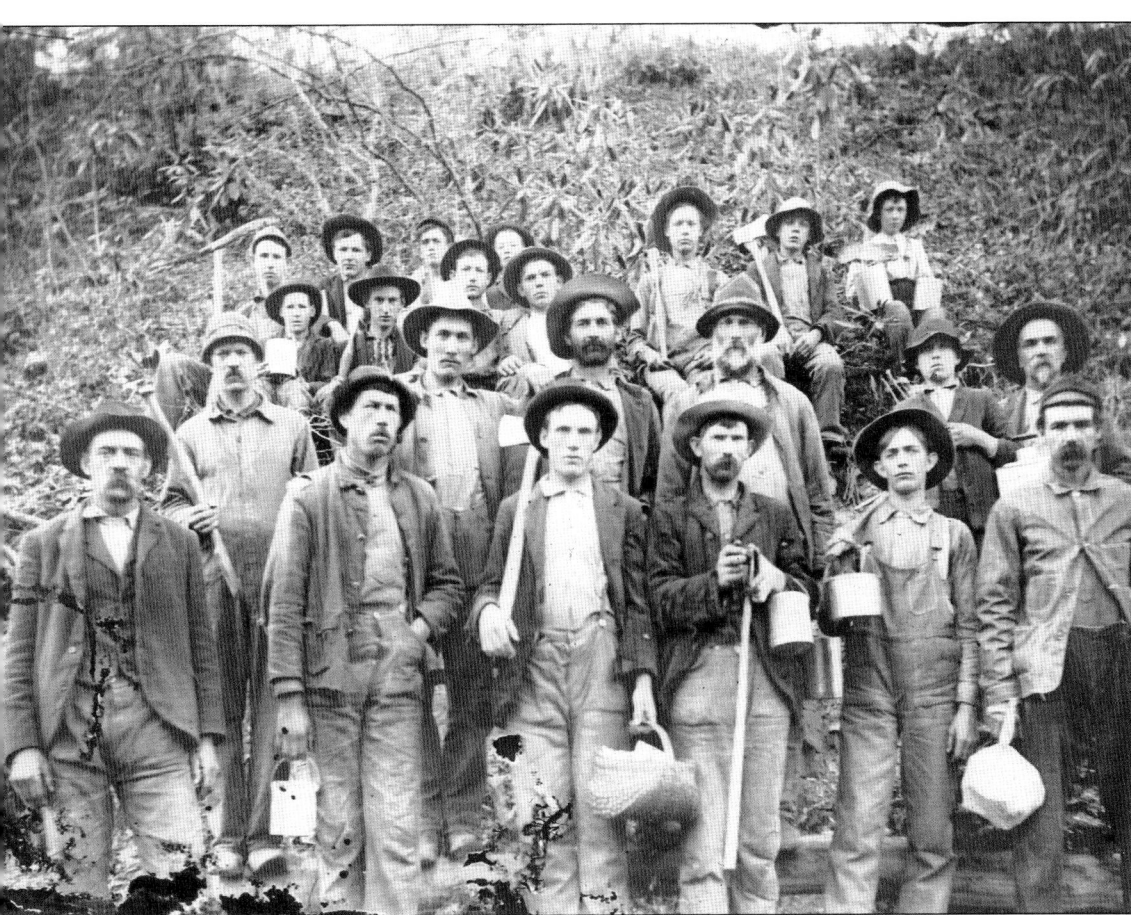

RAILROAD CONSTRUCTION. This is a larger group of men probably engaged in construction of one of the area's timbering railways in the 1890s. Some have suggested that this crew was a timber-cutting group because of the axes. Despite the accoutrements, there are no crosscut saws, typically used to fell large timber in this era. (Courtesy of Rick Davidson.)

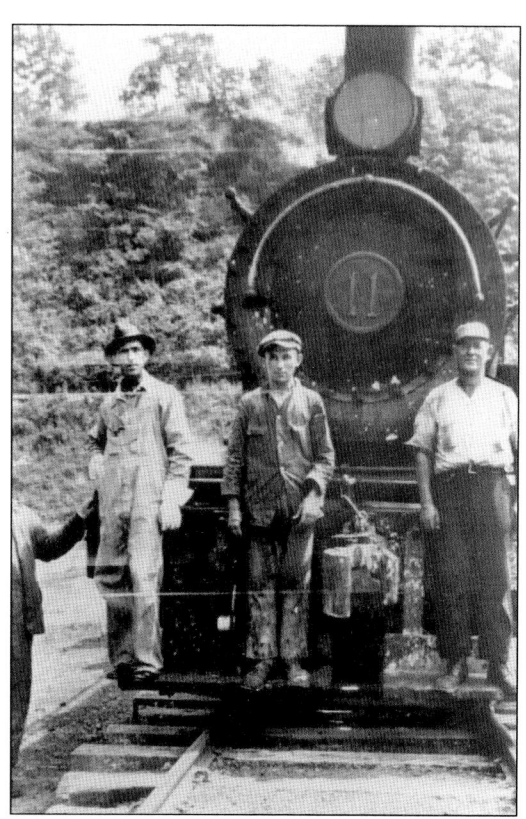

OLD NO. 11. Mathieson engine No. 11, a larger engine than No. 2, is shown here with its crew in the 1940s. This engine was built in Roanoke, Virginia, in 1895 and ran for some time on the main Norfolk and Western lines. No. 11 is the last remaining engine of its type. This engine is currently on display in downtown Saltville.

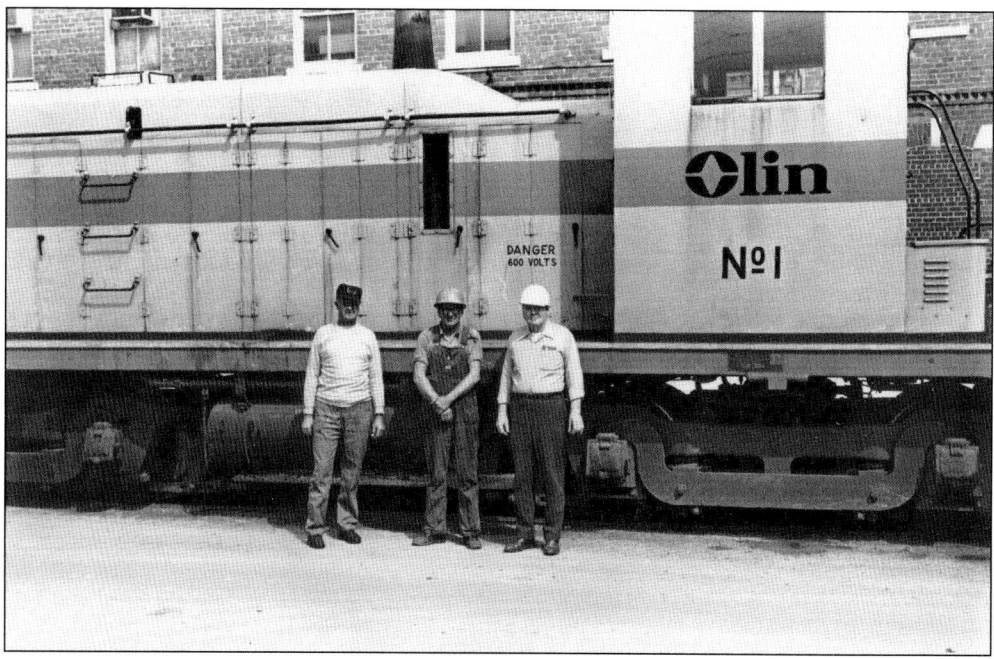

TRAIN MAINTENANCE. This image shows Ed Patrick (left), Otis Null (center), and Andrew Frye (right) in front of Olin's diesel engine No. 1. These fellows were responsible for keeping Olin's rail equipment in proper working order. This photograph dates from about 1970.

Eight
EDUCATION

"Readin', 'Ritin' and 'Rithmetic" have been taught in Saltville since its beginnings. About 1788, General Russell hired a teacher to come to conduct a school. Education in the antebellum South was usually conducted by tutors for families who could afford them or in "old field schools" for the underprivileged children of the community. This appears to be the pattern in Saltville as well. In 1870, George W. Palmer established a school for Saltville's youngsters. This facility was used until 1905, when a new building was built. This was replaced in 1925 by Mathieson, and the new Saltville High School was used until the spring of 1957. The old 1925 school was used as an elementary school for a few years longer. At that time, a new, larger facility was built for secondary education. The new school was named R. B. Worthy High School, in honor of R. B. Worthy, works manager for Olin at the time. This school's physical plant is still in use, though enlarged and renamed Northwood High School in 1987 when Worthy and Rich Valley High Schools were consolidated. Saltville maintained a separate school system until 1980. For many years, the Mathieson organization supplemented the schools' budget buying such things as the first electronic athletic scoreboard in Southwest Virginia.

In the early days, schools were also conducted at Allison Gap, Buckeye, Cedar Branch, McCready's Gap, North Holston, Quarry, and Tumbling Creek.

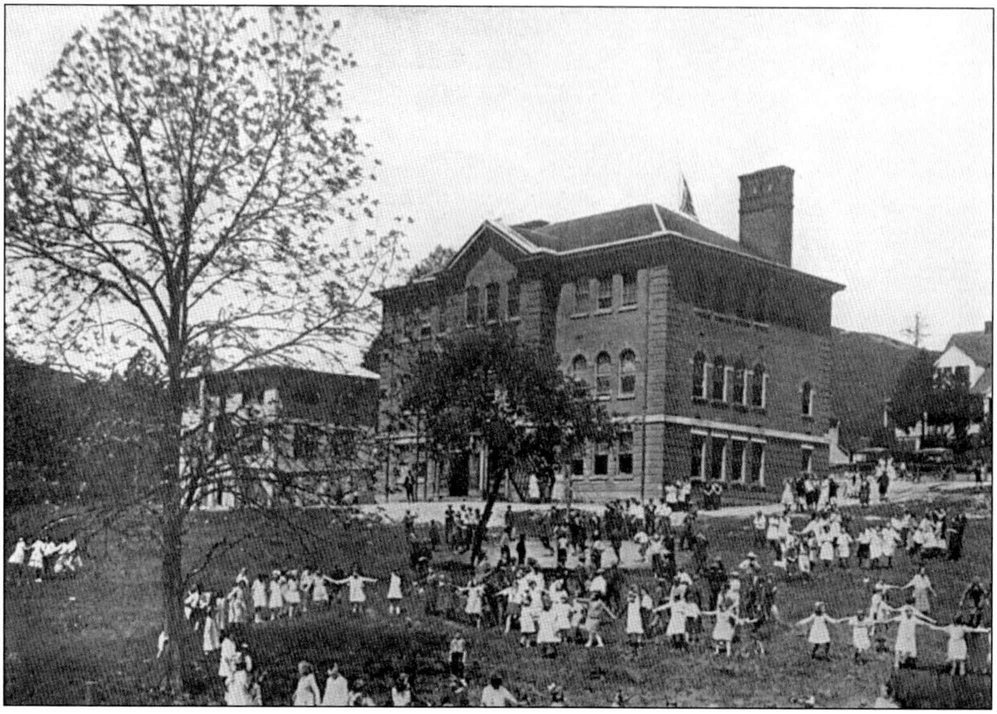

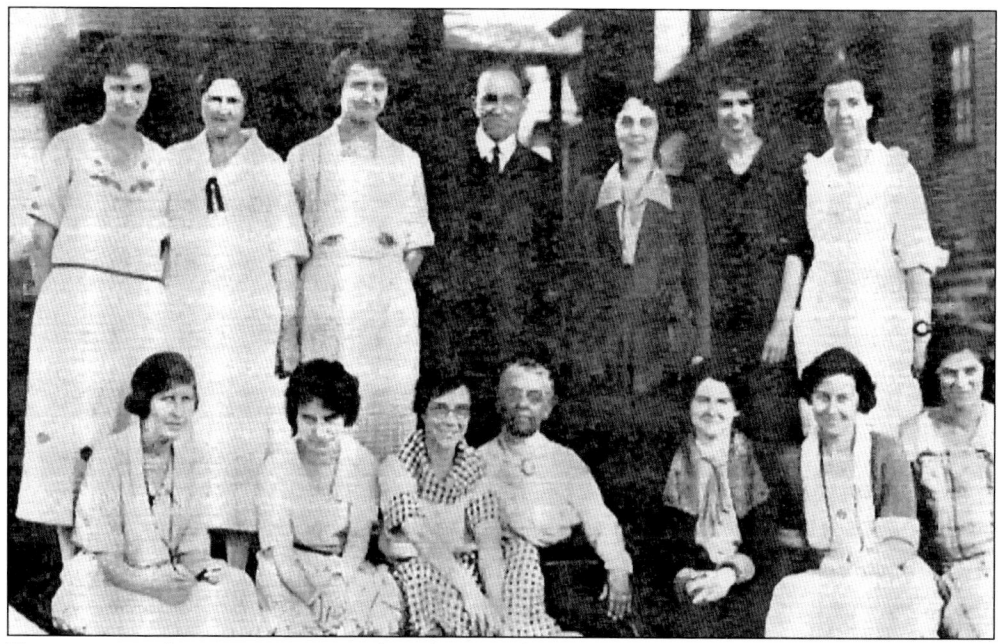

SALTVILLE SCHOOL MAY DAY CELEBRATION. This photograph, taken about 1920, shows the 1905 Saltville School and a group of children dancing around the maypole. (Courtesy of the Saltville Public Library.)

TEACHERS IN SALTVILLE, 1922. This photograph was first printed in the 1922 *Alkalite*, the company's official publication. Fourteen teachers were employed at that time, presumably for 1st through the 11th grades. (Courtesy of Saltville Public Library.)

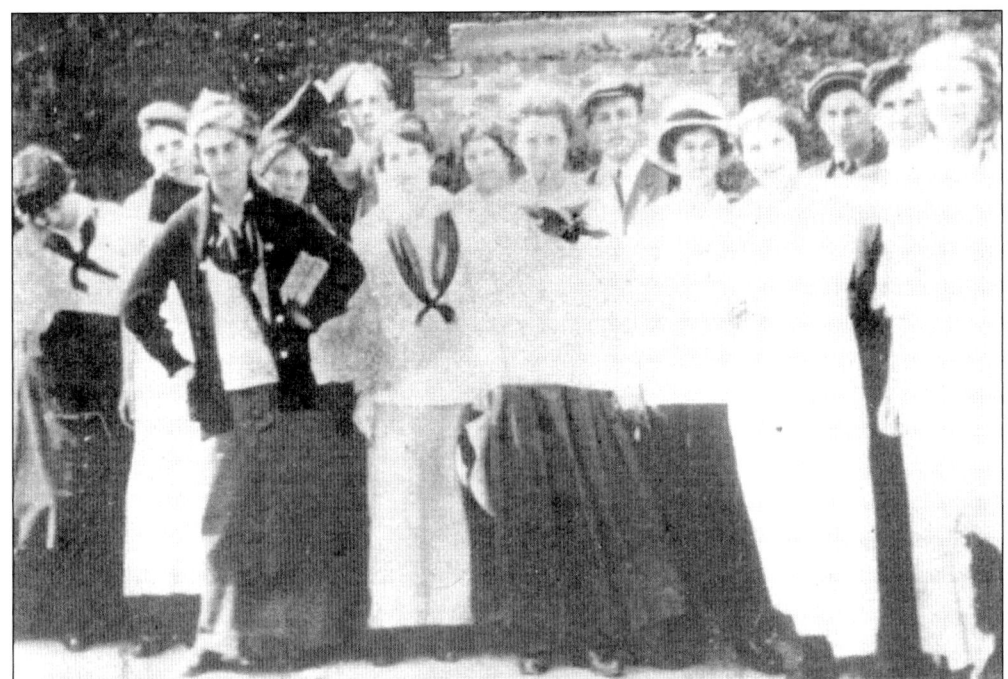

THE 1913 CLASS OF SALTVILLE HIGH SCHOOL. This is the earliest known photograph of a Saltville High School graduating class. (Courtesy of Roger Allison.)

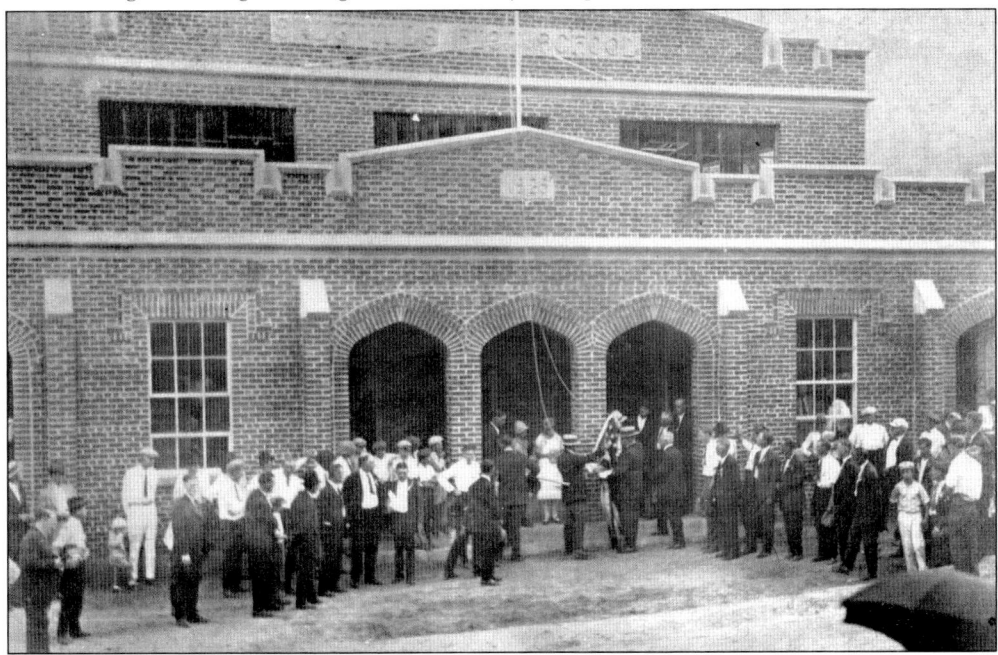

DEDICATION OF THE 1925 SCHOOL. This photograph of the dedication of the 1925 Saltville High School shows the ceremonial raising of the American flag. Speeches and pontifications were made, as they were apt to be on such occasions. The differences in the pontifications made at this ceremony were that the company backed the schools, and they could and did make their promises come true. (Courtesy of Roger Allison.)

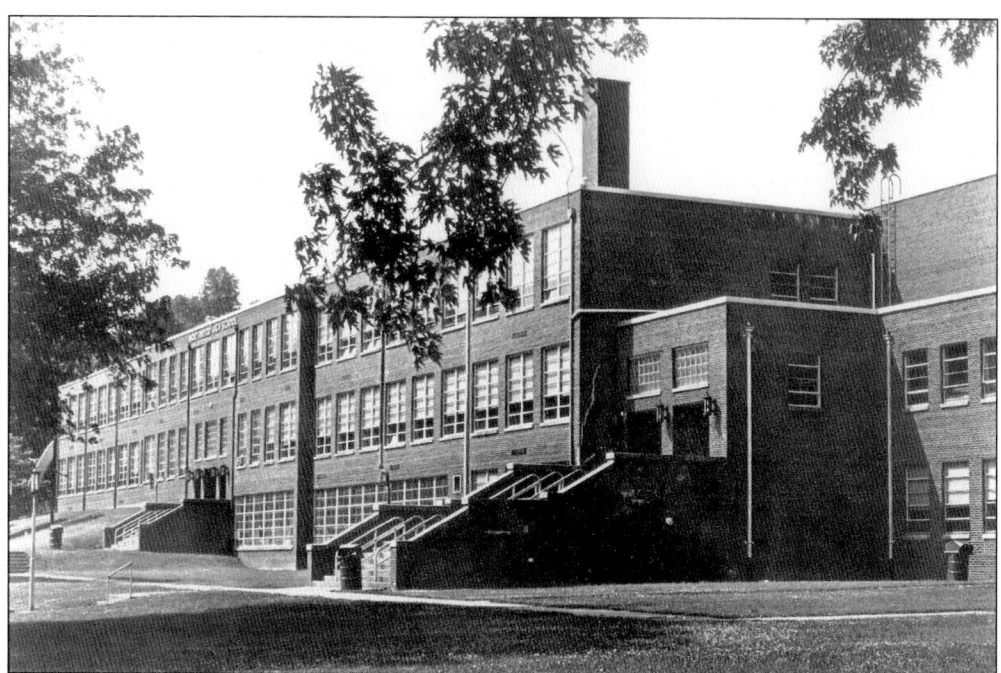

R. B. Worthy High School. This image shows the Northwood High School about 1990. Prior to the name change in 1987, it was known as R. B. Worthy High School. This building was built in 1956. The name change was made because of the consolidation of Worthy and Rich Valley High Schools. (Courtesy of Roger Allison.)

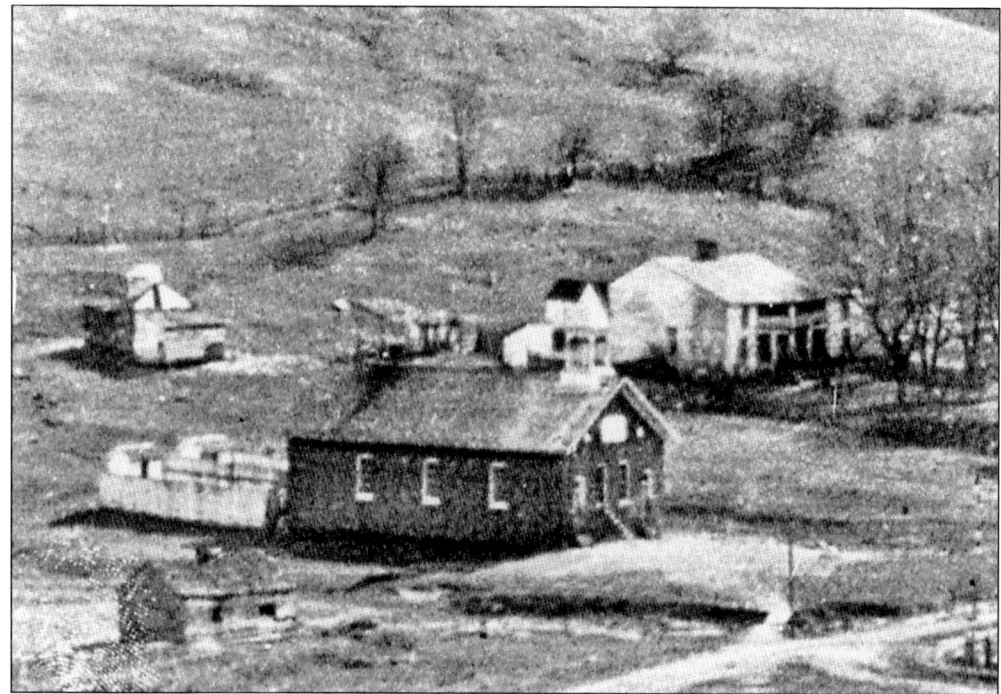

The 1876 Palmer School. This image shows the second postbellum school in Saltville. It was built by George W. Palmer in 1876. This school replaced an 1868 frame school building

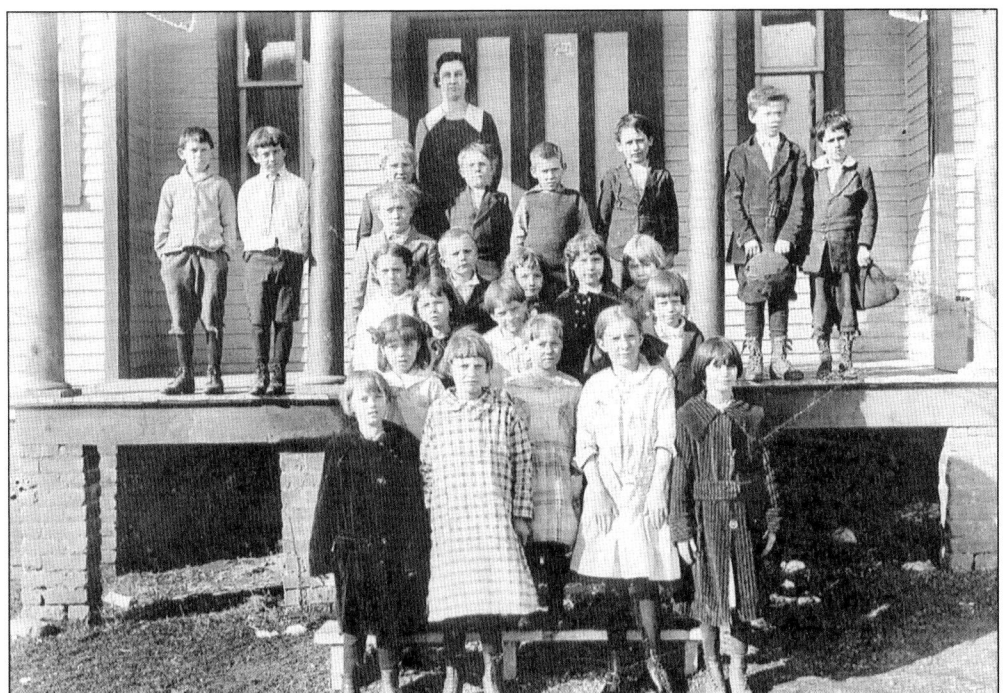

SALTVILLE ELEMENTARY. This photograph shows a group of children who attended the Saltville Elementary School, located at the corner of Henrytown Road and West Main Street. This school was operated from 1905 until 1925. From the appearance of the children, this picture is from the latter part of that period.

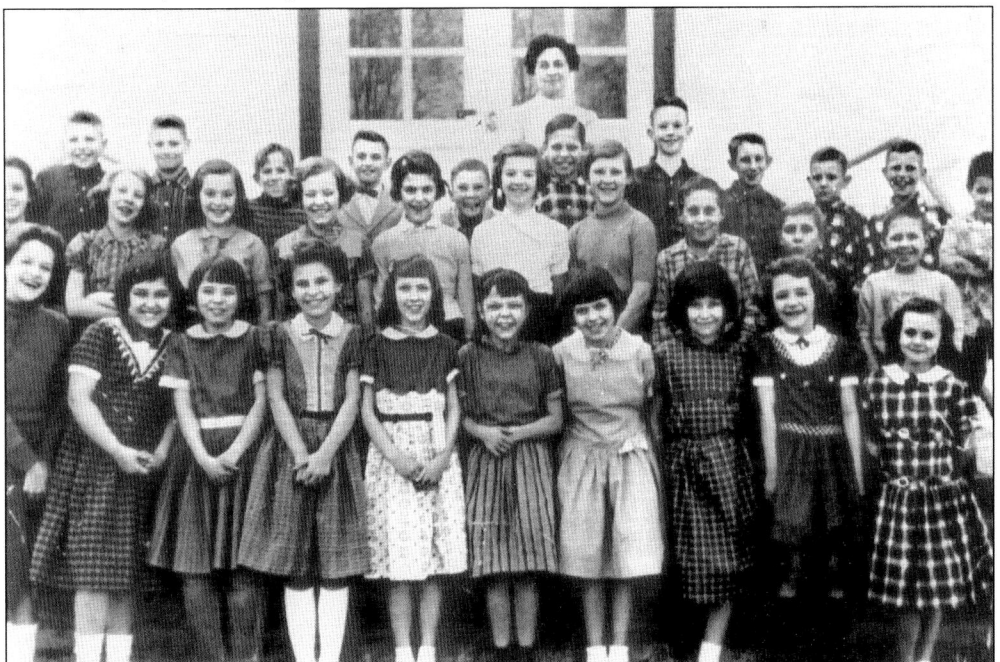

HAPPY CHILDREN. This is a group photograph of the 1956–1957 fourth- and fifth-grade classes of the Plasterco Elementary School.

97

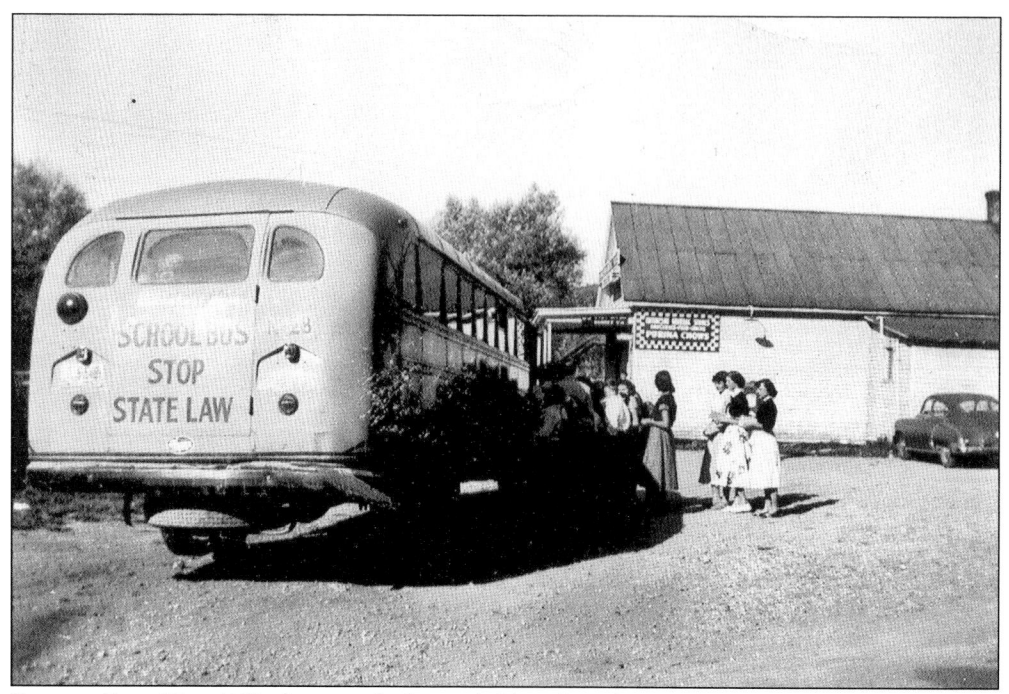

SCHOOL BUS. This 1958 photograph shows children boarding a school bus at the Quarry Store for the two- or three-mile ride to Saltville's schools.

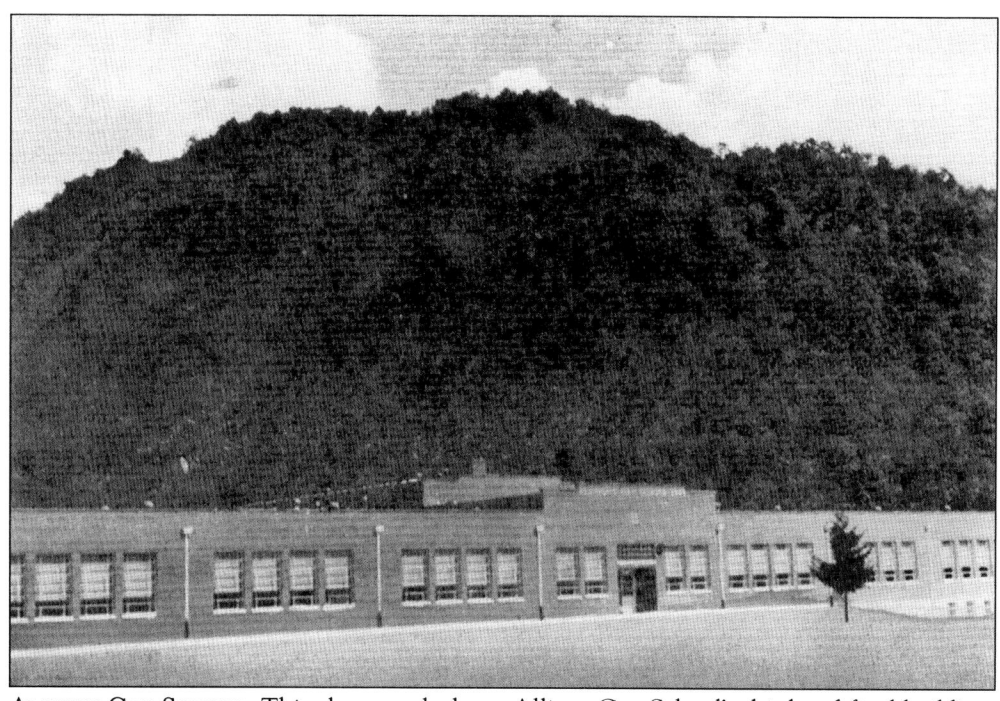

ALLISON GAP SCHOOL. This photograph shows Allison Gap School's third and final building. (Courtesy of Roger Allison.)

Nine
CIVIC LIFE

Every community of any size has a civic life of some sort—churches, town government, charities, or other groups that have banded together for mutual support of each other and their neighbors.

Saltville was chartered as a town under Virginia law in 1894 with a mayor and town council who rule on local issues allowed by statute in the commonwealth. This first charter was replaced by a second charter in 1896. For years, Mathieson nominated candidates for municipal elections, and they were often the only candidates. The present municipal government operates a police department, sanitation department, and department of public works, and has a director of tourism and director of economic development. A volunteer fire department and volunteer rescue squad also serve the community. Saltville has a food pantry to help the less fortunate as well.

Life in small-town Saltville focuses around several churches. The most famous is Madam Russell United Methodist, founded in 1896. The oldest church in the community is Tumbling Creek Primitive Baptist, founded about 1773 and formally established as a church in 1785. Saltville Baptist Church's constitution dates from 1895. The Union Church was constructed for the town in 1873, and it was occupied by Presbyterians and Southern Baptists for some time. This meetinghouse burned about 1977. The Episcopal church was built primarily for the British workers in Saltville in 1896. The Christian church on Allison Gap Road was established in 1913, and Main Street Christian Church was formed in 1918.

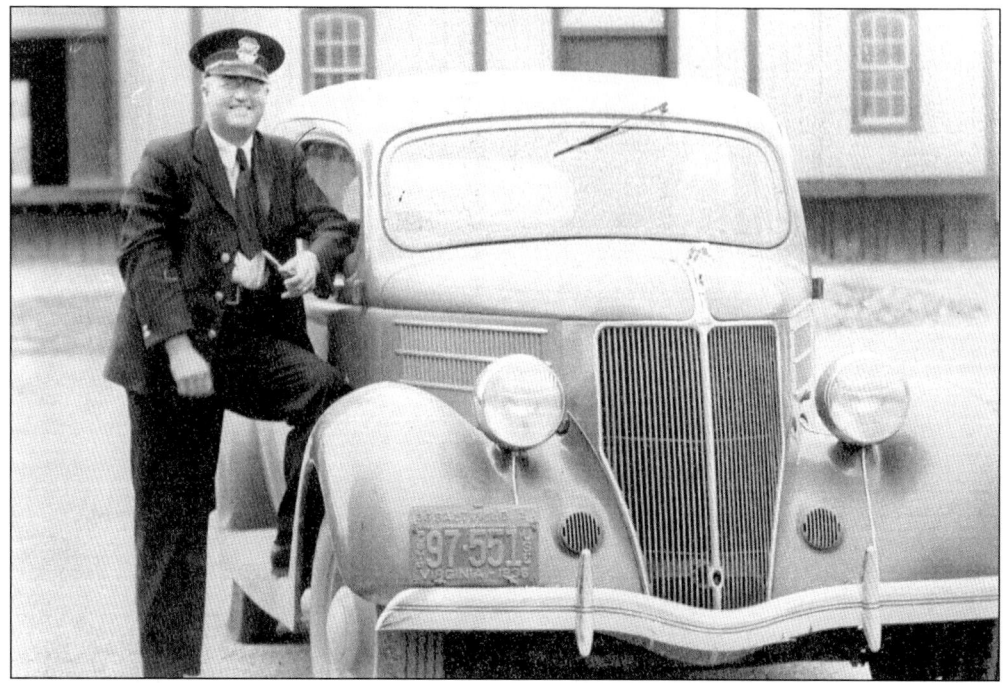

CHIEF OF POLICE W. DALLAS BRANHAM. This image shows the jovial-looking Chief Branham with his brand-new 1936 Ford police cruiser. At this time, the police department consisted of two men. "Jingo" Lambert was the other officer.

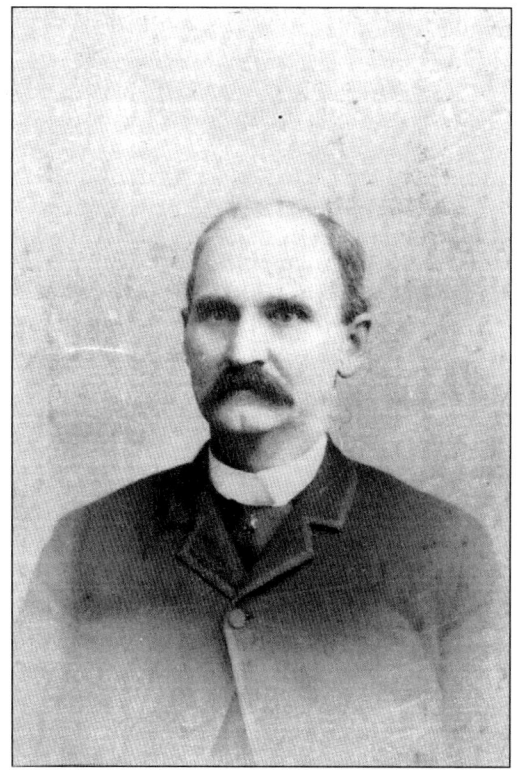

GEORGE W. PALMER. Born in Syracuse, New York, Palmer came to Saltville in the 1850s and remained through the Civil War, despite his Yankee roots. He owned much of the Saltville Valley from 1860 until about 1890. He was the town of Saltville's first mayor and benefactor of the community in numerous ways.

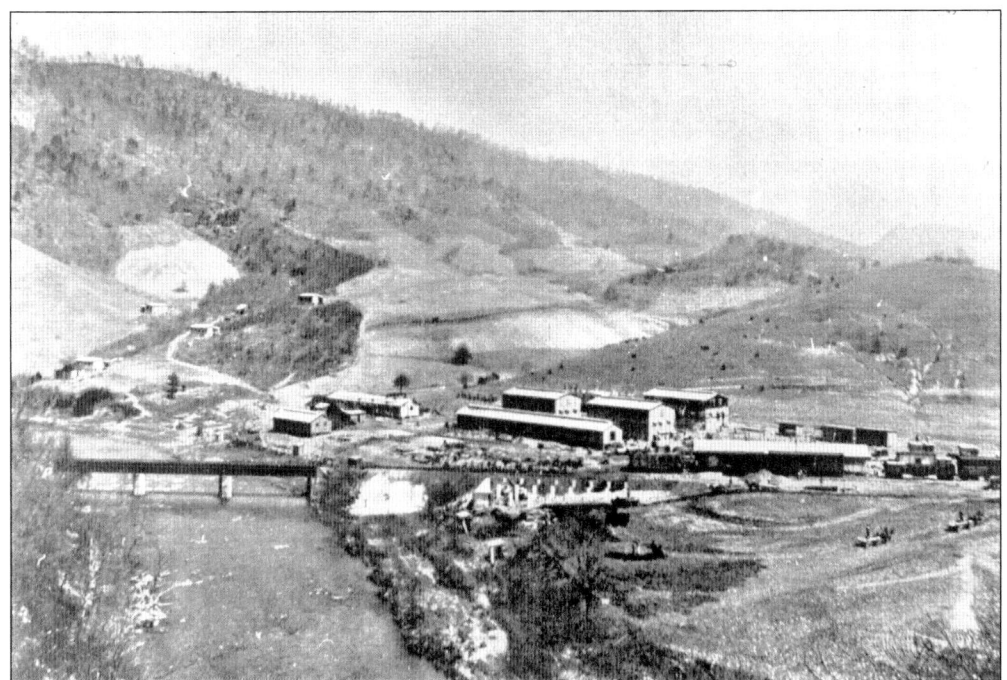

U.S. CHEMICAL PLANT NO. 4. This late-1917 photograph shows the barracks constructed for the 400 men necessary to guard and produce poison gas in World War I. This facility never came into full production before the armistice with the Central Powers on November 11, 1918. It was kept open into 1919 and tested, then dismantled. A 1918 diagram shows several additional buildings that would have been added in the right foreground. (Courtesy of Loretta Hodgson.)

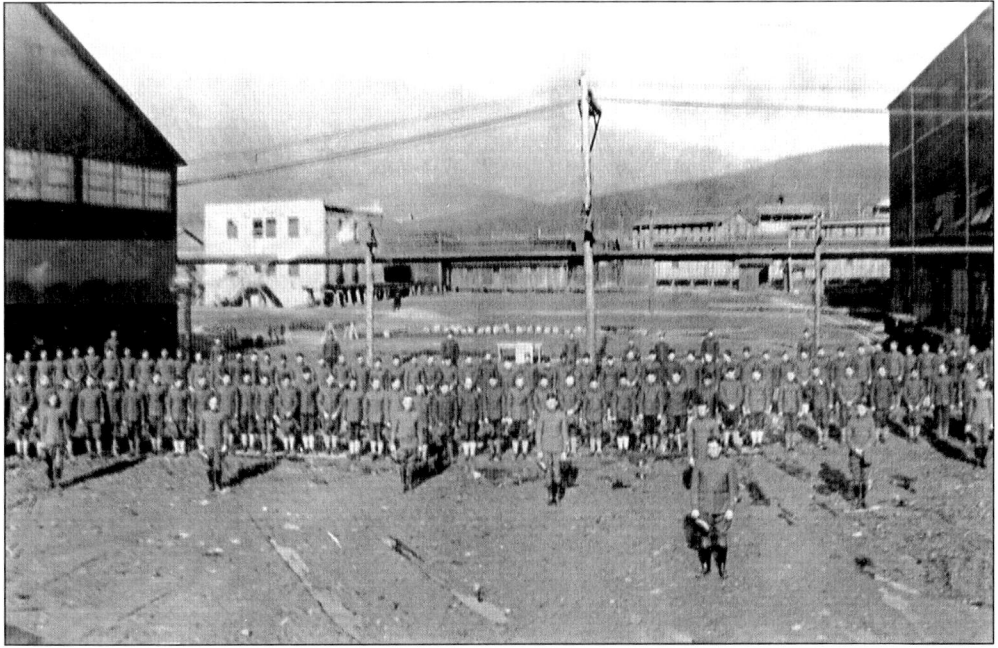

WORLD WAR I GARRISON. This image depicts part of the 400-man garrison stationed at Saltville during the Great War. This unit was part of the U.S. Army's Chemical Corps.

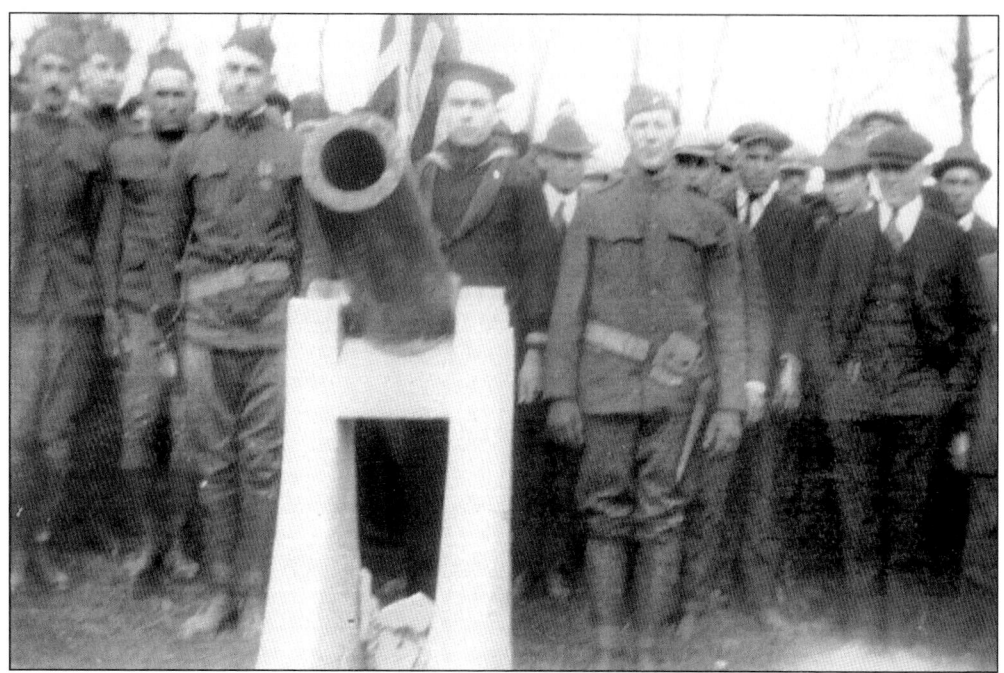

WORLD WAR I VETERANS. This image was made about 1920 and shows a group of World War I veterans dedicating the cannon at the entrance to Elizabeth Cemetery on the east end of town. Marty McIntyre is the man in the sailor's uniform in the center of the photograph.

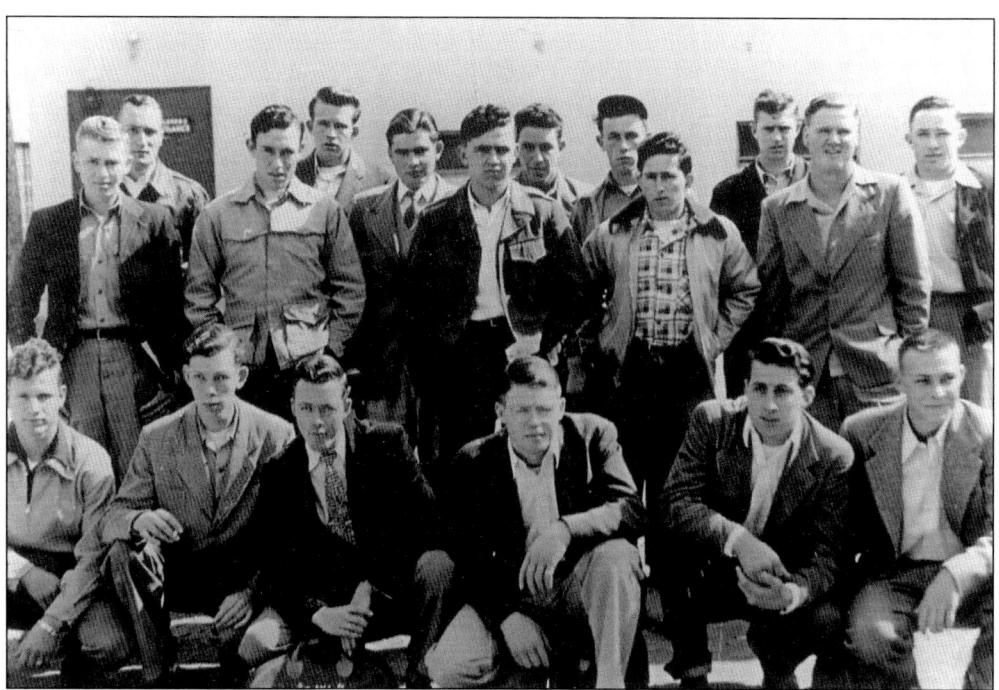

KOREAN WAR DRAFTEES. This group of 18 young men is preparing to leave Saltville for boot camp during the Korean War.

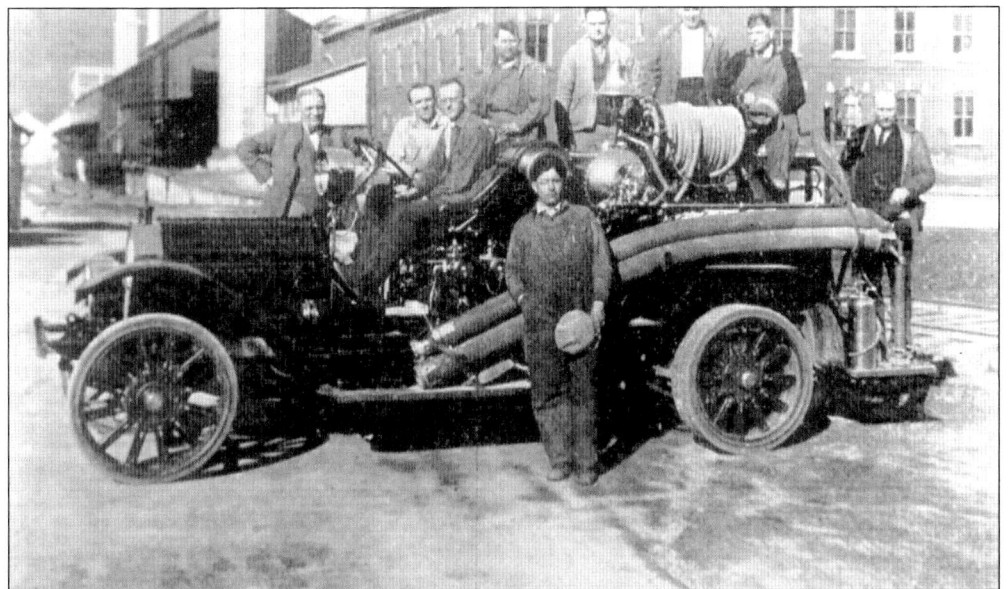

SALTVILLE VOLUNTEER FIRE DEPARTMENT 1925. This group of men made up Saltville's volunteer fire department in 1925. A similar photograph graced the cover of Images of America: *Smyth County*, published in 2005.

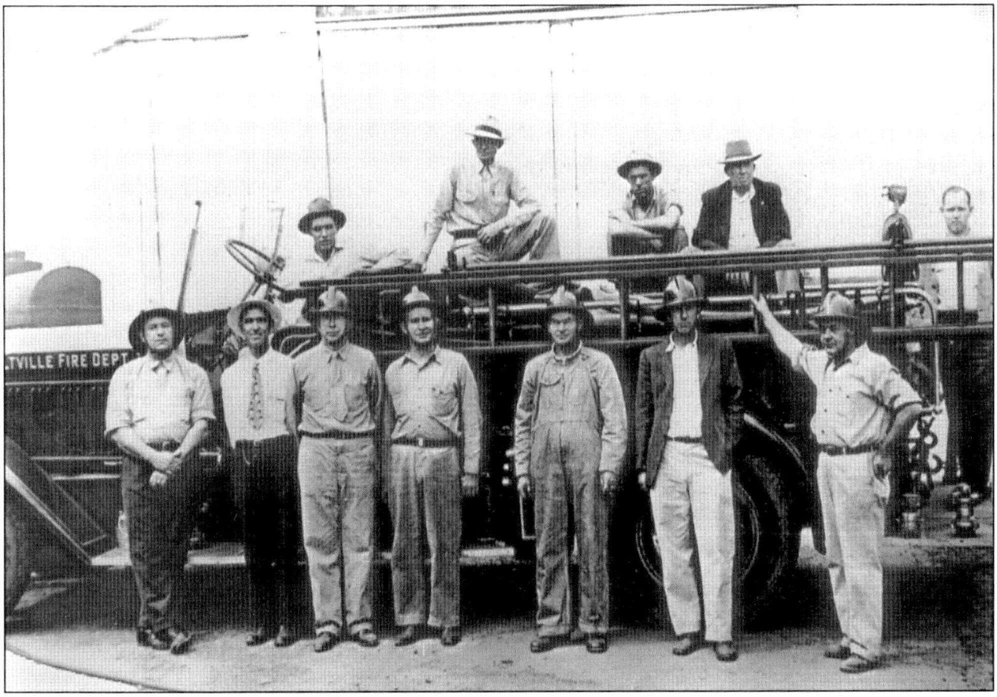

SALTVILLE VOLUNTEER FIRE DEPARTMENT, C. 1955. This photograph of the Saltville Fire Department was taken about 1955. It shows equipment common in the 1950s. Olin bought the most up-to-date equipment for the fire department at that time.

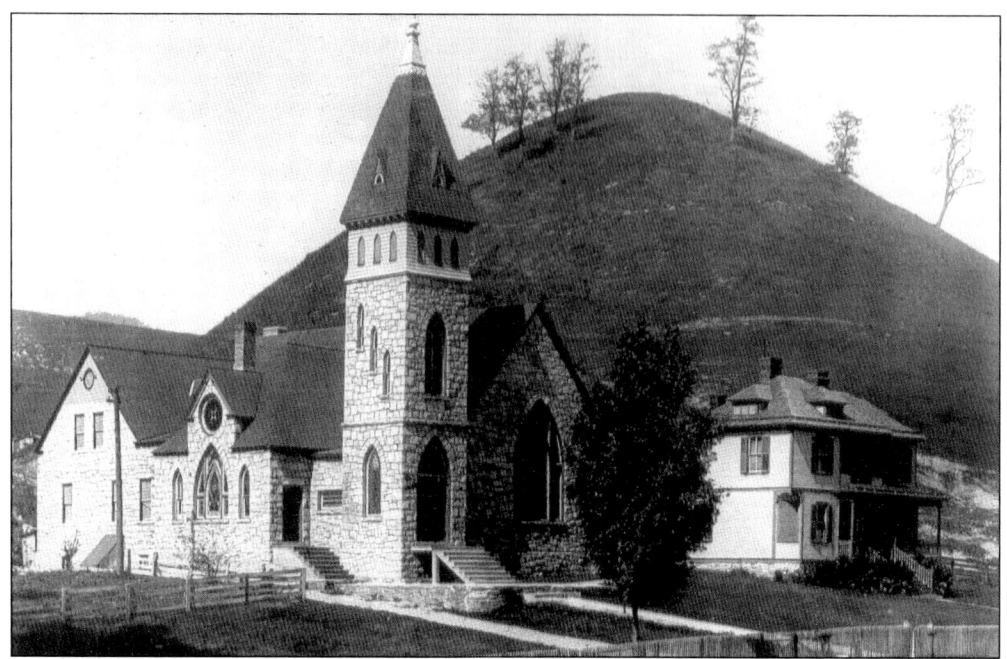

MADAM RUSSELL METHODIST EPISCOPAL CHURCH SOUTH. In the early 1890s, the Methodists who were meeting in the Union Church decided to build their own house of worship. The company made a sizeable donation, and it was supplemented by funds raised by the members. This attractive late-Victorian edifice is the result. The house to the right was the parsonage.

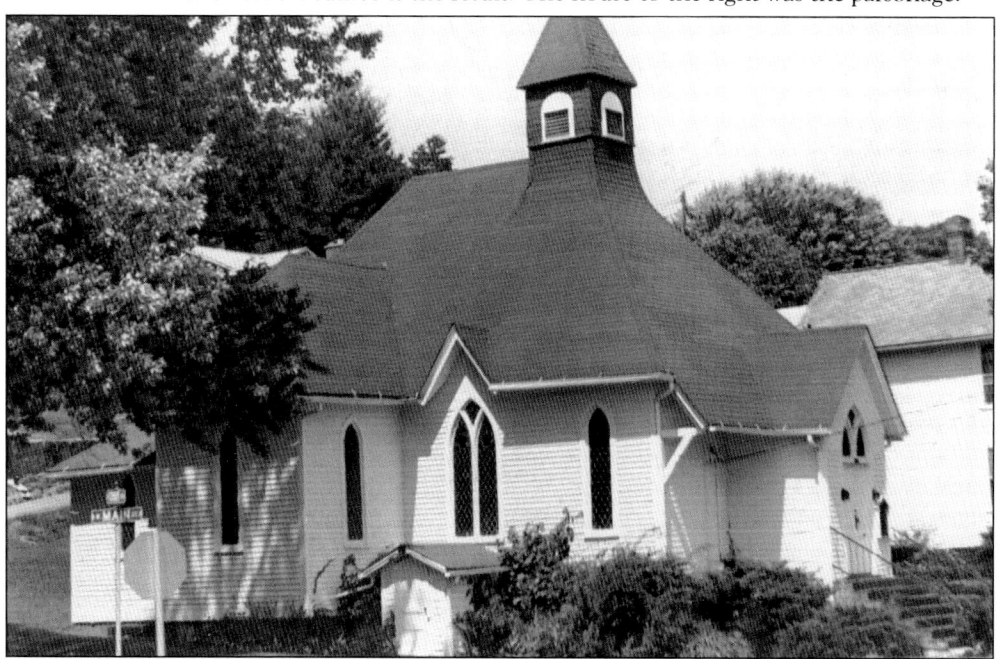

ST. PAUL'S EPISCOPAL CHURCH. St. Paul's and Madam Russell are the two historic downtown churches in Saltville. St. Paul's was erected in 1896 to give the British workers at "the Plant" a place to worship. The church contains a fine pipe organ. Currently services are held here on the second and fourth Sundays of each month.

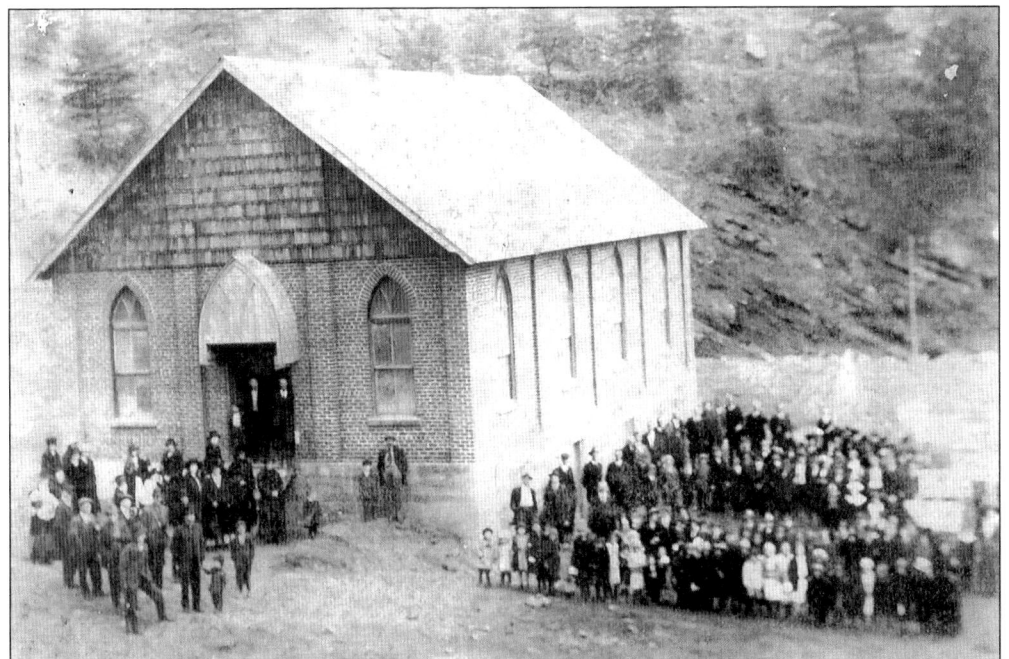

SALTVILLE FIRST CHRISTIAN CHURCH. This image shows the congregation of Saltville First Christian Church in 1918. This church, founded in 1913, is located on Allison Gap Road about a mile from town. The building pictured here has been enlarged over the years, but it still serves its congregation.

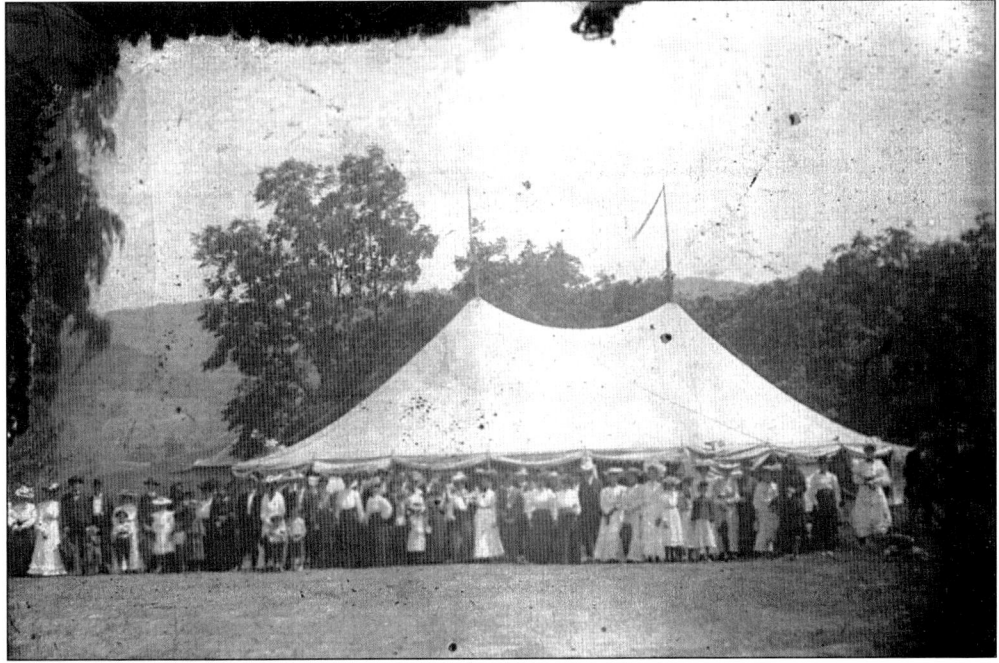

SALTVILLE TENT REVIVAL. Taken in the 1890s, this photograph shows a tent revival somewhere in the Saltville Valley. This large group is well coiffed and elegant for the time and place. (Image made by C. L. Totten, and courtesy of Rick Davidson.)

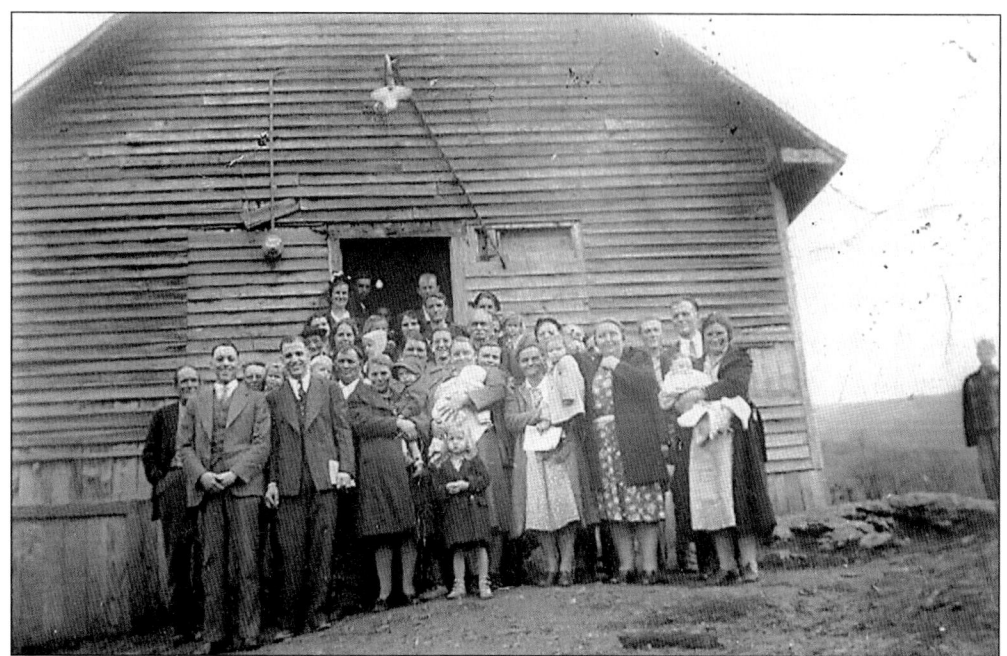

BUCKEYE HOLLOW CHURCH. This 1940s view is of the Buckeye Hollow Pentecostal Holiness Church. This church is located about two miles from the center of town. This structure has been replaced by an up-to-date brick building.

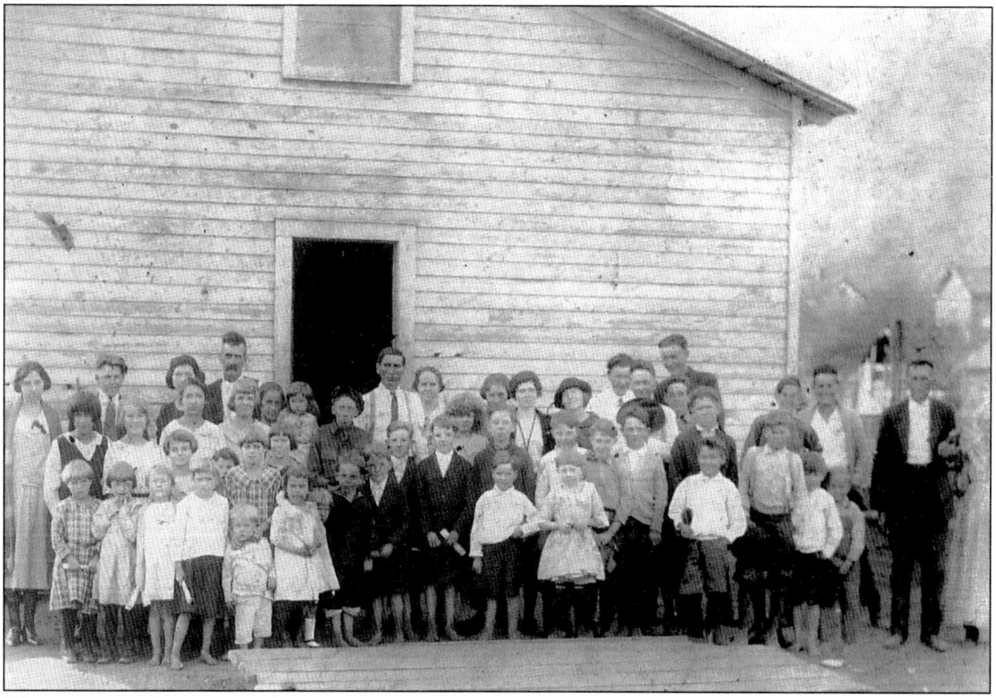

HENRYTOWN CHURCH. This 1927 image is probably of a Bible school group, as mostly youngsters are shown. Note that some of the boys are wearing a jacket, tie, short pants, and no shoes. Shoes were expensive and were not to be worn for events if not absolutely necessary.

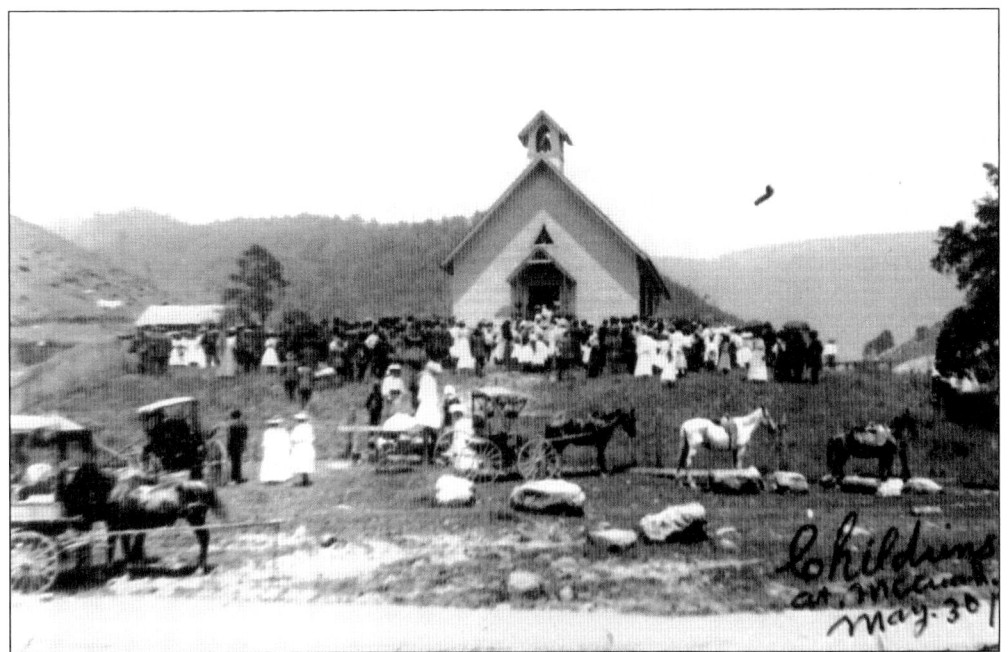

McCready's Gap Methodist Church. This general view shows McCready's Gap Methodist Church on May 30, 1909. The church had a large congregation. A few horses and wagons are present in this scene, but no automobiles. Most people traveled to church on foot. Church attendance in the early 20th century in Appalachia was often as much a social event as a period of worship. This photograph was printed in reverse originally.

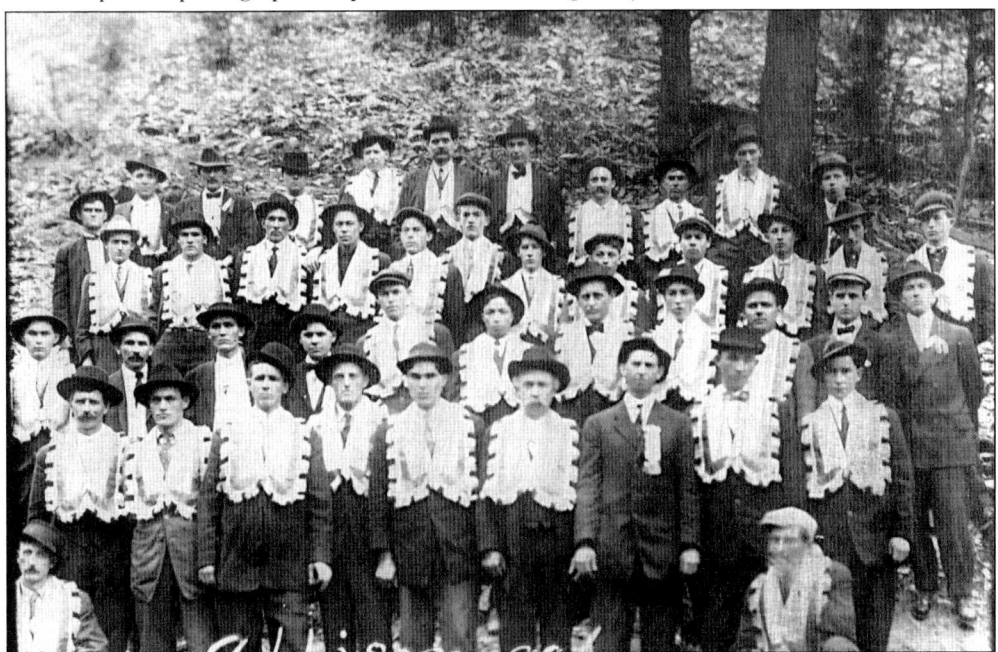

Allison Gap Chapter, Junior Order of United American Mechanics. This is a group photograph of the Junior Order of the United American Mechanics Lodge at Allison Gap in 1913. Note the hats and distinctive vestments the men are wearing.

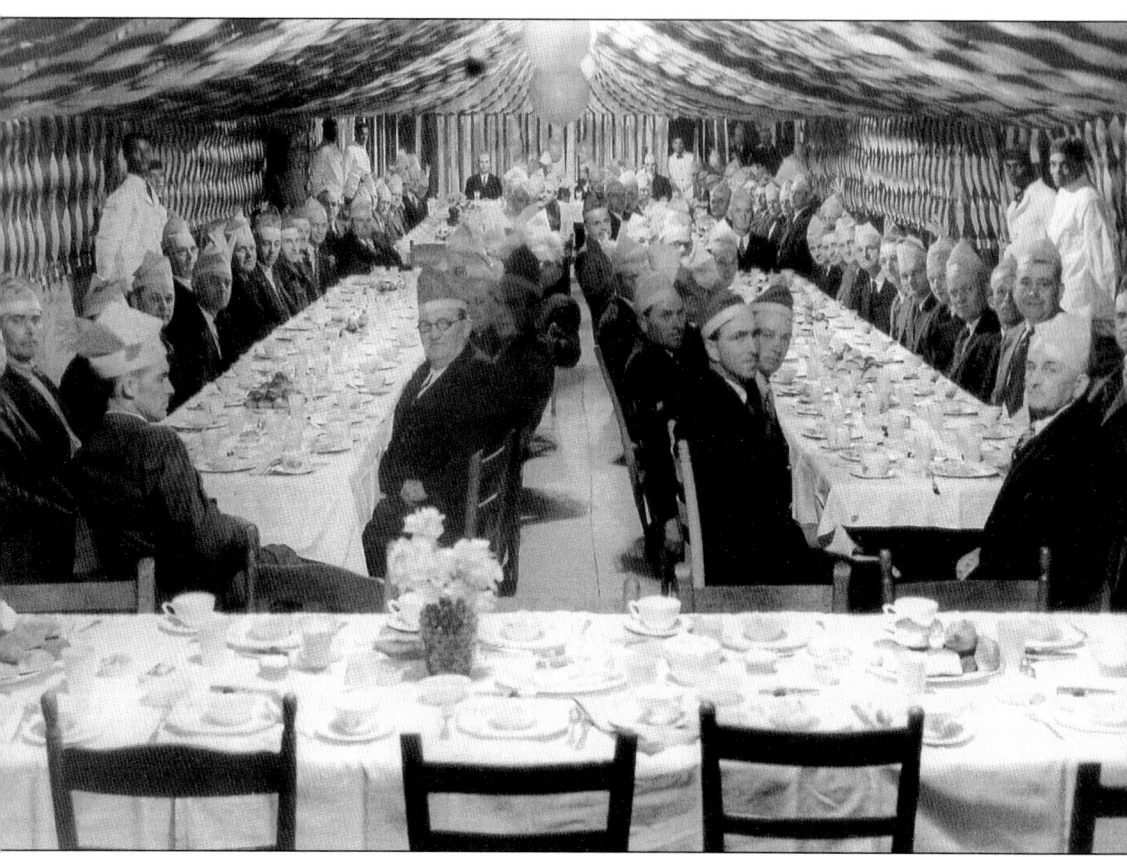

RED MEN'S DINNER. This 1930s photograph shows the Saltville Red Men's Lodge formal dinner. It was a fancy affair for Depression-era Southwest Virginia, but Saltville was a boomtown even then. Note the fellow in the right of the photograph with his face painted. He is believed to be an inductee. African American waiters ring the heavily decorated room.

Ten

RECREATION

All work and no play, as the familiar phrase goes, makes Jack a dull boy. This has not been a problem in Saltville for a very long time. The illustrations in this chapter show many of the activities Saltville residents have participated in for fun. Sports obviously top the list. Mathieson built several recreational facilities for the town over the years. In the 1890s, there was an athletic field where baseball and cricket were played. Around 1920, the company built a baseball facility with seating for 400 spectators. A golf course was constructed in 1923. Saltville High School fielded its first football team in 1919, and they were reckoned to be a local powerhouse for many years. Girls and boys both participated in basketball. A saltwater swimming pool was built in the early 1940s. Billiards and bowling were available in the basement of the Victory Theatre after 1922.

Fishing and hunting were and still are popular pastimes. Others enjoy Civil War reenactments, church socials, or gossiping on the front porch. Such is the life in small-town America and in the Saltville Valley. Saltville has a local theater group that holds semi-occasional performances in a recreated Palmer Mill building. Tickets for their performances are difficult to obtain.

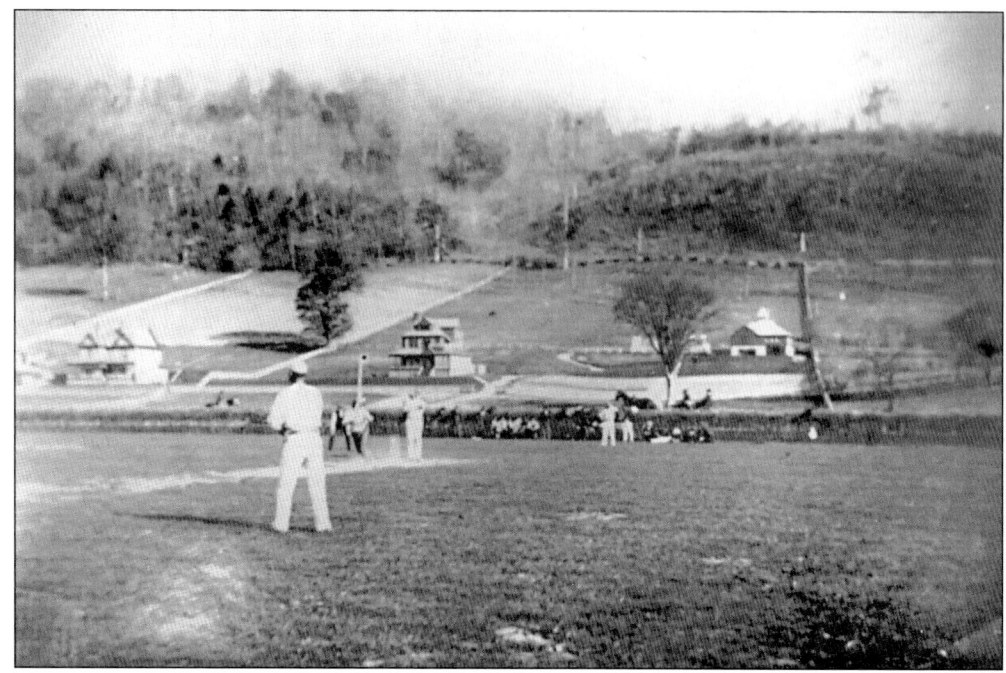

CRICKET IN AMERICA. When the Mathieson family, which started the alkali works, came to America in the early 1890s, they brought many British workers with them. These workers brought their customs and games. Among the more popular games among the British colony at Saltville was cricket, played here on the Saltville Athletic Field about 1895.

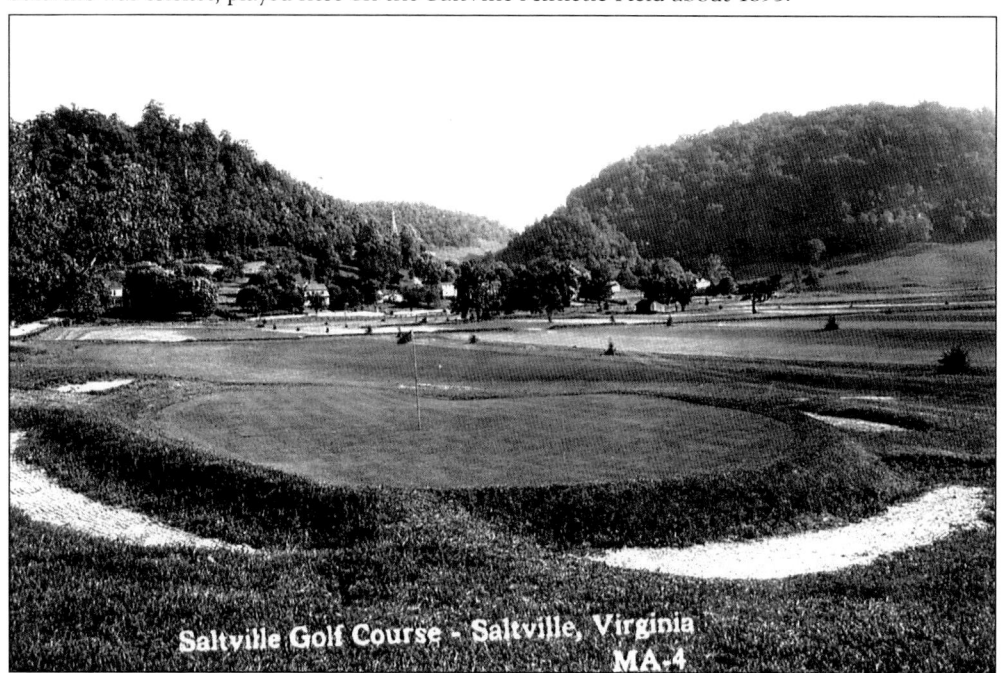

GOLF. The Mathieson Alkali Works built this golf course in 1923 for the white-collar workers at the plant. Teenage boys actively competed for caddy jobs for the sportsmen. This postcard was made in 1925. (Courtesy of Roger Allison.)

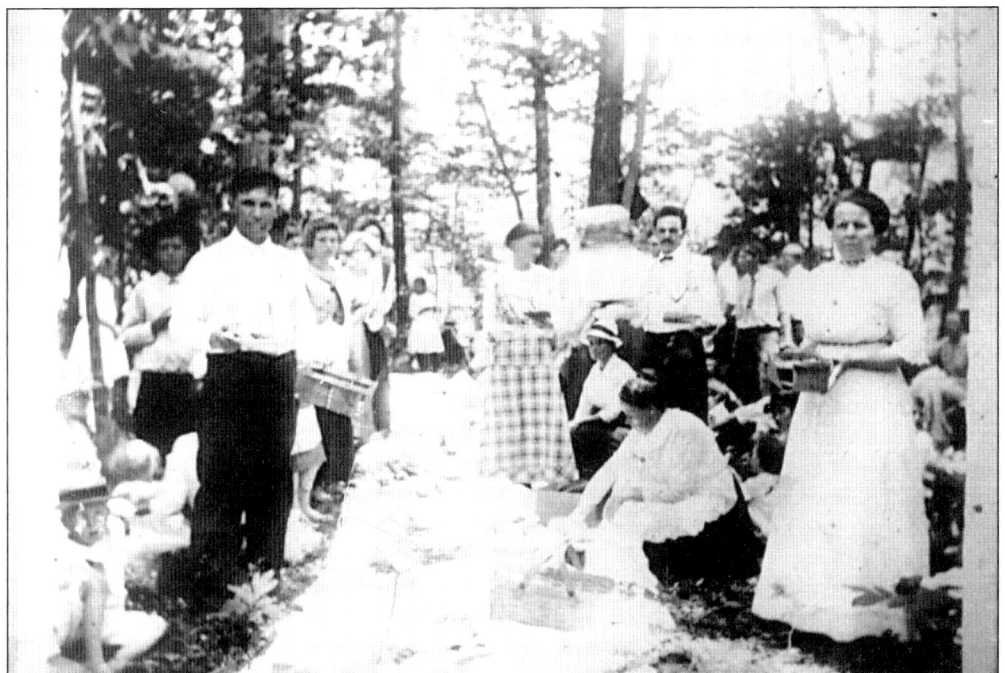

PICNIC. This group from Buena Vista (Plasterco) seems to be enjoying a church social. This photograph dates from the very early 20th century.

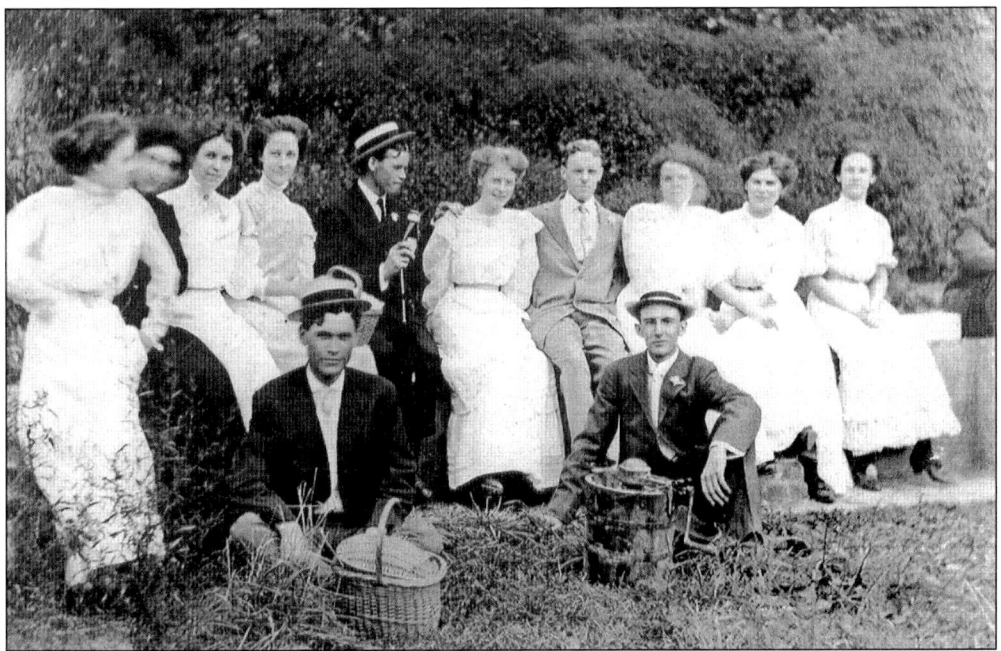

ICE CREAM. This image, made by Dr. James Louis Early about 1912, shows a group of young people sitting along the wall of Palmer Springs. Other photographs show this group going on a picnic, with one chap carrying a watermelon and a menacing knife. After eating their main course, they seem prepared to make some ice cream for desert; note the ice-cream maker in the foreground.

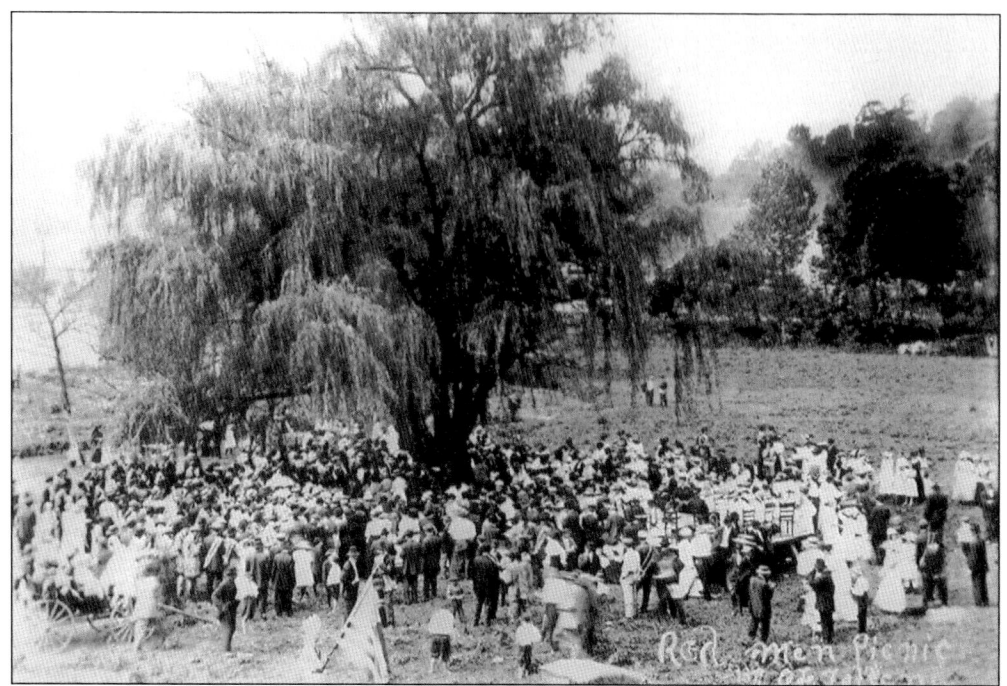

THE RED MEN PICNIC. This photograph shows the members of the Red Men Lodge and their families enjoying a picnic on a bright summer day. The horses and wagons and the long dresses of the women suggest a date of around 1900 for this photograph.

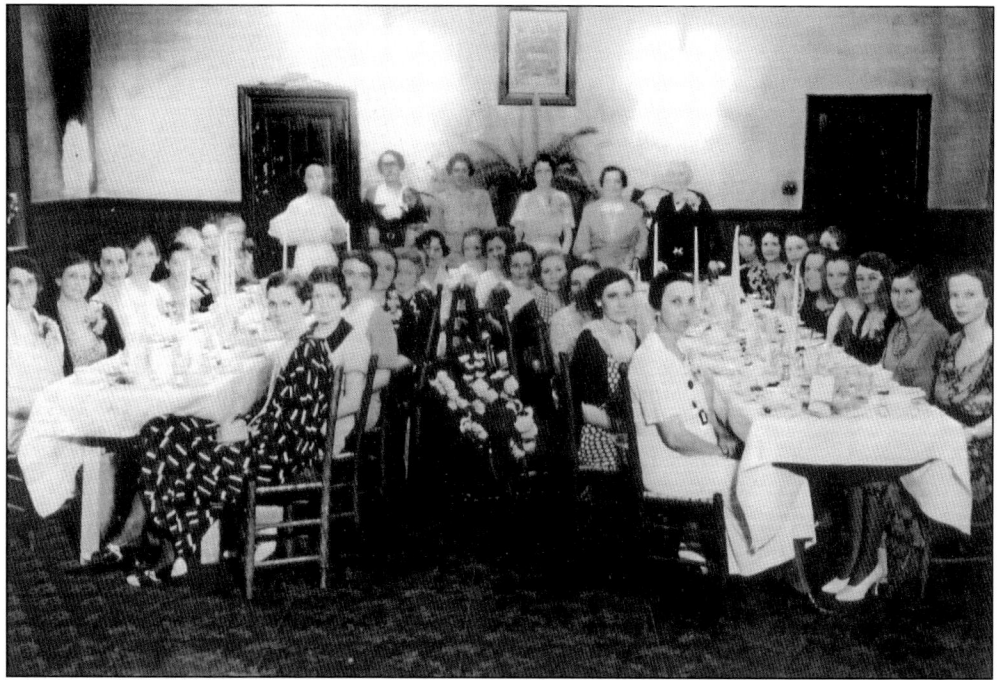

FORMAL DINNER. This photograph taken in the 1930s or 1940s is of some formal dinner in Madam Russell United Methodist Church. The fellowship hall in the basement of the church is the largest gathering place in town.

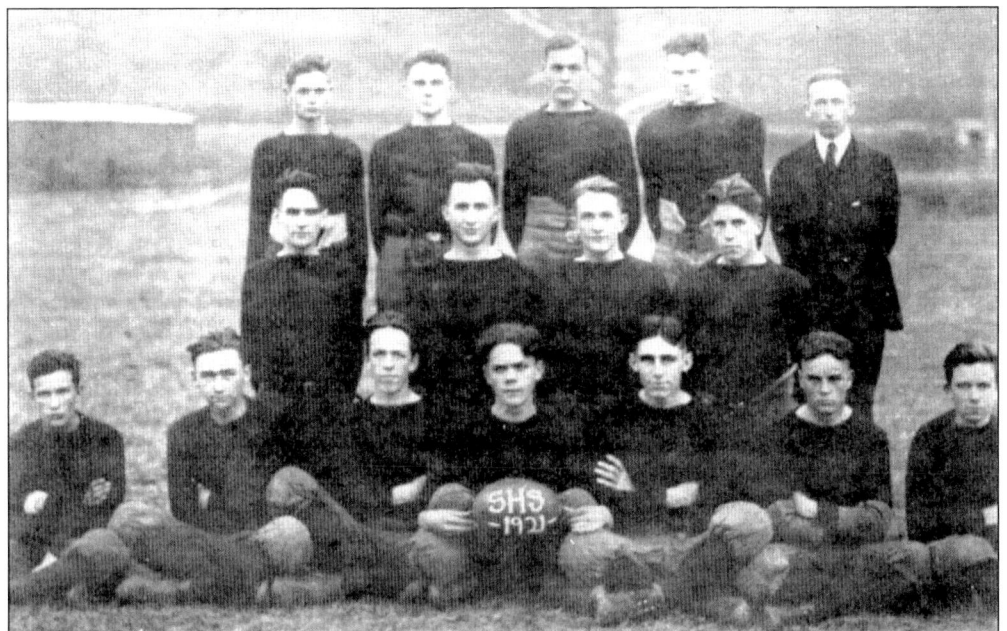

FOOTBALL 1921. This illustration shows the 11 starting members of the 1921 Saltville High School football team. Football began to be played in Saltville in 1919. This is the earliest surviving photograph of a team. Turk Warren is second from right in the front row. (Courtesy of Roger Allison.)

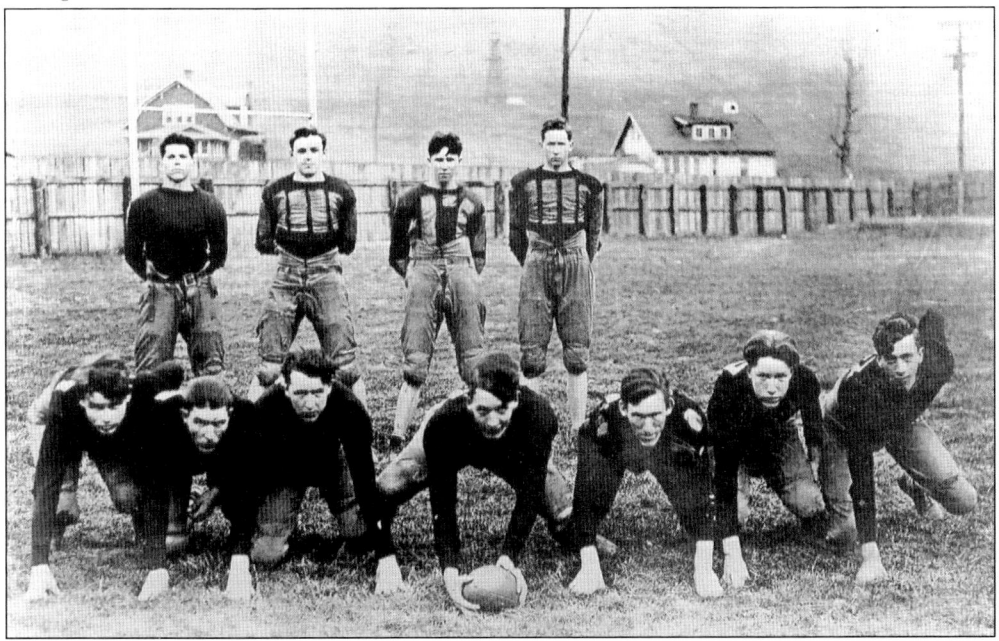

FOOTBALL 1929. This Saltville football team was the 1929 state champion. Those who played on the line from left to right were Randolph Lee, Earl Creggar, Barton Thornton, Ray Neal, Graham Sanders, Charles Davis, and Sanders Campbell. The backfield players, seen in the back row from left to right, were Kent Groseclose, Eldred Walker, Harold Hurt, and Charles Taylor. (Courtesy of Roger Allison.)

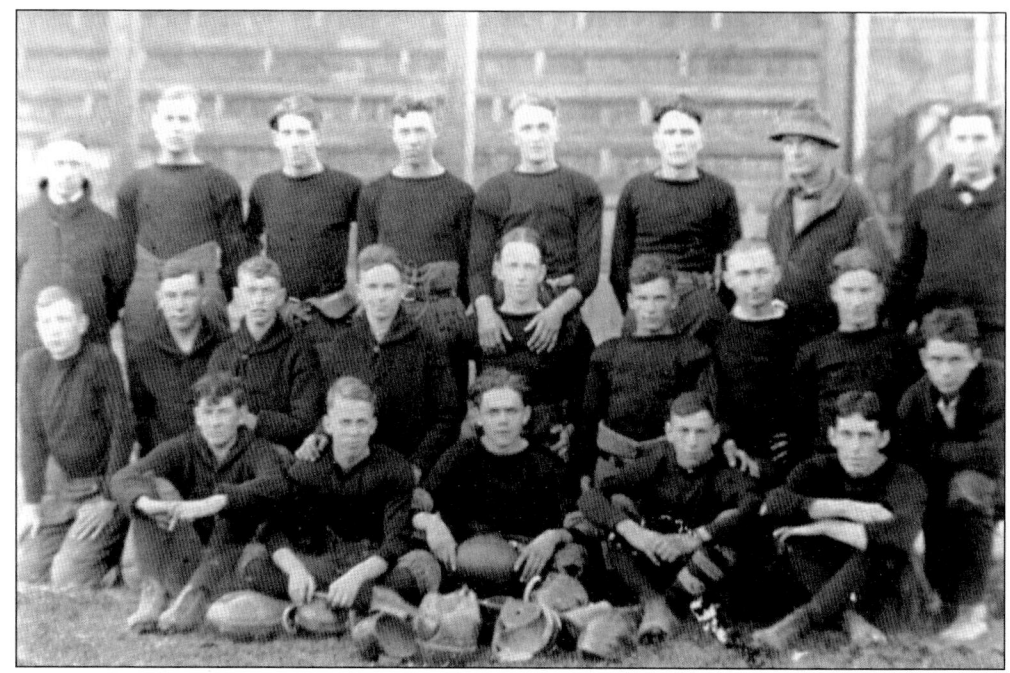

FOOTBALL 1922. Another early Saltville High School football team is shown here. One of the team members is Robert Porterfield, second from right in the first row. He was famous for his connection with Barter Theater, the state theater of Virginia. (Courtesy of Roger Allison.)

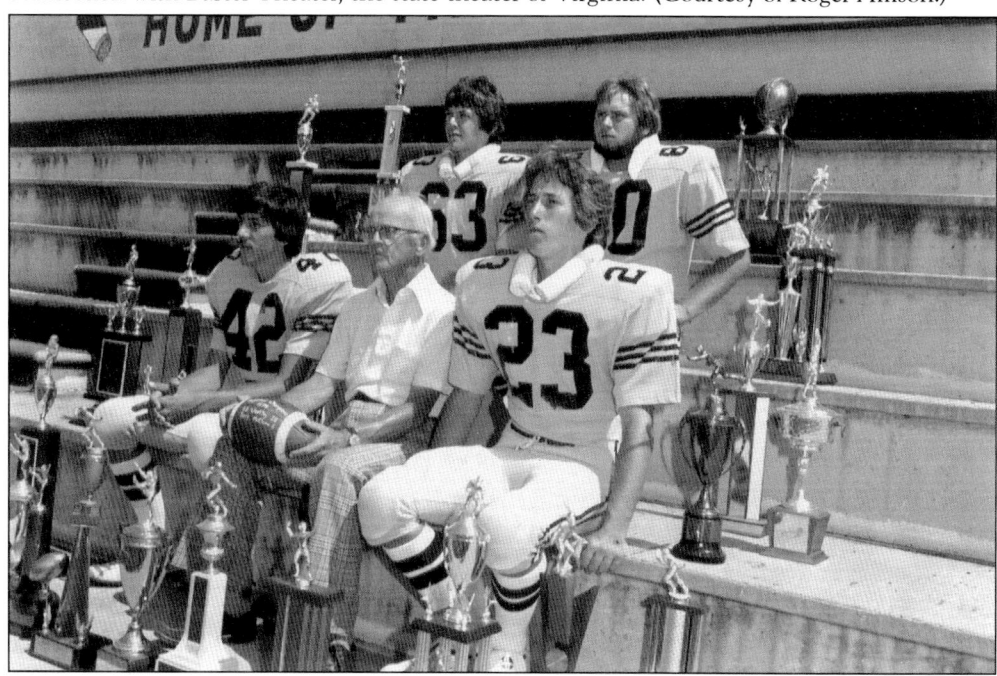

FOOTBALL 1979. In this photograph are four captains of the 1979 R. B. Worthy High School Shakers football team, Scott Poore (left, front), Ricky Hatfield (right, front), John Lee (left, back), and David Kestner (right, back), with Turk Warren (center, front). Warren was one of the captains of the 1919 football team.

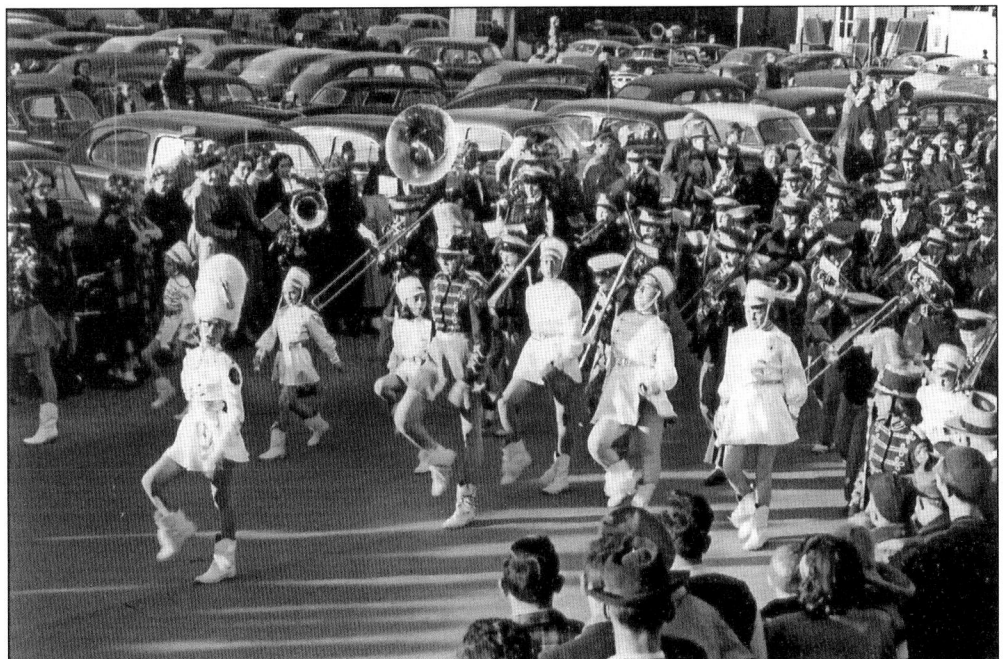

1953 SALTVILLE HIGH SCHOOL HOMECOMING PARADE. This photograph of the Saltville High marching band was taken during the 1953 Homecoming Parade. (Courtesy of Roger Allison.)

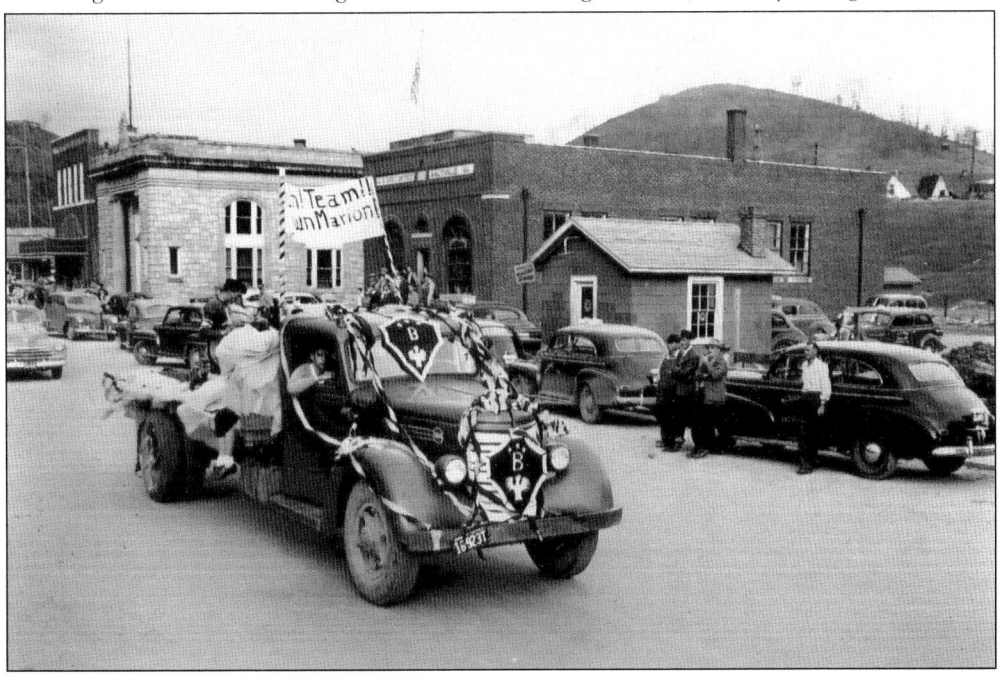

WIN! TEAM! DOWN MARION! Cross-county rivals Marion and Saltville met for Saltville's 1948 homecoming football game. Though it was Saltville's first homecoming, it was not the first meeting between the two teams, and after the Saltville team won the game, the traditional fight between the fans of the Saltville Shakers and the Marion Scarlet Hurricane broke out. (Courtesy of Roger Allison.)

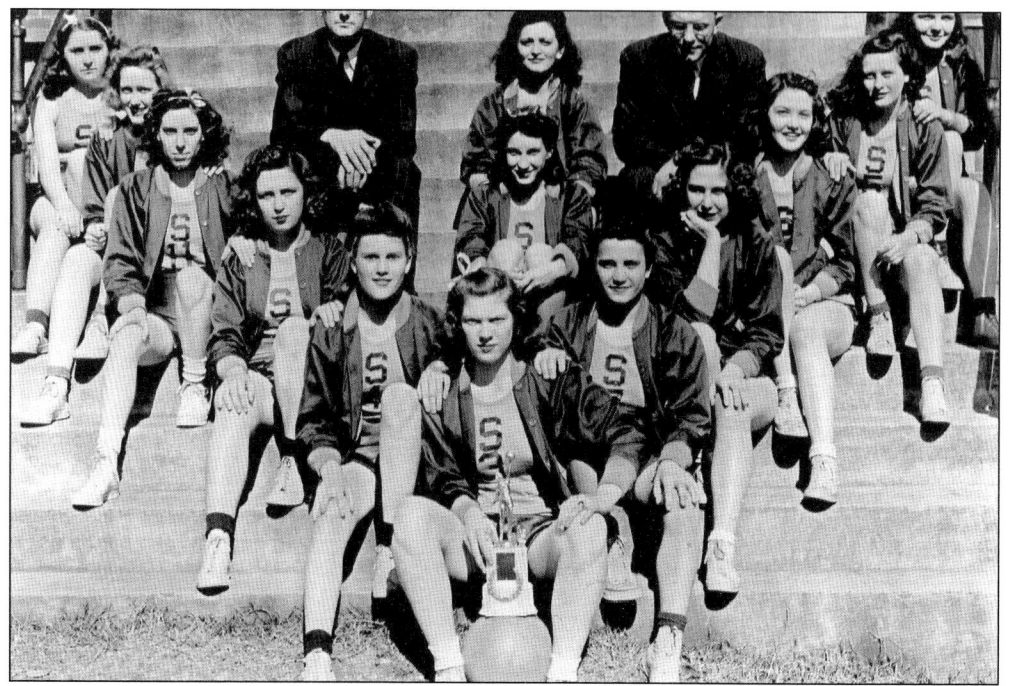

SALTVILLE GIRLS BASKETBALL, 1941. This photograph shows the 1941 county girls high school basketball champions, the Saltville Lady Shakers. (Courtesy of Roger Allison.)

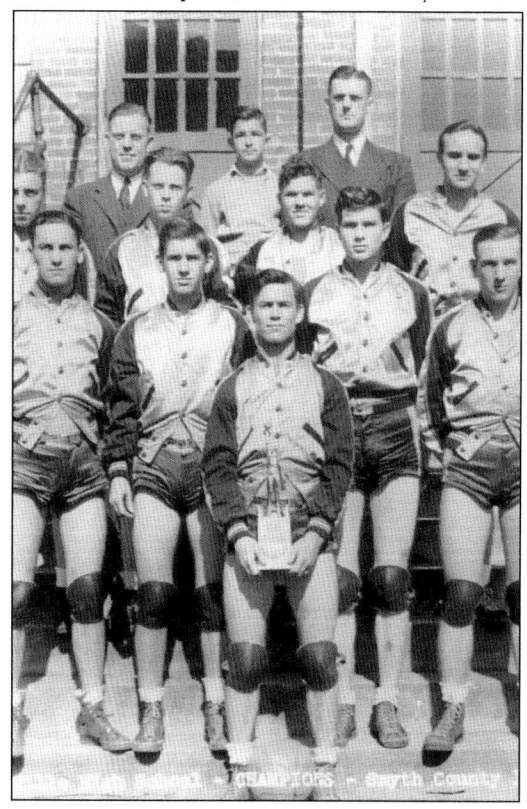

1941 BOYS BASKETBALL. The 1941 Saltville High boys basketball team took home the county championship. Other county schools at the time included Marion, Chilhowie, Sugar Grove, Rich Valley, Allison Gap, and Atkins. (Courtesy of Roger Allison.)

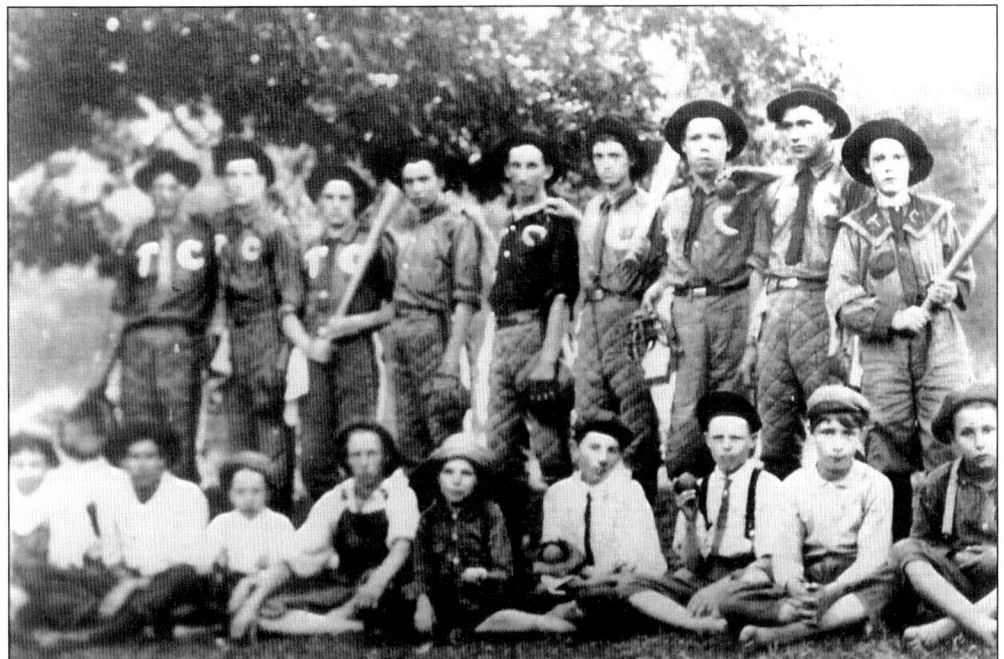

TUMBLING CREEK BASEBALL. This c. 1900 image shows the Tumbling Creek baseball team. Note the T. C. on their shirts and the quilted pants that were worn at that time. Nearly every community had a baseball team, and an informal league developed around Saltville around the close of the 19th century.

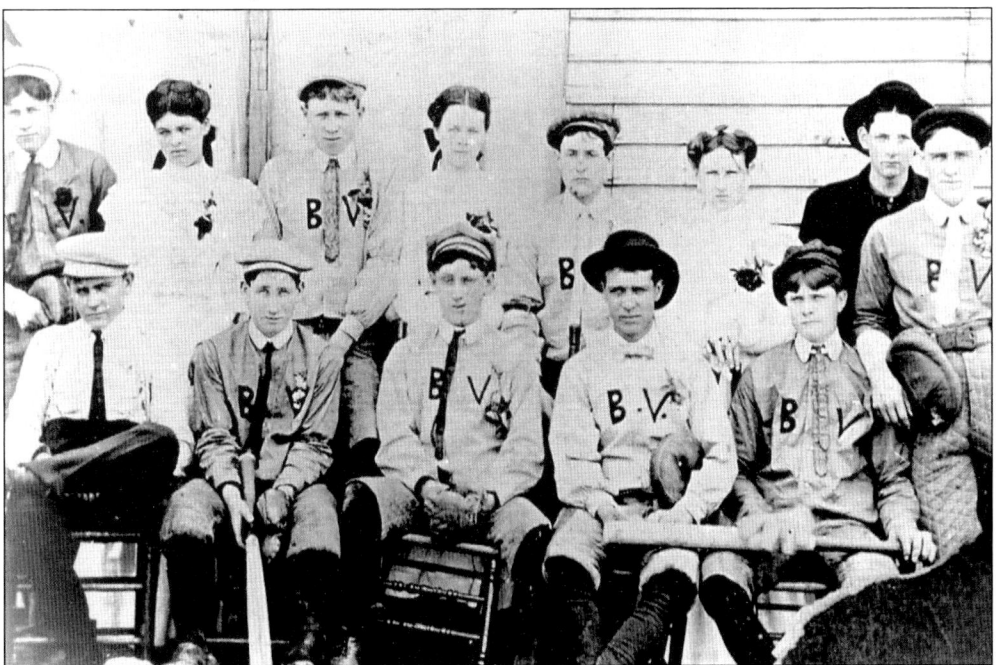

BUENA VISTA BASEBALL. This 1908 photograph of the Buena Vista (Plasterco) baseball team shows some changes in uniform from what is usually expected. The girls in the photograph made the team's clothing. Especially note the hats and the stockings.

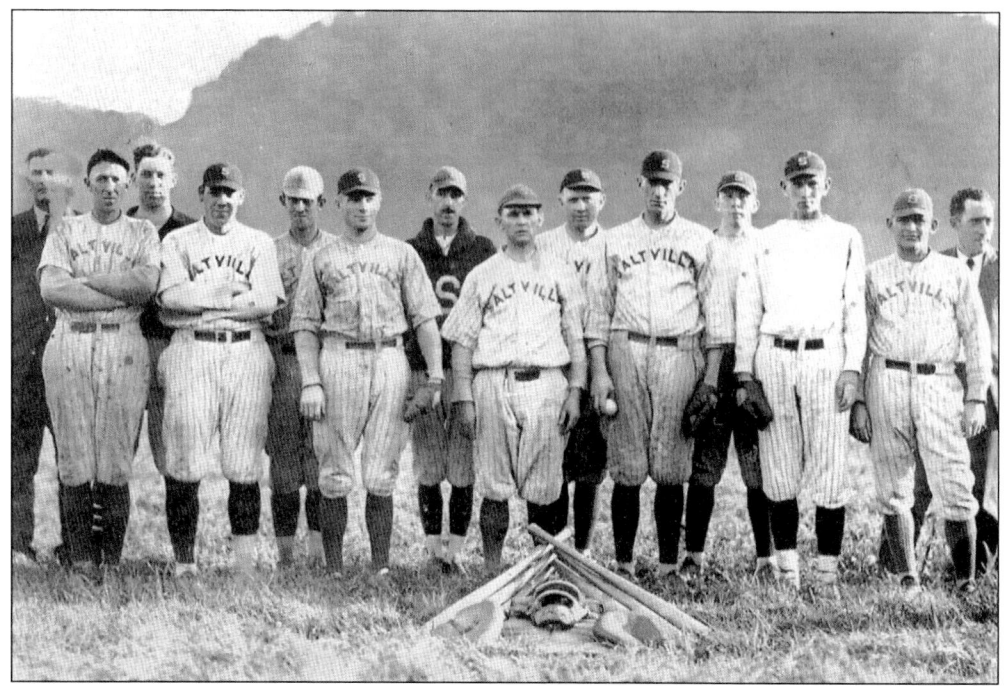

SALTVILLE SEMI-PRO BASEBALL. This photograph of the Saltville Alkalies was taken by C. L. Totten before his death in 1927. Mathieson sponsored the semi-professional Alkalies, who played in the Burley Belt League. Talented college students, usually from nearby Emory and Henry College, were given summer jobs in return for playing on the team.

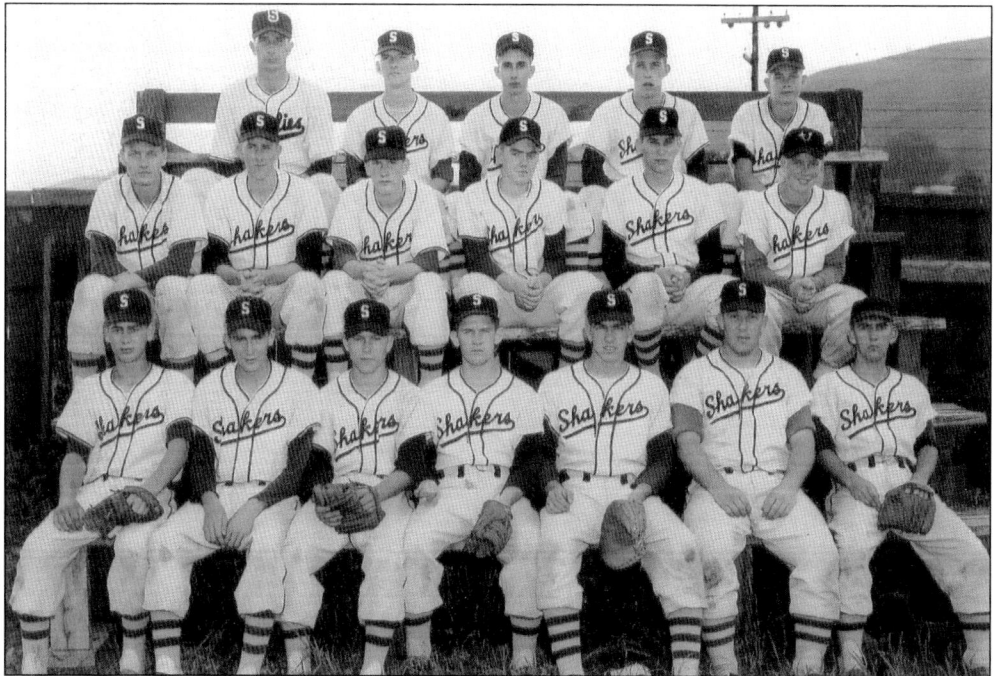

SALTVILLE SHAKERS BASEBALL. This 1956 Shaker team was undefeated. (Courtesy of Roger Allison.)

BASEBALL STADIUM. Mathieson built a baseball stadium for the town in 1920 with seating for 400 spectators. The company actively encouraged their employees to attend these baseball games and gave workers time off to do so. Note the Civil War entrenchment in the foreground. (Courtesy of Roger Allison.)

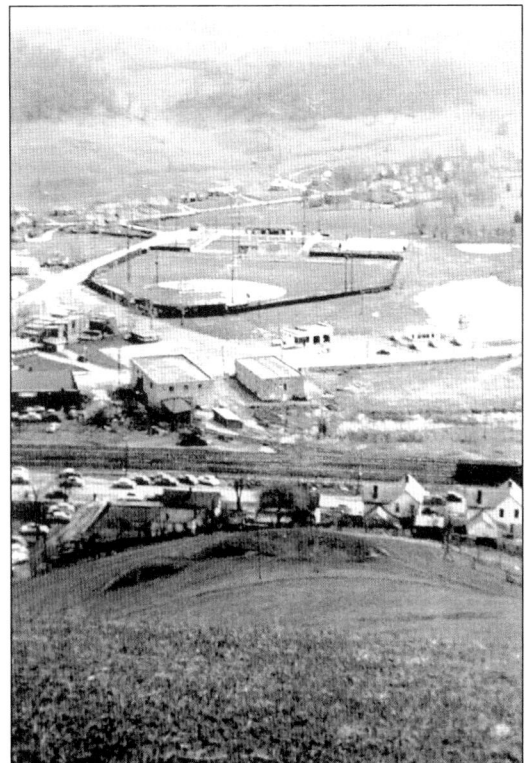

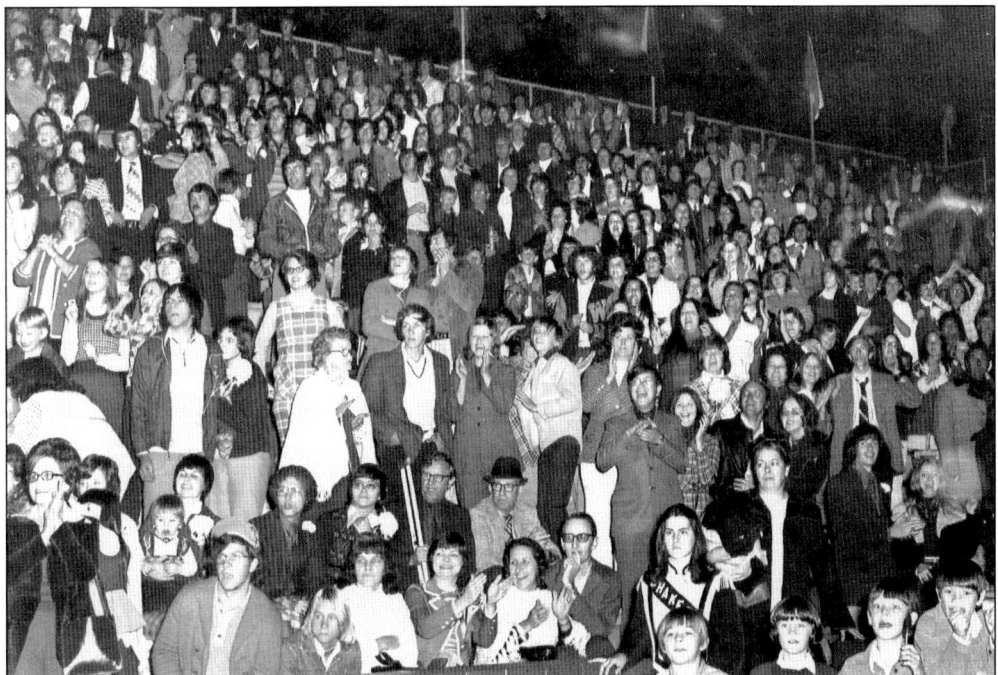

FOOTBALL FANS. This 1970s photograph shows the number of fans who turned out for Shaker games. The population of Saltville is only around 2,500, and the citizens usually pack the stands. (Courtesy of Roger Allison.)

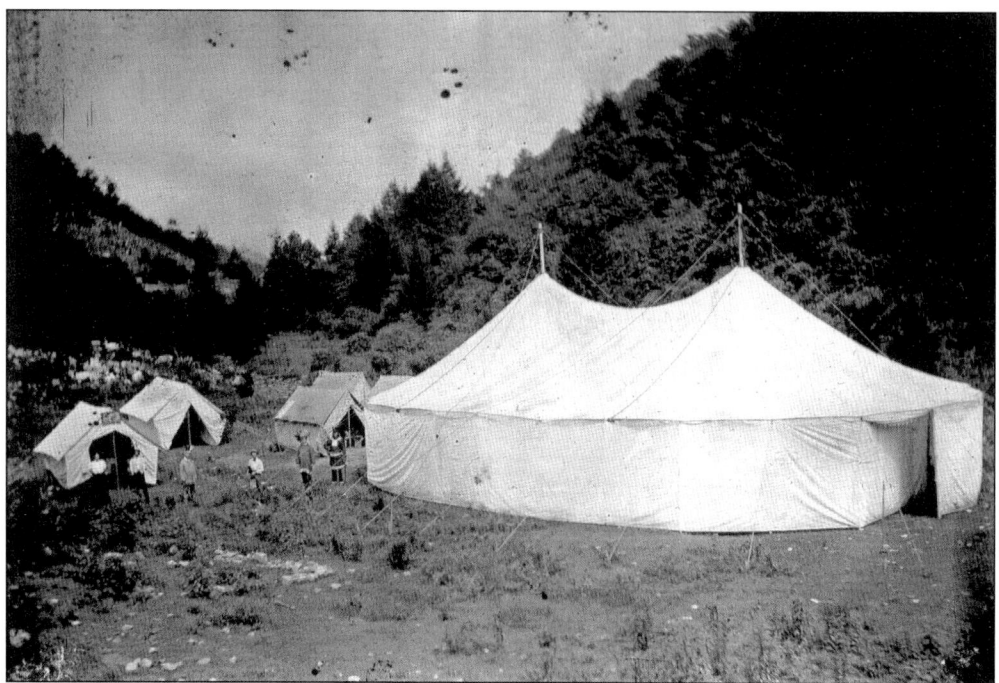

MEDICINE SHOW. This 1890s image by C. L. Totten shows a medicine or Wild West show in the Saltville Valley. Note the large tent in the foreground for the main performance. There are five tents in the background for sleeping quarters for the cast, and probably to peddle some snake oil as well. (Courtesy of Rick Davidson.)

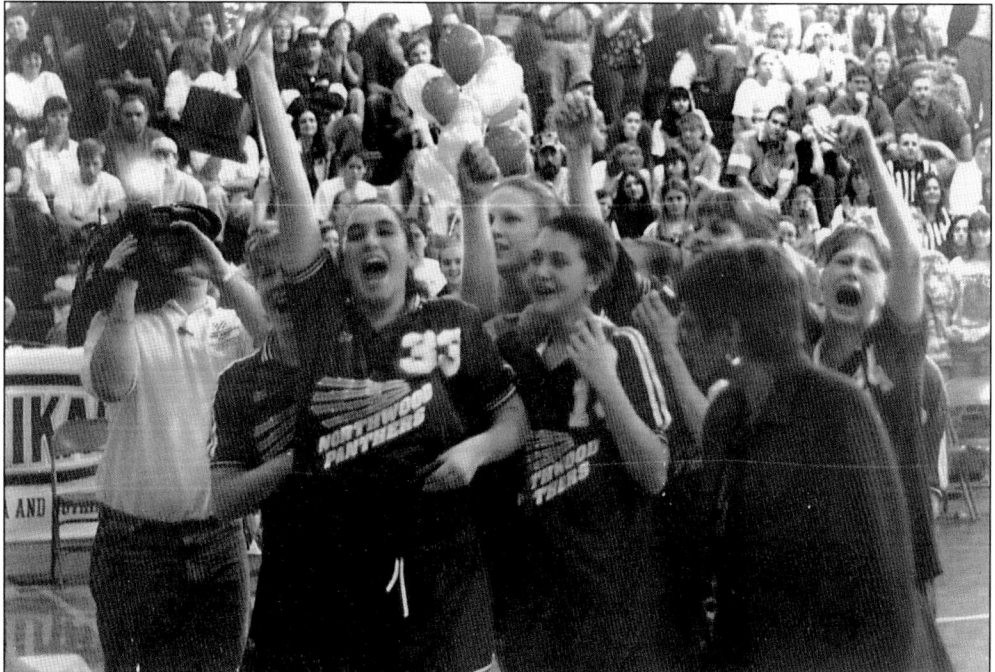

VOLLEYBALL. This photograph was taken after the Northwood High School girls volleyball team won the state championship in 1998. (Courtesy of Roger Allison.)

GIRL SCOUTS. This image, made in the late 1930s or early 1940s, shows a group of Saltville's Girl Scouts. (Courtesy of Roger Allison.)

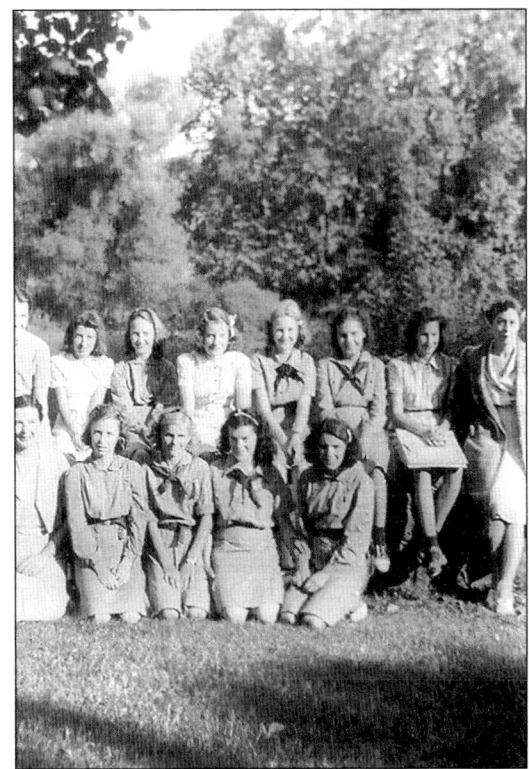

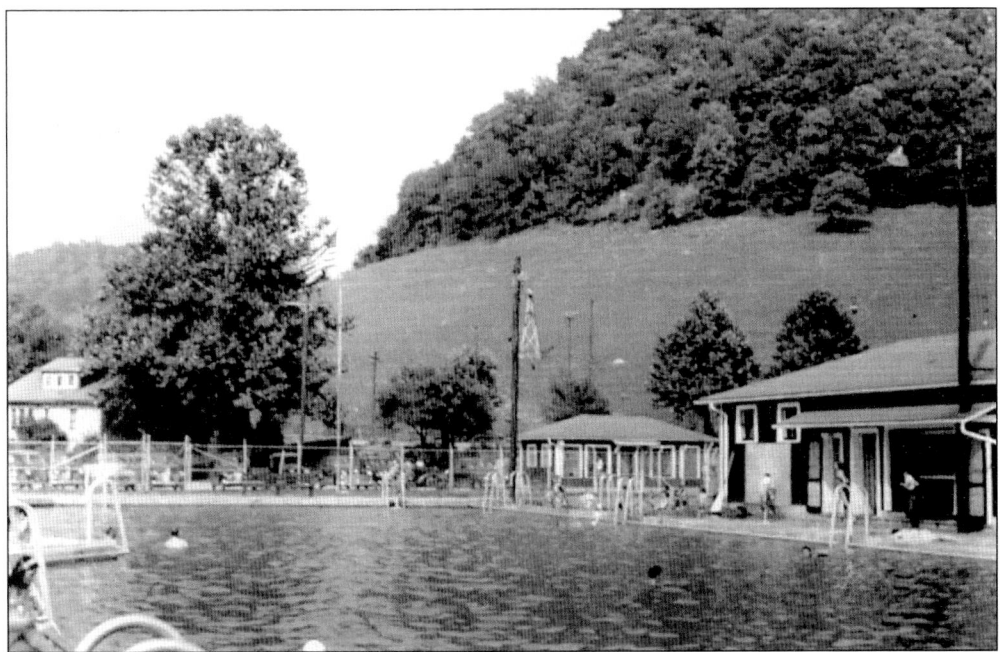

SPLASH. This c. 1946 photograph shows some of the town's children enjoying the salt-water swimming pool. This pool was the first public swimming pool in either Smyth or Washington Counties, Virginia. It was named for Hardy Roberts, a Saltvillian who was killed during World War II at Guadalcanal.

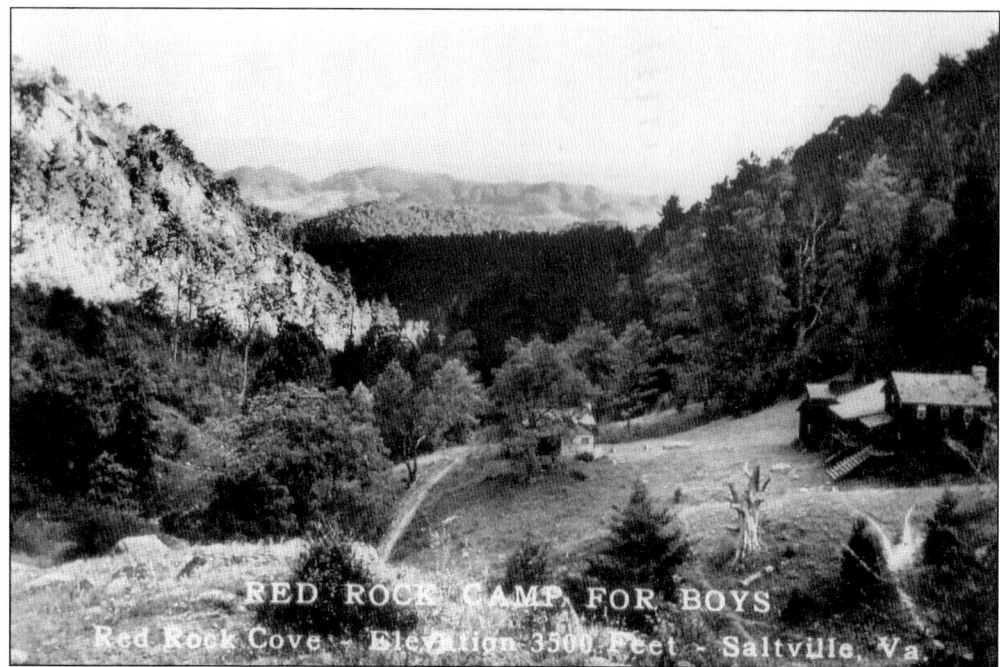

CAMP RED ROCK FOR BOYS. Camp Red Rock, located in the mountains above Saltville and Allison Gap, offered outdoor recreation and art education for boys from 1938 until the mid-1940s. This camp was started by a group of New Yorkers as a place where less fortunate but gifted young artists could come to practice their craft.

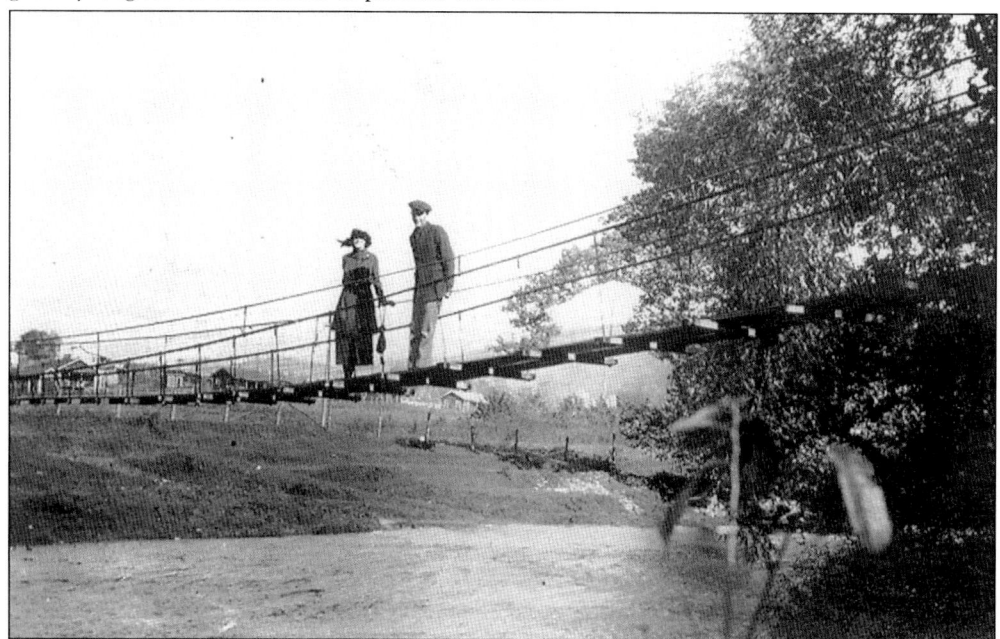

SWINGING BRIDGE. This early-1920s couple seems content to enjoy each others company while the North Fork of Holston River rolls below. The region offers many opportunities for viewing natural beauty. There were several swinging bridges over the North Fork of Holston River near Saltville. This bridge was located at North Holston at River Road.

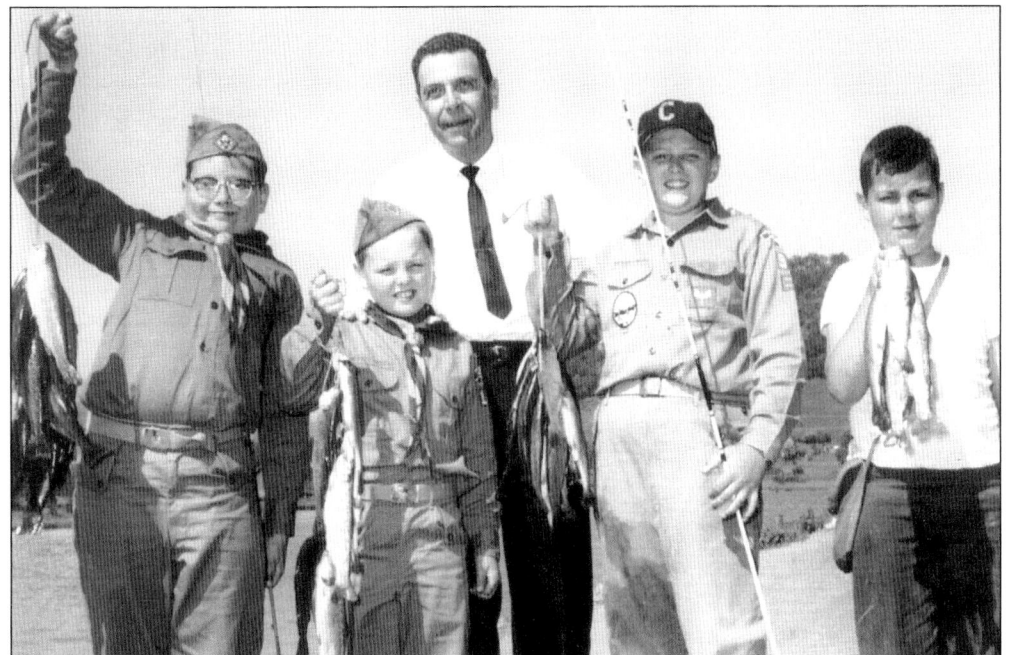

FISHING JAMBOREE. In the period after World War II, the company had the well fields stocked with trout and invited the Boy Scouts in the surrounding area to a fishing jamboree. These lads have had a good day. In this 1950s photograph, Robert Abersold, the plant manager, is in the center of the print.

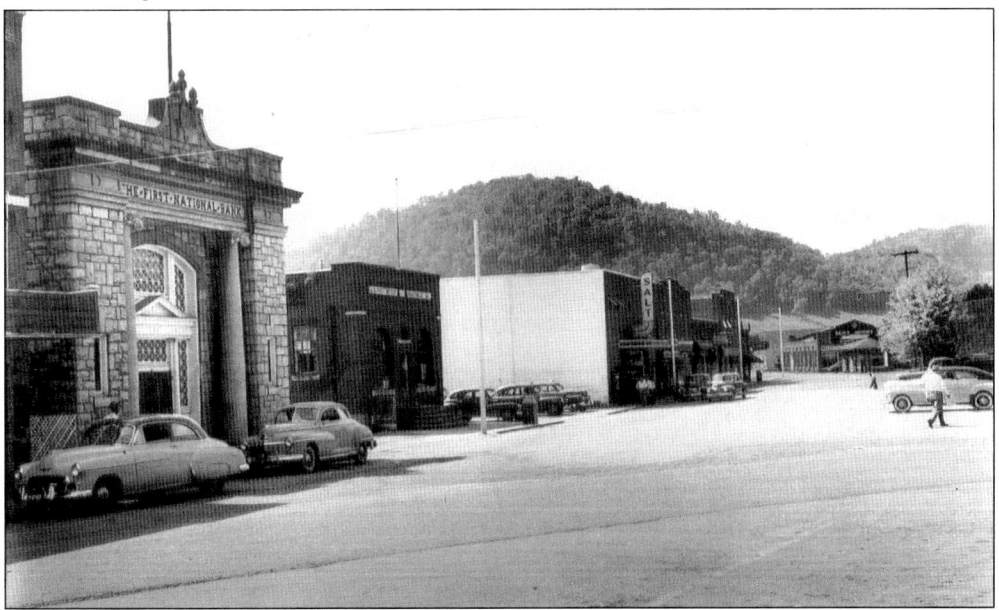

THE SALT THEATER. Saltville's third and final movie house is shown in this c. 1950 image. The Salt Theater was converted into Singleton's Carpet Shop and later into the Museum of the Middle Appalachians in 1998. The Saltville Post Office is shown between the theater and the First National Bank of Saltville. Sauls Motors, later Griffin Motors, a Chevrolet dealership, can be seen in the right center background of this shot.

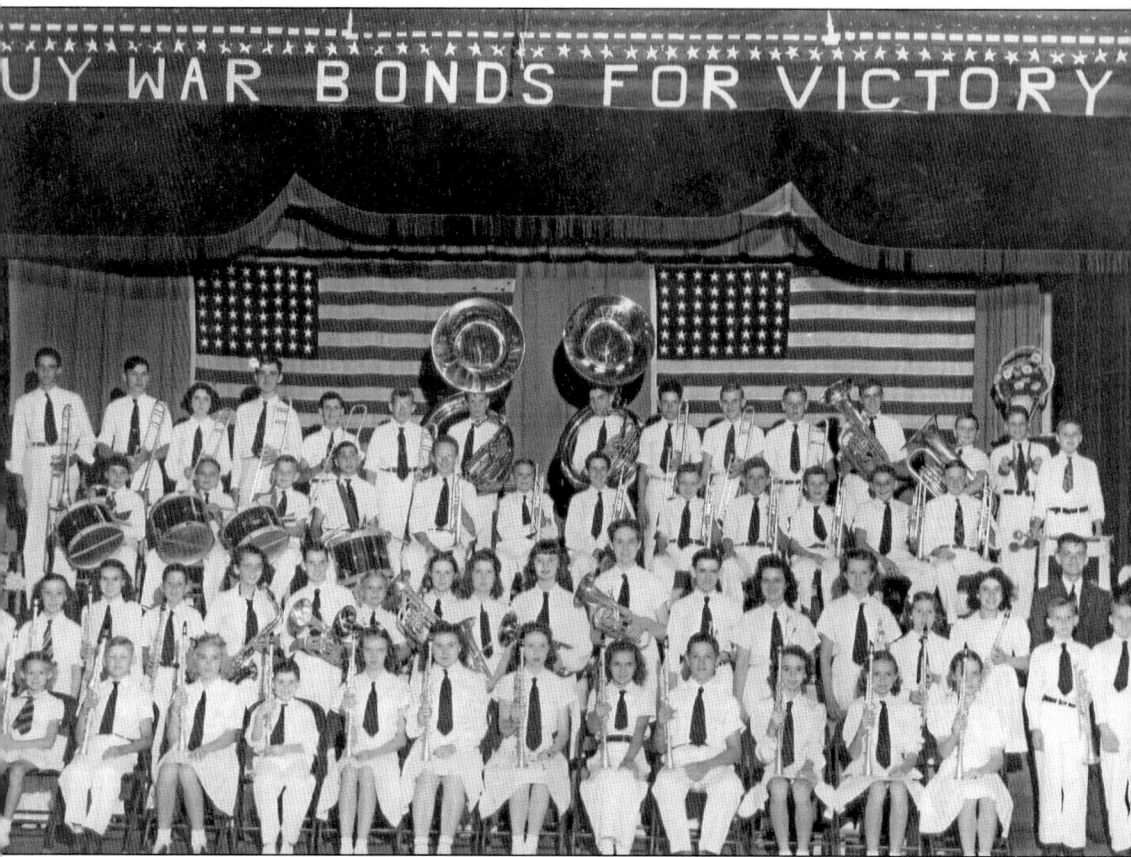

SALTVILLE HIGH SCHOOL'S FIRST MARCHING BAND. This March 1942 image shows the well-groomed Saltville High School marching band. After Pearl Harbor, patriotism ran high, and it is on display in this photograph of the War Bonds campaign. (Courtesy of Roger Allison.)

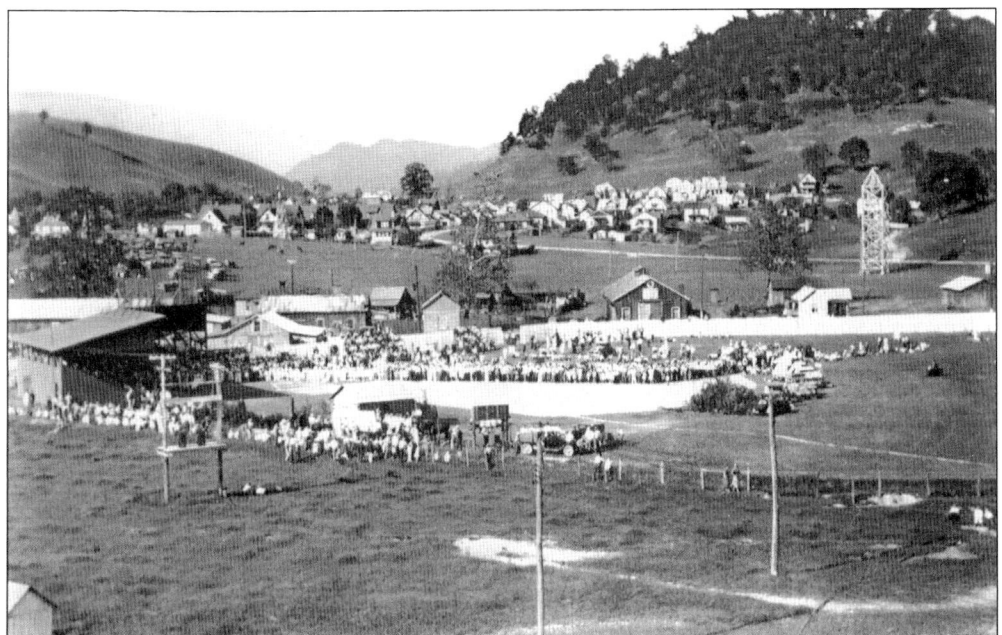

1932 Centennial Celebration. Smyth County was created from Washington and Wythe County in 1832. Quite naturally, a centennial celebration was held on the 100-year anniversary in 1932. A three-day event kicked off in Marion, the county seat, then went to Chilhowie, and ended in Saltville. This shows the kickoff with bands and other entertainment at the baseball field in Saltville.

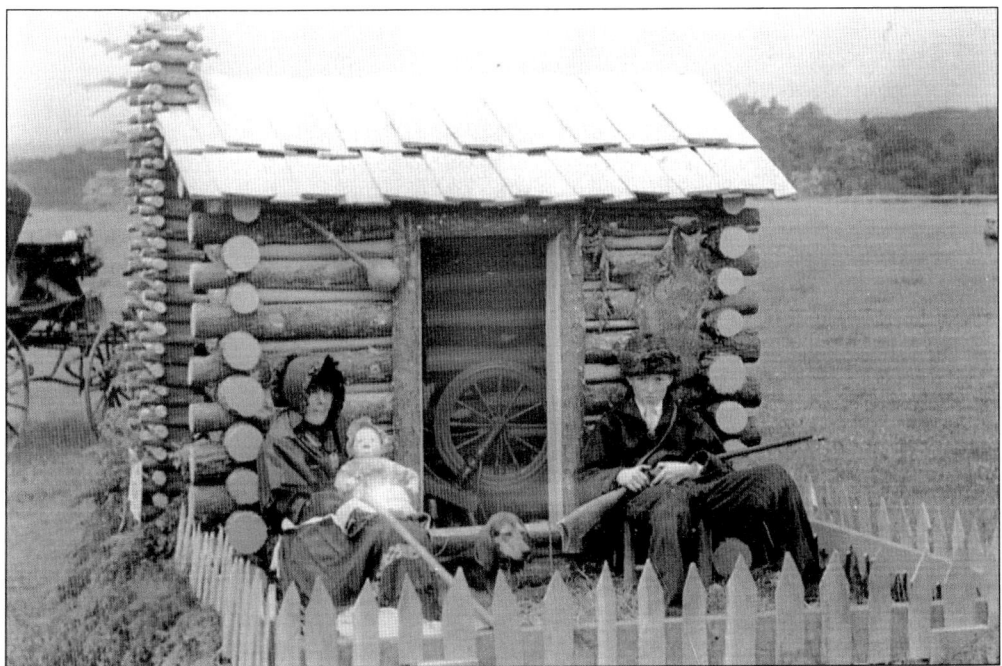

Pioneer Float in the 1932 Parade. This miniature log cabin and its youthful father and mother are meant to show pioneer life in Smyth County a century earlier. Note the dog riding the float and the spinning wheel in the cabin.

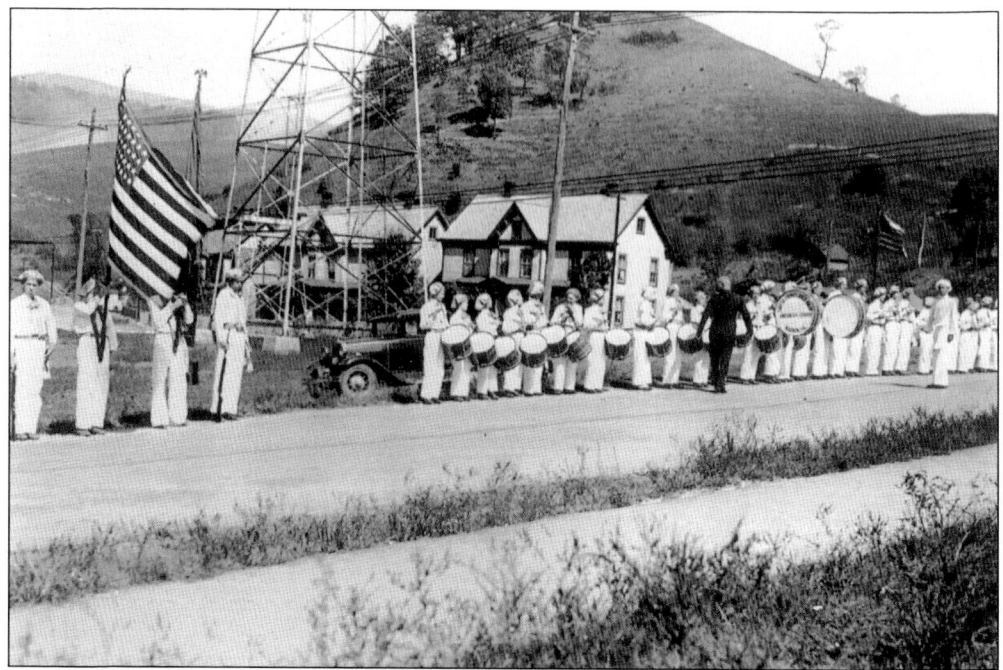

1935 PARADE. This parade was to celebrate what was an important event at the time but which has since been forgotten. This shows parade participants lining up behind a Virginia state trooper. The houses in the back left are British Row, while the marchers are on East Main Street. The base of one of the bucket line towers is the left of the scene.

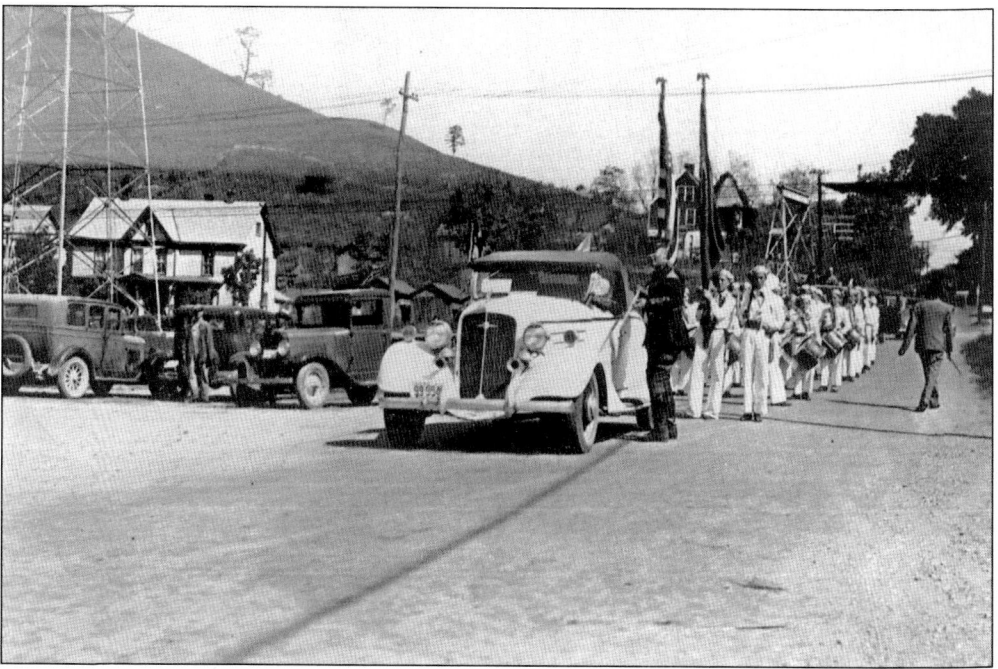

1935 PARADE. Seen here are the color guard with American and Virginia banners and a marching band from the junior chapter of the Marion American Legion post. The duplexes of British Row are shown quite well in this illustration.

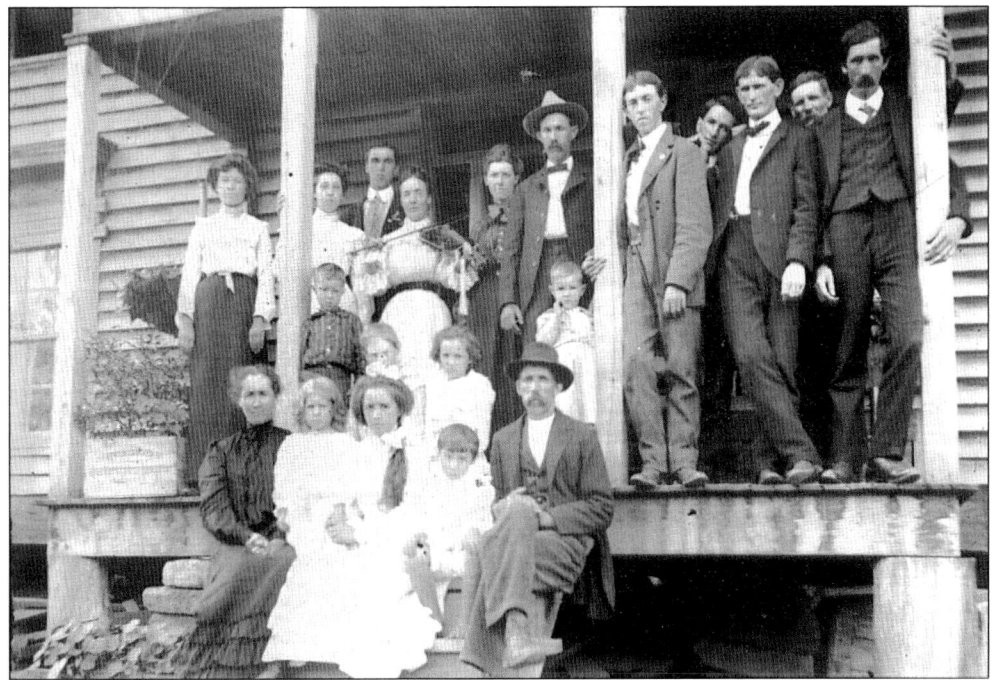

FIDDLIN' WOMAN. This 1890s image shows a large group of people gathered for some celebration. Note the lady in the center of the picture holding a fiddle. (Courtesy of Rick Davidson.)

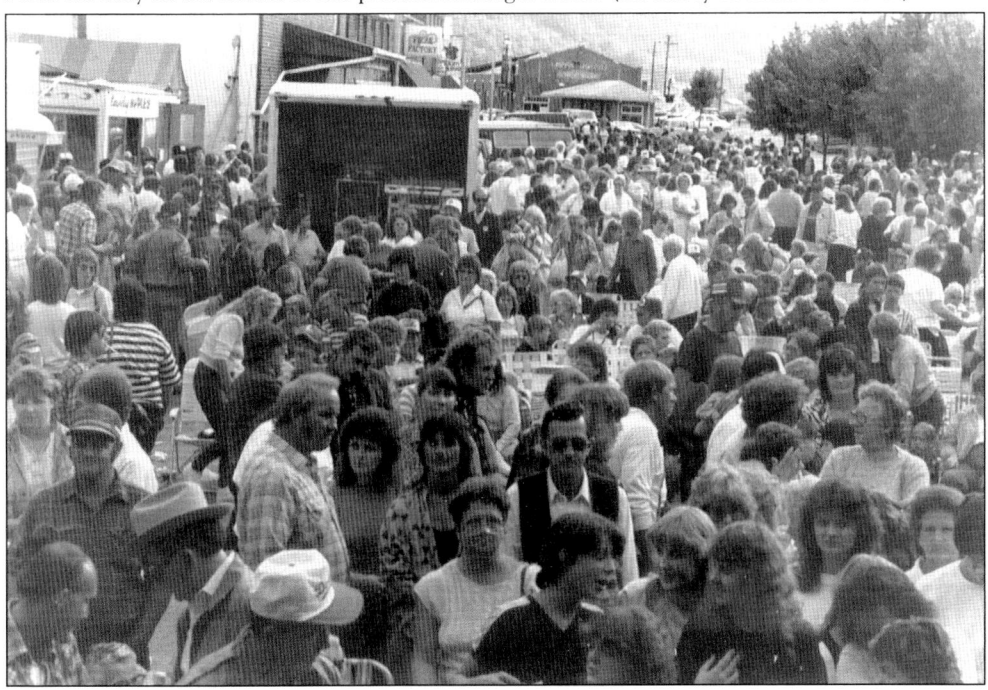

LABOR DAY FESTIVAL. After Olin announced its withdrawal from Saltville in 1971, local businessman Fred Singleton organized a Labor Day festival to raise the spirits of the town. Many nationally known musical groups have been booked for this event. This photograph shows some of the crowds this festival attracts.

BIBLIOGRAPHY

Adams, Dean, ed., et. al. *Heritage of Smyth County, Virginia, 1832–1997*. Marceline, MO: Walsworth Publishing, 1997.

Allison, Roger A. *Saltville Schools, 1788?–1993*. Saltville, VA : The Salt Center, 1993.

———. *A Brief History of Saltville 1896-1996*. Saltville, VA: Saltville Centennial Committee, 1996.

Armstrong, Joan Tracy. *History of Smyth County: Antebellum Years through the Civil War*. Bristol, VA: McFarlane Graphics, 1986.

Byrd, Kimberly Barr and Debra J. Williams. *Smyth County*. Charleston, SC: Arcadia Publishing, 2005.

Des Cognet, Anna. *William Russell and His Descendants*. Lexington, KY: Printed for the family by Samuel F. Wilson, 1884.

Eskridge, Carl V. *The Great Saltville Disaster*. Bristol, TN: King Printing, 1925.

Glanville, Jim, "Conquistadors at Saltville in 1567? A Review of the Archeological and Documentary Evidence." *The Smithfield Review* 8: 70-108. Blacksburg, VA: Pocahontas Press, 2004.

Kent, William B. *A History of Saltville*. Radford, VA: Commonwealth Press, 1955.

Mathieson Alkali Works. *The Alkalite: Anniversary Number*. Saltville, VA: Mathieson Alkali Works, 1922.

Preston, Thomas L. *Historical Sketches and Reminiscences of an Octogenarian*. Richmond, VA: B. F. Johnson Publishing Co., 1900.

———. *A Sketch of Mrs. Elizabeth Russell, Wife of General William Campbell, Sister of Patrick Henry*. Nashville, TN: Publishing House of the M. E. Church, South, 1888.

Saltville, Town of. *Saltville, Virginia Promotional Brochure*. Saltville, VA: Town of Saltville, 1950.

Summers, Lewis P. *History of Southwest Virginia 1746–1786, Washington County, 1777–1870*. Johnson City, TN: Overmountain Press, 1989.

Weaver, Jeffrey C. (Transcriber). *The 1850 Smyth County, Virginia Census*. Clintwood, VA: Mullins Printing, 1989.

Wilson, Goodridge. *Smyth County History and Traditions*. Radford, VA: Commonwealth Press, 1932.